THE AUTHOR

William Empson was born in Yokefleet, in the East Riding of Yorkshire, in 1906. He was educated at Winchester College, then at Magdalene College, Cambridge, where he graduated in Mathematics and subsequently gained a first-class degree in English Literature. While Empson was still at Cambridge, his supervisor, I. A. Richards, encouraged him to develop the brilliant and original ideas which were published in *Seven Types of Ambiguity* (1930) when Empson was only twenty-four. This was followed, in 1935, by *Poems*, and although he produced only one more collection of poetry – *The Gathering Storm*, in 1940 – he is widely regarded as one of the most important poets of his distinguished generation. His influence has been confirmed and extended by his other critical writings, notably *Some Versions of Pastoral* (1935), *The Structure of Complex Words* (1951) and *Milton's God* (1961), all of which have achieved the status of classics. His *Collected Poems* was published in 1955, and a new collection of essays, *Using Biography*, in 1984.

Empson's long teaching career began at the national university in Tokyo, where he lectured in English from 1931–34, and continued, from 1937–39, in Peking. During the Second World War he returned to England to work for the BBC, first in the Monitoring Department and then as Chinese Editor. He was married, to Hetta Crouse, in 1941, and they had two sons. In 1947 Empson returned to Peking, and in 1953 was appointed to the Chair of English Literature at Sheffield University, which he held until his retirement in 1971. He was knighted in 1979, and died in London in 1984.

The Hogarth Press also publishes *Seven Types of Ambiguity*, *The Structure of Complex Words* and *Collected Poems*.

SOME
VERSIONS
OF PASTORAL

William Empson

THE HOGARTH PRESS
LONDON

Published in 1986 by
The Hogarth Press
Chatto & Windus Ltd
40 William IV Street, London WC2N 4DF

First published in Great Britain by Chatto & Windus 1935
Hogarth edition offset from the 1974 Chatto edition
Copyright The Estate of Sir William Empson

British Library Cataloguing in Publication Data

Empson, William
Some versions of pastoral.
1. Pastoral literature, English – English and criticism
I. Title
820'.91   PRI49.P3
ISBN 0 7012 0611 X

Printed in Great Britain by
Cox & Wyman Ltd
Reading, Berkshire

CONTENTS

PREFACE TO 1974 EDITION

This book was first published in 1935, and the first sentence of it will seem a bit raw unless one knows that. I have corrected some mistakes, but could not bring the first chapter up to date, nor even purge successfully the bits in later chapters which now seem to me turgid. However, I still believe in the thesis of the book, and the conclusions drawn from it; I hope I may yet produce convincing evidence for some of them which have been ignored or dismissed as crotchets.

It was not a new idea in 1935 that the love-poetry of Donne claims a defiant independence for the pair of lovers, especially by setting them to colonize some planet made habitable by Copernicus (p. 65). A campaign to exterminate the idea was then in progress, using very little reasoned argument, and its success has naturally made the poems seem pretty trivial to a later generation. I did not realize this, having just got back from three years in Japan, and felt I was working beside my colleagues in recommending our basic tradition; but I regarded Independence as part of the tradition, whereas the revival movement became increasingly attached to the virtues of obedience. After a generation, one may hope for the tyranny of a fashion to relent, if further evidence can be brought against it. I have done some articles which I hope soon to collect and add to.

The analysis of 'They that have power' is perhaps rather wire-drawn, but to show that echoes from the Sonnets hang round Falstaff (p. 87) does at least show that they were not addressed to Herbert. The Sonnets would then be echoing the plays, not the other way round; the middle-aged author, while adulating his childish patron, would compare himself to the disgusting misleader of youth he had recently made famous—a most painful thing, and sure to attract attention. I made no attempt here to use the echoes as evidence for biography, but got round to it at last in my Preface to *Shakespeare Poems* Signet Classics (1968).

The chapter on Milton has been followed up thoroughly in a separate book, *Milton's God* (1961); I still hope to bring out a final edition of that. Professor R. M. Adams, in his book on Milton called *Ikon*, has listed a number of mistakes I made in copying the remarks of Bentley and Pearce (which were copied in the British Museum, and written up in Japan); I am sorry not to have put the mistakes right, but I could not see that they affected the argument. Mr. Christopher Ricks, in *Milton's Grand Style*, showed how much I had missed by not reading further in the eighteenth-century critics of Milton; they went through a development closely parallel to the twentieth-century development, each quite unknown to the other, so that we were like the Aztecs and the Incas. Very likely only one of us had the use of the potato.

W. E.

Proletarian Literature

IT is hard for an Englishman to talk definitely about proletarian art, because in England it has never been a genre with settled principles, and such as there is of it, that I have seen, is bad. But it is important to try and decide what the term ought to mean; my suspicion, as I shall try to make clear, is that it is liable to a false limitation.

As for propaganda, some very good work has been that; most authors want their point of view to be convincing. Pope said that even the *Aeneid* was a 'political puff'; its dreamy, impersonal, universal melancholy was a calculated support for Augustus. And on the other hand proletarian literature need not be propaganda; *Carl and Anna* is simply a very good love-story; it counts as proletarian because no other social world (ideology) is brought in but that of the characters who are factory workers. Of course to decide on an author's purpose, conscious or unconscious, is very difficult. Good writing is not done unless there are serious forces at work; and it is not permanent unless it works for readers with opinions different from the author's. On the other hand the reason an English audience can enjoy Russian propagandist films is that the propaganda is too remote to be annoying: a Tory audience subjected to Tory propaganda of the same intensity would be extremely bored. Anyway it is agreed that there is some good work which a Marxist would call proletarian; the more pressing questions for him are whether some good work may be

3

bourgeois and whether some may not be class-conscious at all.

Gray's *Elegy* is an odd case of poetry with latent political ideas :

> Full many a gem of purest ray serene
> The dark, unfathomed caves of ocean bear ;
> Full many a flower is born to blush unseen
> And waste its sweetness on the desert air.

What this means, as the context makes clear, is that eighteenth-century England had no scholarship system or *carrière ouverte aux talents*. This is stated as pathetic, but the reader is put into a mood in which one would not try to alter it. (It is true that Gray's society, unlike a possible machine society, was necessarily based on manual labour, but it might have used a man of special ability wherever he was born.) By comparing the social arrangement to Nature he makes it seem inevitable, which it was not, and gives it a dignity which was undeserved. Furthermore, a gem does not mind being in a cave and a flower prefers not to be picked ; we feel that the man is like the flower, as short-lived, natural, and valuable, and this tricks us into feeling that he is better off without opportunities. The sexual suggestion of *blush* brings in the Christian idea that virginity is good in itself, and so that any renunciation is good ; this may trick us into feeling it is lucky for the poor man that society keeps him unspotted from the World. The tone of melancholy claims that the poet understands the considerations opposed to aristocracy, though he judges against them ; the truism of the reflections in the church-yard, the universality and impersonality this gives to the style, claim as if by comparison that we ought to accept the injustice of society as we do the inevitability of death.

4

Many people, without being communists, have been irritated by the complacence in the massive calm of the poem, and this seems partly because they feel there is a cheat in the implied politics; the 'bourgeois' themselves do not like literature to have too much 'bourgeois ideology.'

And yet what is said is one of the permanent truths; it is only in degree that any improvement of society could prevent wastage of human powers; the waste even in a fortunate life, the isolation even of a life rich in intimacy, cannot but be felt deeply, and is the central feeling of tragedy. And anything of value must accept this because it must not prostitute itself; its strength is to be prepared to waste itself, if it does not get its opportunity. A statement of this is certainly non-political because it is true in any society, and yet nearly all the great poetic statements of it are in a way 'bourgeois,' like this one; they suggest to many readers, though they do not say, that for the poor man things cannot be improved even in degree. This at least shows that the distinction the communists try to draw is a puzzling one; two people may get very different experiences from the same work of art without either being definitely wrong. One is told that the Russians now disapprove of tragedy, and that there was a performance of *Hamlet* in the Turk-Sib region which the audience decided spontaneously was a farce. They may well hold out against the melancholy of old Russia, and for them there may be dangerous implications in any tragedy, which other people do not see. I am sure at any rate that one could not estimate the amount of bourgeois ideology 'really in' the verse from Gray.

The same difficulty arises in the other direction.

Proletarian literature usually has a suggestion of pastoral, a puzzling form which looks proletarian but isn't. I must worry the meaning of the term for a moment. One might define proletarian art as the propaganda of a factory-working class which feels its interests opposed to the factory owners'; this narrow sense is perhaps what is usually meant but not very interesting. You couldn't have proletarian literature in this sense in a successful socialist state. The wider sense of the term includes such folk-literature as is by the people, for the people, and about the people. But most fairy stories and ballads, though 'by' and 'for,' are not 'about'; whereas pastoral though 'about' is not 'by' or 'for.' The Border ballads assume a society of fighting clans who are protected by their leaders since leaders can afford expensive weapons; the aristocrat has an obvious function for the people, and they are pleased to describe his grandeur and fine clothes. (This pleasure in him as an object of fantasy is the normal thing, but usually there are forces the other way.) They were class-conscious all right, but not conscious of class war. Pastoral is a queerer business, but I think permanent and not dependent on a system of class exploitation. Any socialist state with an intelligentsia at the capital that felt itself more cultivated than the farmers (which it would do; the arts are produced by overcrowding) could produce it; it is common in present-day Russian films, and a great part of their beauty (for instance the one called *The General Line* when it came to England). My reason for dragging this old-fashioned form into the discussion is that I think good proletarian art is usually Covert Pastoral.

Before theorising about this I had best speak of some

recent English artists. A book like Lionel Britton's *Hunger and Love*, one of the few ostensibly proletarian works of any energy that England has to show (I disliked it too much to finish it), is not at all pastoral; it is a passionate and feverish account of a man trying to break his way out of the proletariat into the intelligentsia, or rather the lower middle class into the upper. As such it may be good literature by sheer force, and useful propaganda if it is not out of date by the time it is written, but what the author wanted was the opportunity not to be proletarian; this is fine enough, but it doesn't make proletarian literature. On the other hand nobody would take the pastoral of T. F. Powys for proletarian, though it really is about workers; his object in writing about country people is to get a simple enough material for his purpose, which one might sum up as a play with Christian imagery backed only by a Buddhist union of God and death. No doubt he would say that country people really feel this, and are wiser about it than the cultivated, and that he is their spokesman, but the characters are firmly artificial and kept at a great distance from the author. W. W. Jacobs makes the argument amusingly clear; it is not obvious why he is not a proletarian author, and it would annoy a communist very much to admit that he was. Probably no one would deny that he writes a version of pastoral. The truth that supports his formula is that such men as his characters keep their souls alive by ironical humour, a subtle mode of thought which among other things makes you willing to be ruled by your betters; and this makes the bourgeois feel safe in Wapping. D. H. Lawrence's refusal to write proletarian literature was an important choice, but he was a complicated person; to see the general reasons for it one had best take a simpler example. George Bissill the painter, who worked from childhood in the mines and did some excellent woodcuts of them, refused to work for the *New Leader* (which wanted political cartoons) because he had rather be a Pavement Artist than a Proletarian one. As a person he is obviously not 'bourgeois,' unless being determined not to go back to the mines makes you that. Such a man dislikes proletarian art because he feels that it is like pastoral, and that that is either patronising or 'romantic.' The Englishman who seems to me nearest to a proletarian artist (of those I know anything about) is Grierson the film producer; *Drifters* gave very vividly the feeling of actually living on a herring trawler and (by the beauty of shapes of water and net and fish, and subtleties of timing and so forth) what I should call a pastoral feeling about the dignity of that form of labour. It was very much under Russian influence. But herring fishermen are unlikely to see *Drifters*; for all its government-commercial claim to solid usefulness it is a 'high-brow' picture (that blasting word shows an involuntary falsity in the thing); Grierson's influence, strong and healthy as it is, has something skimpy about it. Of course there are plenty of skilled workers in England who are proud of their skill, and you can find men of middle age working on farms who say they prefer the country to the town, but anything like what I am trying to call pastoral is a shock to the Englishman who meets it on the Continent. My only personal memory of this sort is of watching Spaniards tread out sherry grapes and squeeze out the skins afterwards, which involves dance steps with a complicated rhythm. I said what was obvious,

8

that this was like the Russian Ballet, and to my alarm the remark was translated; any English worker would take it as an insult, probably a sexual one. They were mildly pleased at so obvious a point being recognised, and showed us the other dance step used in a neighbouring district; both ways were pleasant in themselves and the efficient way to get the maximum juice. The point is not at all that they were living simple pretty lives by themselves; quite the contrary; some quality in their own very harsh lives made them feel at home with the rest of civilisation, not suspicious of it. This may well show the backwardness of the country; for that matter there were the same feelings in Russia for the Soviets to use if they could get at them. They seem able to bring off something like a pastoral feeling in Spain and Russia, but in an English artist, whatever his personal sincerity, it seems dogged by humbug, and has done now for a long time. This may well be a grave fault in the English social system, but it is not one an English artist can avoid by becoming a proletarian artist.

It would be as well then to consider a few books written outside England, which are not definite propaganda and might be called proletarian. One would expect the democratic spirit of America to have produced proletarian literature some time ago, but so far as I know the central theme is always a conflict in the author's mind between democracy and something else. (That there must be some kind of social conflict behind good writing is perhaps true, but this is no argument against communism as a political scheme; 'you needn't *make* trouble'; there will be conflicts in any society. It is only an argument against the communist aesthetic.)

9

William Faulkner writes direct moralistic tragedy or melodrama, and tends to take poor or low characters merely because their lives more than most are grindingly and obviously ruled by Fate; this is supposed to make us feel that the same is true of every one. Most writers on Fate play this trick; it uses a piece of pastoral machinery which is generally dignified into bad metaphysics. Whereas in André Malraux's *La Condition Humaine* (*Storm in Shanghai*) the heroes are communists and are trying to get something done, but they are very frankly out of touch with the proletariat; it is from this that they get their pathos and dignity and the book its freedom from propaganda. The purpose behind a Hemingway character is to carry to the highest degree the methods of direct reporting—his stoical simple man is the type who gets most directly the sensations any one would get from the events. This is a very general method for stories of action and has a touch of pastoral so far as it implies ' the fool sees true.' It is irritating when Hemingway implies that his well-to-do heroes should be praised for being boors, but even that is supported by a backwoods pioneer feeling which seems as much aristocratic as proletarian. Céline's *Voyage au Bout de la Nuit* is a more interesting case, not to be placed quickly either as pastoral or proletarian; it is partly the ' underdog ' theme and partly social criticism. The two main characters have no voice or trust in their society and no sympathy with those who have; it is this, not cowardice or poverty or low class, which the war drives home to them, and from then on they have a straightforward inferiority complex; the theme becomes their struggle with it as private individuals. In the first half of the book the hero is crazy, and seems meant to be, from the idea that everybody is attacking him, and in consequence is as brutal as they are. He becomes conscious of this and ashamed of it when he goes off and leaves the girl in Detroit, so sets to work and becomes a doctor. From then on the underdog theme is carried by his double Robinson, whom he is trying to save, and who finally, in a second refusal of a girl's love, accepts death. The hero respects this but is far from the need to imitate it; it somehow releases him and ends the book. Life may be black and mad in the second half but Bardamu is not, and he gets to the real end of the night as critic and spectator. This change is masked by unity of style and by a humility which will not allow that one can claim to be sane while living as part of such a world, but it is in the second half that we get Bardamu speaking as Céline in criticism of it. What is attacked may perhaps be summed up as the death-wishes generated by the herds of a machine society, and he is not speaking as 'spokesman of the proletariat' or with any sympathy for a communist one. It may be true that under a communist government many fewer people would have this sort of inferiority complex, but that does not make a new sort of literature; and before claiming the substance of the book as proletarian literature you have to separate off the author (in the phrase that Gorki used) as a man ripe for fascism.

The essential trick of the old pastoral, which was felt to imply a beautiful relation between rich and poor, was to make simple people express strong feelings (felt as the most universal subject, something fundamentally true about everybody) in learned and fashionable language (so that you wrote about the best subject in the best way). From seeing the two sorts of people combined like this you thought better of both; the best parts of both were used. The effect was in some degree to combine in the reader or author the merits of the two sorts; he was made to mirror in himself more completely the effective elements of the society he lived in. This was not a process that you could explain in the course of writing pastoral; it was already shown by the clash between style and theme, and to make the clash work in the right way (not become funny) the writer must keep up a firm pretence that he was unconscious of it. Indeed the usual process for putting further meanings into the pastoral situation was to insist that the shepherds were rulers of sheep, and so compare them to politicians or bishops or what not; this piled the heroic convention onto the pastoral one, since the hero was another symbol of his whole society. Such a pretence no doubt makes the characters unreal, but not the feelings expressed or even the situation described; the same pretence is often valuable in real life. I should say that it was over this fence that pastoral came down in England after the Restoration. The arts, even music, came to depend more than before on knowing about foreign culture, and Puritanism, suspicious of the arts, was only not strong among the aristocracy. A feeling gradually got about that any one below the upper middles was making himself ridiculous, being above himself, if he showed any signs of keeping a sense of beauty at all, and this feeling was common to all classes. It takes a general belief as harsh and as unreal as this to make the polite pretence of pastoral seem necessarily absurd. Even so there was a successful school of mock-pastoral for so long as the upper and lower classes were consciously less Puritan than the middle.

When that goes the pastoral tricks of thought take refuge in child-cult.

One strong help for the pastoral convention was the tradition, coming down from the origin of our romantic love-poetry in the troubadours, that its proper tone is one of humility, that the proper moments to dramatise in a love-affair are those when the lover is in despair. (Much theorising might be done in praise of this convention ; some of it comes into Poe's absurd proof that melancholy is the most poetical of the tones. For one thing the mere fact that you don't altogether believe in the poet's expressions of despair makes you feel that he has reserves of strength.) Granted this, the low man has only to shift his humility onto his love affairs to adopt the dignity of a courtly convention.

The convention was, of course, often absurdly artificial ; the praise of simplicity usually went with extreme flattery of a patron (dignified as a symbol of the whole society, through the connection of pastoral with heroic), done so that the author could get some of the patron's luxuries ; it allowed the flattery to be more extreme because it helped both author and patron to keep their self-respect. So it was much parodied, especially to make the poor man worthy but ridiculous, as often in Shakespeare ; nor is this merely snobbish when in its full form. The simple man becomes a clumsy fool who yet has better ' sense ' than his betters and can say things more fundamentally true ; he is ' in contact with nature,' which the complex man needs to be, so that Bottom is not afraid of the fairies ; he is in contact with the mysterious forces of our own nature, so that the clown has the wit of the Unconscious ; he can speak the truth because he has nothing to lose. Also the idea that he is in contact with nature, therefore 'one with the universe' like the Senecan man, brought in a suggestion of stoicism; this made the thing less unreal since the humorous poor man is more obviously stoical than profound. And there may be obscure feelings at work, which I am unable to list, like those about the earth-touching Buddha. Another use of the clown (itself a word for the simple countryman) should be mentioned here; the business of the macabre, where you make a clown out of death. Death in the Holbein Dance of Death, a skeleton still skinny, is often an elegant and charming small figure whose wasp waist gives him a certain mixed-sex quality, and though we are to think otherwise he conceives himself as poking fun; he is seen at his best when piping to an idiot clown and leading him on, presumably to some precipice, treating this great coy figure with so gay and sympathetic an admiration that the picture stays in one's mind chiefly as a love scene. It is a far cry from pastoral, but the clown has such feelings behind him among his sources of strength.

Thus both versions, straight and comic, are based on a double attitude of the artist to the worker, of the complex man to the simple one ('I am in one way better, in another not so good'), and this may well recognise a permanent truth about the aesthetic situation. To produce pure proletarian art the artist must be at one with the worker; this is impossible, not for political reasons, but because the artist never is at one with any public. The grandest attempt at escape from this is provided by Gertrude Stein, who claims to be a direct expression of the Zeitgeist (the present stage of the dialectic process) and therefore to need no other relation to a public of any kind. She has in fact a very definite relation to her public, and I should call her work a version of child-cult, which is a version of pastoral; this does not by any means make it bad. The point is to this extent a merely philosophical one, that I am not concerned to deny any practical claim made for what is called proletarian literature so long as the artist had not been misled by its theory; I only call it a bogus concept. It may be that to produce any good art the artist must be somehow in contact with the worker, it may be that this is what is wrong with the arts in the West, it may be that Russia is soon going to produce a very good art, with all the vigour of a society which is a healthy and unified organism, but I am sure it will not be pure proletarian art and I think it will spoil itself if it tries to be.

It seems clear that the Worker, as used in proletarian propaganda, is a mythical cult-figure of the sort I have tried to describe. This is not peculiar to one party. As I write, the Government has just brought out a poster giving the numbers of men back at work, with a large photograph of a skilled worker using a chisel. He is a stringy but tough, vital but not over-strong, Cockney type, with a great deal of the genuine but odd refinement of the English lower middle class. This is very strong Tory propaganda; one feels it is fair to take him as a type of the English skilled worker, and it cuts out the communist feelings about the worker merely to look at him. To accept the picture is to feel that the skilled worker's interests are bound up with his place in the class system and the success of British foreign policy in finding markets. There is an unfortunate lack of a word here. To call such a picture a ' symbol,' like a sign in mathematics, is to ignore the sources of its power; to call it a 'myth' is to make an offensive suggestion that the author is superior to common feelings. I do not mean to say that such pictures are nonsense because they are myths; the facts of the life of a nation, for instance the way public opinion swings round, are very strange indeed, and probably a half-magical idea is the quickest way to the truth. People who consider that the Worker group of sentiments is misleading in contemporary politics tend to use the word 'romantic' as a missile; unless they merely mean 'false' this is quite off the point; what they ought to do is to produce a rival myth, like the poster. In calling it mythical I mean that complex feelings, involving all kinds of distant matters, are put into it as a symbol, with an implication 'this is the right worker to select and keep in mind as the type,' and that among them is an obscure magical feeling 'while he is like this he is Natural and that will induce Nature to make us prosperous.' The point is not that myths ought not to be used but that their use in proletarian literature is not as simple as it looks.

The realistic sort of pastoral (the sort touched by mock-pastoral) also gives a natural expression for a sense of social injustice. So far as the person described is outside society because too poor for its benefits he is independent, as the artist claims to be, and can be a critic of society; so far as he is forced by this into crime he is the judge of the society that judges him. This is a source of irony both against him and against the society, and if he is a sympathetic criminal he can be made to suggest both Christ as the scapegoat (so invoking Christian charity) and the sacrificial tragic hero, who was normally above society rather than below it, which is a further source of irony. Dostoevsky is always using these ideas; perhaps unhealthily, but as very strong propaganda. But I doubt whether they are allowed in pure proletarian literature; the communists do not approve of them, either as tragic or Christian, both because they glorify the independent man and because they could be used against any society, including a communist one.

I am trying here to deal with the popular, vague but somehow obvious, idea of proletarian literature, which is what is influential; there may be a secret and refined definition which disposes of what I have to say. What seems clear from the varying accounts of the position of authors in Russia is that no one definition is generally accepted. Sympathisers tell you there is an arrangement by which authors are expected to do journalistic jobs, writing up conditions in a distant chain of factories or what not, and in their private writing have only to avoid active sedition; this seems healthy if the government would stick to it but not of much critical interest. Gorki, in his speech to the 1934 All-Union Congress of Soviet Writers, made a wider use of the crucial formula of proletarian literature, ' socialist realism.'

> To invent means to extract from the totality of real existence its basic idea and to incarnate this in an image; thus we obtain realism. But if to the idea extracted from the real is added the desirable, the potential, and the image is supplemented by this, we obtain that romanticism which lies at the basis of myth and is highly useful in that it facilitates the arousing of a revolutionary attitude towards reality, an attitude of practically changing the world.

I hope that this use of the word ' myth ' will show that my use of it is not a distortion. The idea of the wheel

going on revolving, even if you add dialectical materialism by saying that this gives it progress along the ground,
is one that a communist must not push too far—revolu-
tionary proletarian literature, in intention at any rate,
is obviously a product of transition; and the second
sentence might be misunderstood as an appeal for lying
propaganda. But the only real trouble about this as
an account of proletarian literature is that it applies
to any good literature whatever. When communists
say that an author under modern capitalism feels cut
off from most of the life of the country, and would not
under communism, the remark has a great deal of
truth, though he might only exchange a sense of isolation for a sense of the waste of his powers; it is certainly
not so completely true as to make the verse from Gray
pointless to a man living under communism. The way
this sense of isolation has been avoided in the past is
by the conventions of pastoral with which I am concerned. (Even Alice in Wonderland, though her
convention corresponds to a failure in the normal
tradition of pastoral, does indeed stand for something
that produces a feeling of solidarity between classes.)
When they say that a proletarian writer is the ' spokesman and representative of the proletariat ' this is something like a definition; but once everybody is proletarian
he is merely the representative of man; and in any case
a representative is conscious that he is not the same as
what he represents. When Radek in his speech at the
same congress appealed for the help of foreign writers
in the production of a great proletarian literature of
' love to all oppressed, hate toward the exploiting class.
. . . Into this literature we will pour the soul of the
proletariat, its passions and its love . . . ' his rhetoric

PROLETARIAN LITERATURE

is meant to shift from a political idea to a universal one. To say that the only way a present-day writer can produce good work is by devoting himself to political propaganda is of course another thing from defining proletarian literature, and in some cases is true. But it seems fair to say that there is some doubt about the definition.

The poetic statements of human waste and limitation, whose function is to give strength to see life clearly and so to adopt a fuller attitude to it, usually bring in, or leave room for the reader to bring in, the whole set of pastoral ideas. For such crucial literary achievements are likely to attempt to reconcile some conflict between the parts of a society; literature is a social process, and also an attempt to reconcile the conflicts of an individual in whom those of society will be mirrored. (The belief that a man's ideas are wholly the product of his economic setting is of course as fatuous as the belief that they are wholly independent of it.) So 'fundamentally true' goes to 'true about people in all parts of society, even those you wouldn't expect,' and this implies the tone of humility normal to pastoral. 'I now abandon my specialised feelings because I am trying to find better ones, so I must balance myself for the moment by imagining the feelings of the simple person. He may be in a better state than I am by luck, freshness, or divine grace; value is outside any scheme for the measurement of value because that too must be valued.' Various paradoxes may be thrown in here; 'I must imagine his way of feeling because the refined thing must be judged by the fundamental thing, because strength must be learnt in weakness and sociability in isolation, because the best manners are learnt in the simple life' (this last

19

is the point of Spenser's paradox about 'courtly'; the Book of Courtesy takes the reader among Noble Savages). Now all these ideas are very well suited to a socialist society, and have been made to fit in very well with the dogma of the equality of man, but I do not see that they fit in with a rigid proletarian aesthetic. They assume that it is sometimes a good thing to stand apart from your society so far as you can. They assume that some people are more delicate and complex than others, and that if such people can keep this distinction from doing harm it is a good thing, though a small thing by comparison with our common humanity. Once you allow the arts to admit this you will get works of art which imply that the special man ought to be more specially treated, and that is not proletarian literature.

It is for reasons like these that the most valuable works of art so often have a political implication which can be pounced on and called bourgeois. They carry an implication about the society they were written for; the question is whether the same must not be true of any human society, even if it is much better than theirs. My own difficulty about proletarian literature is that when it comes off I find I am taking it as pastoral literature; I read into it, or find that the author has secretly put into it, these more subtle, more far-reaching, and I think more permanent, ideas.

It would be interesting to know how far the ideas of pastoral in this wide sense are universal, and I think that to attempt a rough world-view brings in another point about the communist aesthetic. With the partial exception of *Alice* they are all part of the normal European tradition, but they might seem dependent on that, especially as dependent on Christianity. In my account the ideas about the Sacrificial Hero as Dying God are mixed up in the brew, and these, whose supreme form is Christianity, mainly belong to Europe and the Mediterranean. *The Golden Bough* makes a clear distinction between this hero and the Sincere Man as One with Nature, who is also sacrificial so far as national calamity proves that the emperor is not sincere, but refuses to try to separate them; it seems clear that they are at home respectively in the West and the East. On the other hand interest in the problems of the One and the Many, especially their social aspects, is ancient and obvious in the East, and many of the versions of pastoral come out of that. The idea of everything being included in the humble thing, with mystical respect for poor men, fools, and children, and a contrasting idea of everything being included in the ruling hero, were a main strand of Chinese thought by the third century B.C.; before Buddhism and not limited to Taoism. In China the feeling that everything is everything so nothing is worth doing, natural to this mode of thought, was balanced by the Confucian stress on the exact performance of local duties and ceremonies. One can make a list of European ideas with the same purpose, of making the immediate thing real, all of which stress the individual more or less directly and are denied in the East. God is a person; each separate individual is immortal, with the character he has acquired in this life; so one must continually worry about whether he is free; and he is born in sin so that he must make efforts; and because of this only a God, individual like the rest of us, is worthy to be sacrificed to God. These ideas were knocking about Europe before they were

Christian, and the rejection of Christ may well be a less dangerous element in the communist position than the acceptance of Hegel. Gorki said in the early days of the Soviets that the great danger for Russia is that she may ' go East,' a pregnant remark even if the East itself is inoculated against this sort of philosophy. It may be said that men always go in droves, and that all versions of the claim to individualism are largely bogus; but that gives the reason why the prop of individualist theory is needed. Once you have said that everything is One it is obvious that literature is the same as propaganda; once you have said that no truth can be known beyond the immediate dialectical process of history it is obvious that all contemporary artists must prepare the same fashionplate. It is clear too that the One is limited in space as well as time, and the no less Hegelian Fascists are right in saying that all art is patriotic. And the dialectical process proceeds through conflicts, so we must be sure and have plenty of big wars. Of course to talk like this is to misunderstand the philosophy, but once the philosophy is made a public creed it is sure to be misunderstood in some such way. I do not mean to say that the philosophy is wrong; for that matter pastoral is worked from the same philosophical ideas as proletarian literature—the difference is that it brings in the absolute less prematurely. Nor am I trying to say anything about the politics and economics, only that they do not provide an aesthetic theory.

In the following essays I shall try to show, roughly in historical order, the ways in which the pastoral process of putting the complex into the simple (in itself a great help to the concentration needed for poetry) and the resulting social ideas have been used in English literature.

PROLETARIAN LITERATURE

One cannot separate it from the hero business or from the device of 'pantification' (treating the symbol as everything that it symbolises, which turns out to be everything). The book is very far from adequate to such a theme; taken widely the formula might include all literature, and taken narrowly much of the material is irrelevant. Probably the cases I take are the surprising rather than the normal ones, and once started on an example I follow it without regard to the unity of the book. Certainly it is not a solid piece of sociology; for that matter many of the important social feelings do not find their way into literature. But I should claim that the same trick of thought, taking very different forms, is followed through a historical series.

Double Plots

*Heroic and Pastoral in the Main Plot
And Sub-Plot*

I

THE mode of action of a double plot is the sort of thing critics are liable to neglect; it does not depend on being noticed for its operation, so is neither an easy nor an obviously useful thing to notice. Deciding which sub-plot to put with which main plot must be like deciding what order to put the turns in at a music hall, a form of creative work on which I know of no critical dissertation, but at which one may succeed or fail. As in the music hall, the parts may be by different hands, different in tone and subject matter, hardly connected by plot, and yet the result may be excellent; *The Changeling* is the best example of this I can find. It is an easy-going device, often used simply to fill out a play, and has an obvious effect in the Elizabethans of making you feel the play deals with life as a whole, with any one who comes onto the street the scene so often represents; this may be why criticism has not taken it seriously when it deserved to be. Just because of this carelessness much can be put into it; to those who miss the connections the thing still seems sensible, and queer connections can be insinuated powerfully and unobtrusively; especially if they fit in with ideas the audience already has at the back of its mind. The old quarrel about tragi-comedy, which deals with part of the question, shows that the drama in England has always at its best had a certain looseness of structure; one might almost say that the English drama did not outlive the double plot. The matter is not only of theoretical interest; it seems likely that the double plot needs to be revived and must first be understood.

Probably the earliest form of double plot is the comic interlude, often in prose between serious verse scenes. Even here the relation between the two is neither obvious nor constant; the comic part relieves boredom and the strain of belief in the serious part, but this need not imply criticism of it. Falstaff may carry a half-secret doubt about the value of the kings and their quarrels, but the form derived from the Miracle Plays, and Mac's wife in the Nativity is doing something more peculiar. To hide a stolen sheep in the cradle and call it her new-born child is a very detailed parallel to the Paschal Lamb, hidden in the appearance of a newborn child, open to scandal because without a legal father, and kept among animals in the manger. The Logos enters humanity from above as this sheep does from below, or takes on the animal nature of man which is like a man becoming a sheep, or sustains all nature and its laws so that in one sense it is as truly present in the sheep as the man. The searchers think this a very peculiar child, a ' natural ' sent from the supernatural, and Mac's wife tries to quiet them by a powerful joke on the eating of Christ in the Sacrament :

> If ever I you beguiled
> May I eat this child,
> > That lies in this cradle.

This parody must have had its effect on the many critics who have praised the scene, but I don't remember to have read one of them who mentioned it; I suppose those who were conscious of what was affecting them thought it obvious. The effect is hard to tape down; it seems a sort of test of the belief in the Incarnation strong enough to prove it to be massive and to make the humorous thieves into fundamental symbols of humanity.

Wyndham Lewis's excellent book, for one, points out that the Miracle Play tradition gave a hint of magic to Elizabethan drama ; with nationalism and the disorder of religion the Renaissance Magnificent Man took the place of the patron saint, anyway on the stage; hence the tragic hero was a king on sacrificial as well as Aristotelian grounds; his death was somehow Christlike, somehow on his tribe's account, something like an atonement for his tribe that put it in harmony with God or nature. This seems a less wild notion if one remembers that a sixteenth-century critic would be interested in magical theories about kings; he would not be blankly surprised as at the psychoanalyst on Hamlet. In the obscure suggestions of the two plots one would expect to find this as a typical submerged concept, and in fact their fundamental use was to show the labour of the king or saint in the serious part and in the comic part the people, as ' popular ' as possible, for whom he laboured. This gave a sort of reality to the sentiments about the king or saint (*Marriage à la Mode* is an odd example—they needed giving reality there) ; even here the relation between the two parts is that of symbol and thing symbolised.

This in itself can hardly be kept from irony, and the comic part, once licensed, has an obvious subject for its jokes. Usually it provides a sort of parody or parallel in low life to the serious part; Faustus' servant gets dangerously mixed up with the devils like his master. This gives an impression of dealing with life completely, so that critics sometimes say that *Henry IV* deals with the whole of English life at some date, either

29

Shakespeare's or Henry's; this is palpable nonsense, but what the device wants to make you feel. Also the play can thus anticipate the parody a hearer might have in mind without losing its dignity, which again has a sort of completeness. It is hard to feel that Mac's wife was meant to do this, but she is only the less conscious end of a scale, and perhaps no example occupies only one point of it. A remark by Middleton on clowns seems a comment on this process:

> There's nothing in a play to a clown, if he
> Have but the grace to hit on't; that's the thing indeed:
> The king shows well, but he sets off the king.

The ideas of *foil* to a jewel and *soil* from which a flower grows give the two different views of such a character, and with a long ' s ' the words are almost indistinguishable; it may be significant that the first edition of Tamburlane's Beauty speech reads *soil* for the accepted ' foil,' a variant I have never seen listed, but the line is at some distance from interpreting either word. A clear case of ' foil ' is given by the play of heroic swashbucklers which has a comic cowardly swashbuckler (Parolles), not at all to parody the heroes but to stop you from doing so: ' If you want to laugh at this sort of thing laugh now and get it over.' I believe the Soviet Government in its early days paid two clowns, Bim and Bom, to say as jokes the things everybody else would have been shot for saying.

An account of the double plot, then, is needed for a general view of pastoral because the interaction of the two plots gives a particularly clear setting for, or machine for imposing, the social and metaphysical ideas on which pastoral depends. What is displayed on the tragi-comic stage is a sort of marriage of the myths of heroic and pastoral, a thing felt as fundamental to both and necessary to the health of society. In a later part of this essay I shall take the hypostatised hero alone and try to show that his machinery is already like that of pastoral, and more will have to be said about the connections of heroic and pastoral in the essay on the *Beggar's Opera*, where the two halves of the stock double plot are written simultaneously. It will be clear, I hope, that the comic characters are in a sense figures of pastoral myth so far as they make profound remarks and do things with unexpectedly great effects, but I want now to look at some double plots in action without special attention to their clowns.

Some critics have called Green's plays ' a heap of isolated episodes, with clumsy devices to explain the course of the action '; others have said that his invention of the double plot, as apart from the comic sub-plot, required the wide overriding grasp of detail of a brain trained in the law. But I don't know who has tried to say what the point of the method is; why it is an advantage, in the early *Friar Bacon and Friar Bungay*, that the story of King Edward's love for Margaret, the keeper's daughter, and his magnanimity in letting himself be cut out by the Earl of Lincoln, should be told side by side with the story of Bacon and the Brazen Head; why, if these stories have nothing to do with each other, they should form a unity by being juxtaposed.

One connection is that Margaret and Bacon, like Faustus and Tamburlane, are low-born people who by their own qualities have obtained respect and power; both stories are democratic and individualist. But such powers are dangerous (*Faustus* was a rival meant to outdo *Bacon*); at one point there is a very firm parallel between Margaret and Bacon to make this clear. It has been called a specially shameless piece of episodic writing that Edward should forgive the Earl of Lincoln so early as the third act, thus leaving time, while the earl is ' testing ' her by pretending to break it off, for two country gentlemen to become rivals for her hand and kill each other in a duel. In any case this is the repetition of a situation with new characters to show all its possibilities; also how wise the king has been, and how humble Margaret is still, and how it is a fatal hubris for mere gentry to love this demigoddess, and how they are sure to do so in any pause of the story. But its main use is to compare her to Bacon. While the duel is going on two scholars at Oxford have asked to see their fathers in Bacon's perspective glass; they see them kill each other, so they kill each other too. Bacon cracks his glass and forswears necromancy, and we next see Margaret preparing to turn nun; they are well-meaning, but their powers are fatal. (One may add that she marries the earl, and that Bacon uses his powers at least once more to have his servant carried off by the devil.) This incident had to come late, not till we have learned to respect them both will we find it natural to compare them; it had to be applied to minor lovers of Margaret, or it would spoil the happy ending. So if you start with the two legends and the intention of making this comparison Green's ' episodic ' plot is the only possible one.

On seeing the calamity the friars say :

BUNGAY. O strange stratagem !
    [as if it was intentional].
BACON. See, friar, where the fathers both lie dead.
    Bacon, thy magic doth effect this massacre.

The sense must be ' Not a trick of mine intended to kill the sons; the fathers are really dead. Still I have killed the sons with my magic.' This stress is then on *this* (' not the fathers'). But the rough impression is that Bungay is accustomed to villainy and that Bacon admits he has killed all four. His magic is somehow the same as Margaret's magic, which has also killed all four.

The process is simply that of dramatising a literary metaphor—' the power of beauty is like the power of magic ' ; both are individualist, dangerous, and outside the social order. But it is so strong that it brings out other ideas which were at the back of the metaphor. It lets Margaret's continual insistence that she is humble and only the keeper's daughter make her into a sort of earth-goddess, and Bacon's magic, though not from Black Magic like Faust's, is from an earth-magic he must repent of; his pupil Bungay actually defends the claims of the earth-spirits, in an argument with the foreign magician Vandermast, against Vandermast's more ethereal spirits of the fire. Here at least M. Saurat's theory of the influence of the cabbalists is not fanciful, for they are quoted, and Bungay is making just that claim for the value of matter—

> I tell thee, German, magic haunts the ground

which M. Saurat takes as the essential novelty of the Renaissance. (Matter is not evil and made from nothing but part of God from which God willingly removed his will; one can therefore put more trust in the flesh, the sciences, the natural man and so on.)

The effect on the friars is to make them ' jolly,' connected with low life or the people as a whole. That is why Bacon depends on his servant Miles at the crucial

33

moment of preparing the head; it shows the importance of the common people for this sort of magic, and yet we are to feel that Miles was right (so that he too is the fool who becomes the critic) in letting the head spoil. Also it was not very wicked of Bacon to let the devil carry him off; it is only an earth-devil and it suits him; he rides on its back. And it does not seem an irrelevant piece of flattery when Bacon produces a final prophecy in praise of Elizabeth; it was this Renaissance half-worship of Elizabeth and the success of England under her rule that gave conviction to the whole set of ideas. One need not suppose that Green invented these implications any more than the stories themselves; what I want to point out is that the double plot was an excellent vehicle for them, if only because it could suggest so powerfully without stating anything open to objection.

There are two elements here, both normal to the form; used in the same way, though incomparably more intelligently, in *Troilus and Cressida*. The two parts make a mutual comparison that illuminates both parties (' love and war are alike ') and their large-scale indefinite juxtaposition seems to encourage primitive ways of thought (' Cressida will bring Troy bad luck because she is bad '). This power of suggestion is the strength of the double plot; once you take the two parts to correspond, any character may take on *mana* because he seems to cause what he corresponds to or be Logos of what he symbolises. The political theorising in *Troilus* (chiefly about loyalty whether to a mistress or the state) becomes more interesting if you take it as a conscious development by Shakespeare of the ideas inherent in the double-plot convention.

It is with this machinery that Troilus compares the

sexual with the political standards, and shows both in disruption. The breaking of Cressida's vow is symbolical of, the breaking of Helen's vow is cause of, what the play shows (chiefly by the combat between Hector and his first cousin Ajax) to be a civil war; Shakespeare's horror of this theme, which history so soon justified, may in part explain the grimness of his treatment (all large towns in the plays are conceived as London); and it is because of this that the disloyal elements in the Greek camp, Ajax and Achilles, compared to Cressida, disloyal because of Briseis, seem only to carry further the social disruption caused by Helen. (Cressida is called Briseida in the first version of her story.) From his name, as its rising hope, and because both are victims of women, Troilus becomes a symbol of Troy; as he is loyal to Cressida, so Troy is not broken up by disloyalties like the Greek camp. Yet its isolation is the product of a disloyalty, against hospitality in the theft of Helen, and this is somehow like the original mistake in his choice of Cressida; there is a pathetic irony and fitness in his support of Paris, cuckold supporting cuckold-maker, in the council scene.

If you say he was no husband, that he should deserve this title, then the only reason he wasn't was to make him more like Paris, the private affair more like the publicly important one. But the point is as obscure here as in Chaucer. Critics talk about the 'troubadour convention,' but in its normal form the woman adored was already married. Certainly the play is not interested in marriage so much as in the prior idea of loyalty, but it was to the interest of these lovers to marry so as to have a claim against being separated. Dryden's quarrel

35

scene in which Troilus heroically gives her up for the sake of Troy makes a much more coherent situation, but Shakespeare wanted to make them wild flowers, almost ignorant of the storm that destroyed them, and only as it were naturally parallel to it. Morton Luce said that III. ii. was meant as a regular betrothal—regular enough for these heathens, anyway—and if so 'I take to-day a wife' (II. ii. 61) may be meant as simple statement rather than dramatic irony. Probably Shakespeare saw no reason to decide which.

One effect of this is that the whole weight of Shakespeare's 'everpresent fear of the breaking of the floodgates,' the whole Pelion of theory ranged through the speeches of Ulysses, is piled by mere juxtaposition onto Cressida; her case has to be taken as seriously as the whole war because it involves the same sanctions and occupies an equal position in the play. We are made to feel she ought to have known this, ought to have been hushed into virtue by comparing herself with the whole war, whereas in fact one of its minor results was that she was tempted to be unfaithful; and this acts as a dramatic irony; she does not see herself as we are made to do. And one may apply to her the speeches of Ulysses to the disaffected heroes, Achilles and Ajax; like them, she is cut off from her tribe and her happiness as much by folly as disloyalty, and more than either by 'the bitter disposition of the time'; from either side the ironies between them show both their helplessness and the disasters that it caused.

Critics have said that though noble elements exist in *Troilus* it is not organised round them, they seem swamped and isolated; a rather one-eyed complaint; whether or no this is a moral fault it is the point and

36

theory of the play. Its central and most moving expression is Ulysses'

> let not virtue seek
> Remuneration for the thing it was

said sincerely enough to Achilles, to make him fight though he is undervalued; he becomes a sympathetic figure in his talk about this; fight he does, and kills Hector so unfairly as to excite horror. (His talk has been called out of character; it does not aim at character but at manipulation of our sympathies.) We have seen Hector spare many men under much lesser disadvantages, but he must not expect generosity because he is generous; Troilus has told him that his generosity is weakness, and Achilles himself that it is a form of vanity. This same irony hangs over Troilus and his love affairs; it is the two great speeches about time, this to Achilles and that of Troilus' farewell to Cressida, which force us to compare their situations though in themselves they are so unlike. He has objected in the council scene that value *does* dwell in ' particular will ' (the phrase echoes through the play in perpetual puzzles of language); not in the object loved but in the force that takes it for a symbol; in the glory of possessing Helen, not in Helen herself; in what his love for Cressida *was*, therefore, not in a remuneration from his fidelity, and his disillusion shows not that his statement was wrong but that he must take its consequences. People complain that the play is ' bitter '; it is not to be praised for bitterness but for a far-reaching and exhausting generosity, which is piled up onto the pathos of Cressida.

So that in a way, though he puts so much weight on her faults, Shakespeare despises her less than his comtators have; except indeed in a scene that drives home the parallel. After all her outbursts and protestations, after that last pathetic question turned back on him out of curiosity, ' my lord, will you be true ? ' ('It is hard to believe even that people like you are; I know I shall not be, but perhaps you will ') Cressida is led from Troy, and we hear the blast of a Greek trumpet marking truce; the truce in which she is exchanged, and in which Hector by chivalric combat defends the glory of the Trojan ladies. The moment before she arrives at the Greek camp the same blast again is now seen, a hooting satire, being blown on its trumpet, and immediately she prances round kissing everybody; she must have covered the ground in two minutes; it forces us with something of the brutality of a pun to see with what extreme and as if mechanical buoyancy she has changed. The incident is nonsense, surely, as character-study; it is not the Cressida who was embarrassed by her own tongue in the love scenes who could achieve this change of front without a brief period of self-torture. Shakespeare indeed is always willing to take the dramatic assumptions wholeheartedly; all his people change their minds on the stage and use heightened language where the rest of us use lapse of time; but the reason we have this fearfully striking joke about it here is that Cressida is somehow parallel to public affairs and this is her one public occasion.

People sometimes complain about *Troilus* that it contains not like so many of Shakespeare's plays one, but two unpleasant characters, as who should say ' I expect a dog to have some fleas, but these are too many.' At least there is only one flea to each story, one mocker each to love and heroism; I do not know whether this reflection is any comfort to the complainers. But

when Mr. Robertson, for instance, says that the remarks
of Thersites cannot possibly be what the Bard wrote
or wanted (so that they must be by Chapman—as far
as I remember) one must look for a definite answer;
I think that a final answer, obtained by pursuing rather
queer points of language, is that the verbal ironies in
the comic character's low jokes carry on the thought of
both plots of the play. It is one of the strange things,
chiefly about Shakespeare, but in some degree about
most Elizabethans, that this is not irrelevant; I believe
myself what the notes say about the mad talk of Ophelia,
that it had most elaborate connections with the story,
though I have never heard a modern actress make it
seem anything but raving. I propose to look at a pun
on *general*, used seven times in this play and seldom
elsewhere, for which the superb and well-punctuated
first words of Thersites act as a sort of official explanation; and if you call this mere verbal fidgets, I reply
that one source of the unity of a Shakespeare play,
however brusque its handling of character, is this co-
herence of its subdued puns.

> AJAX. Thersites.
> THERSITES. Agamemnon, how if he had Biles (ful) all ouer
> generally.
> AJAX. Thersites.
> THERSITES. And those Byles did run, say so; did not the
> General run, were not that a botchy core?
> AJAX. Dog.
> THERSITES. Then would come some matter from him; I see
> none now.

The irony of the word is that though it connects the
hero to the people it implies a failure of his rule; a
general commands an orderly force such as the people
ought to be, but the general is a mob. The core of the

state here is botchy and dissolving into the primitive matter of chaos, and the comparison to syphilis is an appeal from the plot about heroism to the plot about love. When Thersites next uses the word its irony has turned against him. (He is railing at the pride of Ajax when chosen to fight Hector.)

> I said, good-morrow Ajax; and he replyes, thankes Aga-memnon. What think you of this man, that takes me for the Generall? He's grown a very landfish, languageless, a monster.

There is too much rather than too little in his language. Thersites, as the barking dog, the critic, is the general to whom excellence is caviare; Ajax is the monster, 'not presented in all love's pageant,' which takes one general for the other. And the real monster that gibbers behind that lovely phrase of Troilus is Pandarus's bone-ache.

This same pun is put to solemn uses of political theorising.

> The specialty of rule hath been neglected
> And look, how many Grecian tents do stand
> Hollow upon the plain, so many hollow factions.
> While that the general is not like the hive
> To whom the foragers shall all repair,
> What honey is expected? Degree being vizarded,
> The unworthiest shows as fairly in the mask.

Troilus' last words seem to look back to this:

> You vile abominable tents
> That proudly pight upon our Phrygian plains,
> Let Titan rise as early as he dare,
> I'll through and through you.

It is no use stabbing them; they are hollow like ghosts. Everything is dissolving and the sun itself rises as a titan against heaven.

The general is given the personal *whom*, but the state is being personified; Ulysses is speaking to a general, but it is the general good which is like a hive. Shakespeare indeed thought that the hive had a king, but not that he had rational means of control; the hive is a symbol both of absolute regal power and of a mysteriously self-regulating social order. The general seems opposed to, but may repeat, the *specialty of rule* (so too the opposite key phrase *particular will*); and there is the same doubt in the pun on *mask*. For *degree* may mean 'persons of quality' or 'the idea of social hierarchy' (the rulers or the whole state); the *mask* may be what covers the face of the courtier, or the symbolic dance of ordered function (or the dance of abandonment) in which the whole of society is engaged. Much of the language of *Troilus*, I think, is a failure; it makes puzzles which even if they can be unravelled cannot be felt as poetry; but even so, what they are trying for is a pun of this sort applying both to the hero and the tribe.

The word which has acquired all this energy (other uses are in I. iii. 321, 341; V. vi. 4) is brought out again for the central joke against Cressida. For a second time we hear the one blast of the trumpet that calls a false truce and a sham fight, and she flounces into the Greek camp:

> AGAMEMNON. Most dearly [expensively?] welcome to the Greeks, dear lady.
> NESTOR. Our general doth salute you with a kiss.
> ULYSSES [who made the last speech about general]. Yet is the kindness but particular;
> Twere better she were kissed in general.

So they all do. It is one of the crucial points of contact between the two themes of the play.

Nor is it only the puns and the double plot which make this comparison between a person and the state, between a personal situation and a political one.

> There is a mystery, with whom relation
> Durst never meddle, in the soul of state
> Which hath an operation more divine
> Than tongue or pen may give expressure to.

Phrases forged for Mr. W. H. (the play has many reminiscences of the Sonnets) are here given to the Greek army. It may be only to frighten Achilles that Ulysses so firmly makes a god of the state here, but the play is full of gods who are found out. Hector tells Troilus

> Tis mad idolatry
> To make the service greater than the god

but he dies in its service, whether it was Helen or glory, and Troilus himself makes his disillusion a political (as well as a cosmical) matter.

> If there be rule in unity itself
> This is not she . . .
> Bifold authority, where reason can revolt
> Without perdition, and loss assume all reason
> Without revolt . . .
> The Bonds of heaven are slipped, dissolved, and loosed.

(It is the answer to his jibe at Helenus; ' you fur your gloves with reason, brother priest '). We are forced here to connect the two plots, and at once there is the universal break-up of the last scenes; only the Colossus Pandarus is left standing, a thundercloud over the wreckage of the camps, to rain down his bone-ache in answer to the prayers of Thersites.

Such an identification of one person with the whole moral, social, and at last physical order, was the standing device of the metaphysicals; it fits in very easily with the 'tragic king—comic people' convention, and I think that is what allowed it to be put to so strange and so tragic a use here.

1 *Hen. IV* is a plain case of 'tragic king-comic people'; this made a solid basis on which to plant other ideas. But what is obvious about it on the stage is true of the ideas let loose by the double plot; the parts tend to separate. There are three worlds each with its own hero; rebel camp, tavern, and court; chivalric idealism, natural gusto, the cautious politician. The force and irony of the thing depends on making us sympathise with all three sides so that we are baffled when they meet; this makes an unmanageable play, and I think is only possible because the prince belongs to all three parties. Obviously he belongs both to Falstaff's and the King's— he is very like his father; the same arguments, supported by the same metaphors, make the one pretend friendship with Falstaff, the other adopt a dignified seclusion. But when he meets Hotspur the two seem alike, and probably Ernest Jones would call their scenes a 'decomposition' of one person; Shakespeare falsified history to make the two splendid creatures the same age and set them killing each other. The prince is the go-between who can talk their own language to each; ''a would have clipped bread well'; he is absorbed into the world of Hotspur as parasitically as into that of Falstaff, and as finally destroys his host there.

Something very curious is going on when Falstaff and Hotspur meet. The great scene in which their ideals are opposed to one another shows Douglas, in an anticipation of Macbeth irrelevantly stirring to the imagination, searching the battlefield for Henry, and meeting (it is the chronicle series in little) innumerable simulacra, a non-personal budding of kings.

> my name is Douglas,
> And I do haunt thee in the battle thus
> Because some tell me that thou art a king
> 　　　[*the* king, suggest commentators, intelligently].

> Why didst thou tell me that thou wert a king?
> HOTSPUR. The king hath many marching in his coats.
> DOUGLAS. Now, by my sword, I will kill all his coats,
> I'll murder all his wardrobe, piece by piece,
> Until I meet the king.

> Another king.　They grow like Hydra's heads;
> I am the Douglas, fatal to all those
> That wear those colours on them; what art thou
> That counterfeitest the person of a king.

Among these falling and phantom kings the clown Falstaff takes his tumble; the stage directions insist that he is 'killed' by Douglas at the same moment as the prince kills Hotspur. Like inseparable twins the hero's two chief rivals fall together; Harry has both parts in his wardrobe. The reigning house are usurpers, the clothes of kings only (nobody doubts that is what Douglas meant by the last line quoted); and that is why the world is crawling with false authorities like Falstaff.

This play is as full as *Troilus* (where the double plot gives more reason for it) of that curious use of the language of love about fighting, pointed out by Wyndham Lewis, which one cannot call a peculiar perversion of Shakespeare's now that it has been accepted by so many generations as a superb expression of the poetry of war. Marlowe does not strike this note, though both more pugnacious and more homosexual, and though he doesn't Shakespeare usually gives it the Marlowan line.

44

Perhaps the simplicity of that style, which always seems
so very sure of the grandeur of whatever it is mentioning,
had always seemed to Shakespeare somehow touching and
ill-considered.   (By the way, supposing this is true, and
supposing *e.g.* Mr. Robertson's tests for authorship were
genuinely ' scientific,' they would the more certainly
deceive him.)

> Come, let me taste my horse
> Which is to bear me like a thunderbolt
> Against the bosom of the Prince of Wales.
>
> Cousin, I think thou art enamoured
> Of his follies
> yet once ere night
> I will embrace him with a soldier's arm
> That he shall shrink under my courtesy.
>
> Sound all the lofty instruments of war
> And by that music let us all embrace.

Falstaff accepts this connection with the same twist as
Thersites; we see him wandering about the battlefield,
cheering on, with obscene approval, the groups of fighters.
The main effect is to take the dignity out of the rebels;
'war is only another lust; Hotspur is as wicked as Falstaff.'

> FAL. Well said Hal, to it Hal.   Nay you shall finde no Boyes
> play heere, I can tell you.
>   (Enter Douglas, he fights with Falstaffe, who falls down as
>   if he were dead.   The Prince killeth Percie.)

Hotspur dies after being allowed a few grand lines.   The
prince's remarks about the two rival heroes stretched
before him are then arranged to apply to both, by a
series of puns applying both to fatness and greatness.

> When that this body did contain a spirit
> A Kingdome for it was too small a bound,
> this earth that bears thee dead
> Bears not alive so stout a gentleman.

45

We are forced to feel seriously here about lines that this hideously clever author writes frankly as a parody; the joke turns back from Falstaff against Hotspur. For Falstaff has already made this joke his own.

> FAL. Hal, if thou see me down in the battle, and bestride me, so; 'tis a point of friendship.
> PRINCE. None but a Colossus can do thee that friendship. Say thy prayers, and farewell.

Falstaff hands the prince the joke readymade; what he means is that he is too great for the prince not to betray him. Indeed the prince implies that he is a traitor like Hotspur (in the joke about his ' deer ' being disembowelled) as he leaves the bodies together.

Falstaff then jumps up and proceeds to pluck bright honour from the pale-faced moon; wounds the dead Hotspur euphemistically in the ' thigh ' (again the punishment of a traitor) and claims the reward for having killed him. The words of the prince to his brother, as he comes back, again apply to John Falstaff as well as another hero.

> Come, brother John, full bravely hast thou fleshed
> Thy maiden sword.

Hotspur is the most attractive of Shakespeare's soldiers; no man anything like him in the tragedies has such a death-scene. The double-plot method is carrying a fearful strain here.

In Dryden's *Marriage à la Mode* the two plots are no less sharply different, and on the face of it there is much less ' criticism of life,' much less of the strength that could unite them. Heroic Tragedy and the Comedy of Manners had been worked out; each needed to be judged by its proper rules; it seems odd that they didn't destroy each other. Indeed Cibber used to make 'regular' comedies, when this sense of convention had become a real tyranny, by jamming together two Restoration sub-plots. Dryden apologised for using the two together in the preface to his *Troilus*; it was the audience, not the theorists, that had the sense to demand it.

The clash makes both conventions less unreal; Saintsbury made the essential point, that the heroic part shows the comic heroes are not mere 'carpet knights.' All this Restoration insolence presumed courage, and was easier when it could be shown casually. Yet it has a more searching effect, almost like parody, by making us see they are unreal; the heroic characters' belief that they are of more than human breed has a certain infantile petulance, as when Palmyra prefers to die than to disagree with a father she has just met, the comic characters' experimental wish to satisfy all parties comfortably has a certain pimpish complacence, not least when they decide to keep the virtue they despise. (The play connects the one frame of mind with incest, the other with sodomy —the comic women dress up as boys, the princely lovers seem always to have thought they were brother and sister.) The extraordinary use of the word *die* is a crucial point. The bawdy sense is officially insisted on by that excellent song, 'Now die, my Alexis, and I will die too,' which is placed not among the comic people but in mockery of a jealous heroic person, one of those always ready to die for a point of honour. Dryden had no feeling that the parody in the word was a danger to his heroics, which are coarse or solid enough to use it.

> Oh, there's a joy to melt in her embrace,
> Dissolve in pleasure,
> And make the gods curse immortality
> That so they could not die.

47

Melantha's slang use of it is at bottom insolent; ' of course I don't really feel these sentiments, I pretend them because I am refined. An absurd enough exaggeration may make this point clear even to you.' Clashes are arranged between this and the heroic invocation of death, which is also an exaggeration to fix a sentiment.

> MEL. . . . how he looks, madam! now he's no prince, he is the strangest figure of a man.
> PALM. Away, impertinent! my dear Leonidas.
> LEO. My dear Palmyra.
> PALM. Death shall never part us; my destiny is yours.
> (He is led away to execution.)
> MEL. Impertinent! Oh I am the most unfortunate person this day breathing. . . . Let me die, but I'll follow her to my death, till I make my peace.

Peace it would be. Leonidas himself uses her phrase.

> Keep me from saying that, which misbecomes a son,
> But let me die, before I see this done.

And so far from making the heroic use of it ridiculous this gives a certain pathetic beauty to its use by Melantha.

> Stay, let me read my catalogue—suite, figure, chagrin,
> naivete, and let me die, for the parenthesis of all.

If you count in the bawdy sense it is a fairly complete catalogue of the sentiments of both worlds of the play.

Swinburne said of *The Changeling* that ' the underplot from which it most absurdly and unluckily derives its title is very stupid, rather coarse, and almost vulgar,' after which it is no use saying, as he does, that it is Middleton and Rowley's greatest play, ' a work which should suffice to make either name immortal '; the thing might have good passages but would be a bad play. And however disagreeable the comic part may be it is of no use to ignore it; it is woven into the tragic part very thoroughly. Not that this interferes with the accepted view that the comic part is by Rowley and most of the tragic part by Middleton; the sort of unity required depends on the order of the scenes, which they would presumably draw up together, and on ironies which they could work out separately.

The chief reason why modern critics have passed over the comic part is that it forces one to take the unembarrassed Elizabethan view of lunatics, and though still alive in the villages this seems mere brutality to the cultivated. They were hearty jokes, to be treated like animals, and yet were possessed by, or actually were, fairies or evil spirits; they had some positive extrahuman quality; they might say things profoundly true. No doubt it was crude to keep a lunatic as a pet, but we may call Shakespeare and Velasquez in evidence that the interest was not as trivial as it was brutal; and though no other Elizabethan could write the part of the madmancritic as Shakespeare could, so that their lunatics are less pleasant than his, this was chiefly for lack of his surrealist literary technique; they could assume the same attitude to lunatics in the audience as he could. People nowadays can swallow the idea in terms of painting or metaphor but to feel it at first hand about a realistic stage lunatic is too much. Certainly if the chorus of imbeciles here was merely convenient or merely funny the effect would be disgusting; but the madhouse dominates every scene; every irony refers back to it; that is why the play is so much nearer Webster than either of its parts.

Though their tones are different the two plots are very alike; in both the heroine has been married for social convenience to a man she does not love, so that there is a case for her if she cuckolds him. In the comic story she gets enough fun out of her lovers to keep up her spirits without being unfaithful to him even in detail; no doubt this is coarse and flat enough, but the contrast is not pointless. Beside the tragic characters she is sane; living among madmen she sees the need to be. This in itself compares the madmen to the tragic sinners, and a close parallel is used to drive it home. The idea of the changeling, a child stolen into the fairies' world, a fairy child replaced for it, makes you feel that the shock of seeing into a mad mind is dangerous; it may snatch you to itself. This shock is in all the discoveries of the play. When Antonio, disguised as a lunatic, makes love to Isabella, she breaks after three lines of his rhetoric into hearty laughter: ' you're a fine fool indeed . . . a parlous fool '; he is a changeling the other way round, she finds, but that is the same thing; he may snatch her into his world. It is in the next scene, so that we are forced to compare them, that we have the discovery the critics have praised so justly in isolation :

> Why tis impossible thou canst be so wicked
> Or shelter such a cunning cruelty
> To make his death the murderer of my honour.

The real changeling from which the play ' derives its title ' is De Flores.

One need not look at all the jokes about the jealous madhouse keeper; they simply repeat that love is a madness. There is a more striking parallel between De Flores and the subordinate keeper Lollio, who has some claim to be counted among the fools. He demands ' his share ' from Isabella as a price for keeping his mouth shut about Antonio, just as De Flores does from Beatrice. This is not irony but preparation ('device prior to irony'); coming in the scene after De Flores commits the murder and before he demands his reward it acts

as a proof of Isabella's wisdom and a hint of the future
of Beatrice. Isabella threatens to make Antonio cut
Lollio's throat, which does not impress him; when the
tragic scene they foreshadow is over we find them smack-
ing the threats at each other as casually as ever. I don't
say that this is delicate, but it is a relief; Isabella is a
very impressive creature; and the assumption in the
tragic part that Alsemero will take his maid's virginity
without discovering she is not his wife is more really
brutal than anything in the asylum scenes.

The two stories get their connection of plot from the
two lovers of Isabella, who leave Beatrice's court to be
disguised as madmen and are brought back with other
madmen to amuse it in the masque at her wedding.
This was not merely a fine show on the stage but the
chief source of the ideas of the play. The antimasque
at a great wedding, considered as subhuman, stood for
the insanity of disorder to show marriage as necessary,
considered as the mob, ritually mocked the couple (for
being or for not being faithful, innocent, etc.), both to
appease those who might otherwise mock and to show
that the marriage was too strong to be hurt by mockery.
We have been shown the chief thing the madmen of
the play stand for, when Isabella seemed likely to take
Antonio seriously.

> (Cries of madmen are heard without, like those of birds
> and beasts.)
> LOLLIO. Cuckoo, cuckoo.
> ANTONIO. What are these?
> ISABELLA. Of fear enough to part us.

Fear parted Beatrice from Alsemero, the husband won
falsely; the madmen brought in to be mocked form,
for her as for Isabella, an appalling chorus of mockers,

and assimilate her to themselves. The richness of the thought here does not come from isolated thinking but from a still hearty custom; to an audience which took the feelings about a marriage masque and a changeling for granted the ideas would arise directly from the two plots.

So the effect of the vulgar asylum scenes is to surround the characters with a herd of lunatics, howling outside in the night, one step into whose company is irretrievable; looking back to the stock form, this herd is the 'people' of which the tragic characters are 'heroes.' Beatrice too becomes a changeling;

> I that am of your blood was taken from you

she tells her father. Morally a child such as the fairies can steal, and fearing De Flores as a goblin, she puts him to a practical use to escape him; he could then steal her; she must realise his way of feeling and be dragged into his world. It is the untruth of the appeal that makes it so terrible, and the hint of the changeling idea given by the other plot that makes us accept it. As a finale this connection is at last made obvious; the venomous courage of De Flores is united to the howling of the madmen.

> BEA. Alsemero, I'm a stranger to your bed.
>   Your bed was cozened on the nuptial night,
>   For which your false bride died.
> ALS. Diaphanta?
> DE F. Yes, and the while I coupled with your mate
>   At barley-break; now we are left in hell.
> ALS. We are all there, it circumscribes us here.

We have heard about barley-break before. 'Catch there, catch the last couple in hell' scream the lunatics in the darkness at the back of the stage, when Antonio discloses his plot to Isabella; the two parts are united, and they are all there together.

II

I shall add here some remarks about irony and dramatic ambiguity, arising out of the double plots, and only connected with pastoral so far as they describe a process of putting the complex into the simple. If the foregoing account of the double plots is at all true the process seems to leave room for critical theorising.

There are two elements in the type of joke made by Bim and Bom or Parolles. In part you treat the reader as an object of psychology and satisfy two of his impulses; in part you make him feel, as a rational being, that he can rely on your judgment because you know both sides of the case. But this is not in itself irony; you do not appeal to *his* judgment and he need not realise what you are doing. There is a good crude example in *The Atheist's Tragedy*. Castabella has been forced to marry the son of D'Amville, who has sent her lover Charlemont away; the son is dying, and too weak to consummate; she speaks of this as her only comfort in affliction. Levidulcia, in the next words of the play, tries to seduce Sebastian, and when he leaves her walks off with the servant Fresco, with the reflection

> Lust is a spirit, which whosoe'er doth raise
> The first man to encounter boldly, lays.

If you had been thinking this before, and feeling that Castabella's chastity was a little extravagant and heroical, then the contrast would show that the author knew it already; it is not that he is ignorant of human nature, but that Castabella really was very chaste. And again it is in part a less rational matter of satisfying impulses; after you have made an imaginative response of one kind to a situation you satisfy more of what is included in your own nature, you are more completely interested in the play, if the chief other response possible is called out too. The two may seem inextricable; at its crudest the device has something of the repose of wisdom as well as the ease of humour. But clearly Mac's Wife's parody was more ' psychological ' than rational.

Also the device sets your judgment free because you need not identify yourself firmly with any one of the characters (the drama of personality is liable to boil down to this); a situation is repeated for quite different characters, and this puts the main interest in the situation not the characters. Thus the effect of having two old men with ungrateful children, of different sorts, is to make us generalise the theme of Lear and feel that whole classes of children have become unfaithful, all nature is breaking up, as in the storm. The situation is made something valuable in itself, perhaps for reasons hardly realised; it can work on you like a myth.

One would expect this to come naturally to the Elizabethans because their taste must partly have been formed on those huge romances which run on as great tapestries of incident without changing or even much stressing character, and are echoed in the *Arcadia* and *Faery Queen*; any one incident may be interesting, but the interest of their connection must depend on a sort of play of judgment between varieties of the same situation. Thus there is a lady in the *Arcadia*, unnamed, who induces the king her husband to suspect of treason the prince her stepson; a magnificent paragraph explains all the devices by which this was achieved. Twenty folio pages later, after some one has told another story, the knights come to the castle of a queen called Andromana, who tries to

seduce them and finally allows them to joust for the
pleasure of watching, by which means they escape. It
is with pleasure and some interest that one finds, on
considering who her relations are, that this is the same
lady, but it is quite unimportant; in both parts she is
only developed enough to fill the situation. Bianca in
Women Beware Women is treated very like this, only
more surprisingly; she is first the poor man's modest
wife, then the Duke's grandiose and ruthless mistress;
the idea of ' development ' is irrelevant to her. Nor is
this crude or even unlifelike; it is the tragic idea of the
play. She had chosen love in a cottage and could stick
to it, but once seduced by the Duke she was sure to
become a different person; what is ' developed ' is a
side of her that she had suppressed till then altogether.
The system of ' construction by scenes ' which allows
of so sharp an effect clearly makes the scenes, the incidents,
stand out as objects in themselves, to be compared even
when they are not connected.

The Levidulcia example, because absurdly simple,
may be taken another way; the two responses here are
so sharply opposed that a representation of one involves
a sort of negative notion of the other. The more
interesting situations arise when the two sets of people
in the same situation act differently rather than in two
ways already fixed as opposites; here after all the contrast
is mainly designed to make Levidulcia absurdly wicked
and cynical, one of the Atheists that cause the Tragedy.
A low member of the audience, however, might give
an ironical cheer, meaning ' she is the other half of the
truth.' I should call this version the ' device prior to
irony,' since it does not imply a judgment; it is clearly
at the back of an ironical joke, and when alone carries

something of the richness of a joke though not its surprise. This notion seems important for dealing with double plots, where there is a great deal of dramatic irony which need hardly be noticed and has no sharp ' point '; it gets a strong effect merely by making you feel there is ' a great deal *in* ' the situation. To understand this one needs a wider notion of irony, which I shall now pursue for a time off stage.

An irony has no point unless it is true, in some degree, in both senses; for it is imagined as part of an argument; what is said is made absurd, but it is what the opponent might say. There may be an obscure connection here with the reason why critics who agree about the degree of merit of the *Jew of Malta* can disagree about whether or not it is a joke, why so much of Handel can become funny without ceasing to be beautiful. It is not the joke that is fundamental but the conflict, and there is something like a conflict in the maintenance of a satisfying order.

> Would you keep your pearls from tramplers,
> Weigh the license, weigh the banns;
> Mark my song upon your samplers,
> Wear it on your knots and fans.

It is very hard to know what Smart himself felt about this excellent verse. There must be some sort of joke in the idea of the young lady flaunting a fan with ' weigh the banns ' on it, and striking terror through the ballroom, but the joke may be against *banns* or *fans*. (The advice was not too fantastic; the *Beggar's Opera* songs were put on fans.) The song is about a conflict between delight in the courageous trivialities of pleasure and terror of the forces a triviality may let loose; there is too little doubt of its force for a doubt about its ' sincerity.' Either a conscious overstatement was meant to add to the courage, and so the gaiety, of the pleasure, or the underlying terror of Smart's melancholia became too strong for the gaiety of the form; these are two sides of the same thing, and yet whichever you take there is an irony against the other. Any mutual comparison between people who would judge differently has a latent irony of this sort, if only because if it is the material from which either irony could be made.

To do this on the stage might be regarded as combining the normal halves of the double plot into one. The quality Mr. Eliot described in Marlowe and Jonson seems to depend on it; Restoration heroic gives more obvious if more puzzling examples. The reason why the plays are satisfying though so unreal is that they are so close to their parodies; the mood of parody is hardly under the surface, only as it were officially ignored. Morat will not allow Nourmahal to kill Aurungzebe:

> NOURM. What am I, that you dare to bind my hand?
> So low, I've not a murder at command!

How bitter, how belittling, how destructive of the heroic attitude, this line might be in Pope; and yet the same feeling here somehow makes the reality of its dignity. The sentiment and the 'pseudo-parody to disarm criticism,' usually separated into the two plots, are combined in one.

Here the effect is, I suppose, known to be a clash, felt to be odd, by the author, but the same thing may be done without any suggestion of irony. Swinburne's *Before a Crucifix* gets all its beauty of metaphor from the Christian ideas it sets out to destroy, and its rhetoric is no less clear and strong when you have noticed the fact. The whole point of Housman's *Last Poems*, xxvii., is to deny the Pathetic Fallacy, to say that man is alone and has no sympathy from Nature; its method is to assume the Pathetic Fallacy as a matter of course.

> The diamond tears adorning
> Thy low mound on the lea,
> These are the tears of morning,
> That weeps, but not for thee.

It may weep for pains reassuringly similar to those of humanity, whether consciously or not, or actually for those of man though not of one individual. That the dew might not be tears at all the poetry cannot imagine, and this clash conveys with great pathos and force a sense that the position of man in the world is extraordinary, hard even to conceive. Dr. Richards in *Science and Poetry* said that this trick was played in order to hide facts the poet pretended to accept, and no doubt it often is, but I can see no weakness in its use here. That excellent story in Hugh Kingsmill's *Frank Harris* about the meeting with Professor Housman shows how misleading his irony can be, and how excellent the poetry remains after you have been misled; it seems normal to this sort of ' perfect ' verse that, because so much has been polished away from the original feeling, it will satisfy a great variety of feelings, and because of its perfection of ' form ' will attract them.

The ironies I have quoted are clearly very different from that of *Jonathan Wild*, which appeals fiercely and singly to the readers' judgment, but I think they are only near the other end of a scale; and a scale on which no irony occupies only one point. It is a commonplace that irony is a dangerous weapon because two-edged, so that Defoe was arrested by his own party, and that there are usually partial ways of enjoying an irony, so that Gulliver makes a book for children. I shall take a comfortable example where one can see this at work.

> Fish say, they have their stream or pond,
> But is there anything beyond?
> This life cannot be all, they swear,
> For how unpleasant, if it were . . .
> Oh never fly conceals a hook,
> Fish say, in the eternal brook;
> But more than mundane weeds are there,
> And mud, celestially fair;
> Fat caterpillars drift around,
> And Paradisal grubs are found;
> Unfading moths, immortal flies,
> And the worm that never dies.

I take it many people like this playful thing by Rupert Brooke as making fish seem vain (touchingly absurd) but otherwise just like people (to try to imagine them as fish makes the universe seem inhuman, indifferent to people); they feel good from sympathising with fish, and agreeably superior to them because we are right about heaven and fish wrong. ('Anyway it is not true that fish talk like this, so the poem is not serious, and why should one read cynicism where there is so much tenderness?') A later stage would recognise the scepticism about human knowledge but take it as an essentially 'poetical' mood, Poe's 'tone of melancholy'; a false pretence of humility, like pastoral, designed only to give strength. This too does not find it a shock to theology; indeed finds in its readiness to conceive doubt something of the ease of certainty. I should say that both these pleasant interpretations were active in the author's mind and a source of the courage of the poem's gaiety; the tone of banter seems even to imply some sense of teasing his audience with the possible interpretations, or laughing at them for accepting the pleasant ones, like the fish. Not that the poem is unusually subtle; this sort of analysis would apply to quite crude work.

It is the same machinery, in the fearful case of Swift, that betrays not consciousness of the audience but a doubt of which he may himself have been unconscious. 'Everything spiritual and valuable has a gross and revolting parody, very similar to it, with the same name. Only unremitting judgment can distinguish between them'; he set out to simplify the work of judgment by giving a complete set of obscene puns for it. The conscious aim was the defence of the Established Church against the reformers' Inner Light; only the psycho-analyst can wholly applaud the result. Mixed with his statement, part of what he satirised by pretending (too convincingly) to believe, the source of his horror, was 'everything spiritual is really material; Hobbes and the scientists have proved this; all religion is really a perversion of sexuality.'

The language plays into his hands here, because the spiritual words are all derived from physical metaphors; as he saw again and again how to do this the pleasure of ingenuity must have become a shock to faith. *Spirit* in English is mixed with the chemical sense—'the profounder chemists inform us that the strongest spirits may be extracted from human flesh' (the fanatics are lustful) and with its special sense of alcohol (intoxicated with the spirit, the fanatics are drunk); its root derivation is from wind or breath (inspired by the breath of God or the wind of the spirit the fanatics are windbags, and for special contempt may be told they are farting, as in Ernest Jones and the Vedas). In a state of 'enthusiasm' they are 'possessed' by devils or an animal impulse;

they ought to possess it. 'Beside themselves' with ecstasy they are mad. When 'profound,' being deep, they are low, being dark, they are senseless, or dropping they perform a bathos. When 'sublime,' being airy, they are unsubstantial (the spiritual is a delusion), being high, they are unsafe or become the mob in the gallery. There was no word with which some such trick could not be played.

It worked as well for literary criticism; there, too, faith must repress the pride of reason, and in a given case must rely on the mysterious act of judgment. There, too, delicacy had no safety but to insult the crowd. Pope said this very charmingly (to the fury of his nineteenth-century editor) when asked to reconcile Horace and Longinus, to reconcile 'the true sublime thrills and transports the reader' with

> let not each gay turn thy fancy move
> For fools admire, but men of sense approve.

'Longinus' remark was truth, but like certain truths of more importance, it required assent from faith, without the evidence of demonstration.' Swift had not the light touch required for this sort of faith.

> I desire of those whom the learned among posterity will appoint as commentators upon this elaborate treatise, that they will proceed with great caution upon certain dark points wherein all who are not *vere adepti* may be in danger to form rash and hasty conclusions, especially in some mysterious paragraphs, where certain *arcana* are joined for brevity sake, which in the operation must be divided. And I am certain that future sons of art will return large thanks to my memory for so grateful, so useful an *innuendo*.

They may show caution by searching for the meaning or by not telling it. First the *arcana* are what are so carefully divided in 'The Mechanical Operation of the Spirit'; 'a supernatural assistance from without' and 'the spirit we treat of here, proceeding entirely from within'; secondly they are the 'lewdness and nastiness,' divided in the two operations of the penis, which have already been compared to the first in the comparison of conscience to a pair of breeches. 'Joining for brevity's sake' is a habit both of the hated sensuality and the controlling reason (especially in the Augustan style); they too by this similarity are fearfully and inextricably joined. It is urgent for Swift to take the first two as opposites; he does not see much irony in pretending the second two are alike; yet if you accept the blasphemy against nature the blasphemy against spirit is a sort of corollary. The insinuating horror of the style (the remarks for posterity which pretend to be irony are quite true) so joins them as to defile all four. What Swift was trying to say is a minor matter; he was rightly accused of blasphemy for what he said; his own strength made his instrument too strong for him.

The fundamental impulse of irony is to score off both the arguments that have been puzzling you, both sets of sympathies in your mind, both sorts of fool who will hear you; a plague on both their houses. It is because of the strength given by this antagonism that it seems to get so safely outside the situation it assumes, to decide so easily about the doubt which it in fact accepts. This may seem a disagreeable pleasure in the ironist but he gives the same pleasure more or less secretly to his audience, and the process brings to mind the whole body of their difficulty with so much sharpness and freshness that it may give the strength to escape from it. It is when the ironist himself begins to doubt (late in Butler's *Fair Haven*) that the far-reaching ironies appear; and by then the thing is like a dramatic appeal to an audience, because both parties in the audience could swallow it. The essential is for the author to repeat the audience in himself, and he may safely seem to do nothing more. No doubt he has covertly, if it is a good irony, to reconcile the opposites into a larger unity, or suggest a balanced position by setting out two extreme views, or accept a lie (more or less consciously) to find energy to accept a truth, or something like that, but I am not concerned with these so much as with the machinery by which they are put across. I think it must be conceived as like a full-blown 'dramatic ambiguity,' in which different parts of the audience are meant to interpret the thing in different ways.

The two phrases 'dramatic irony' and 'ironical cheers,' both concerned with an audience, take a wide view of irony as a matter of course. Dramatic irony, as the term is used, need only make some point (not a simple comparison) by reminding you of another part of the play. And the best ironical cheers do not mean 'obviously you are wrong' but 'obviously we can grant that; taking the larger view, your argument is in our favour.' When Levidulcia brings out her couplet, those who take it as an irony against her hiss; those who feel it needed saying give an ironical cheer. The effect is like humour in its breadth, though like irony in its tension; humour need only say 'it is cheering to watch her, she shows we are right by being so obviously wrong,' whereas the cheer means 'it is discreditable, but it is the other half of the truth.' Language seems to agree with me here, that double irony is somehow natural to the stage.

The value of the state of mind which finds double irony natural is that it combines breadth of sympathy with energy of judgment; it can keep its balance among all the materials for judging. The word *sympathy* here is suspicious; it may range from ' able to imagine what some one feels and so understand him ' to ' prepared to be sorry for him, because you are safe and superior'; indeed it may have shrunk towards the second. People say that Pope's satire has too little sympathy to be good, but sympathy in the first sense it certainly has. The Elizabethan feeling can be seen most clearly in the popular rogue pamphlets, which express warm sympathy for the villains while holding in mind both horror for their crimes as such and pity and terror for the consequences. Stories of successful cheats are ' merry ' because the reader imagines himself as the robber, so as to enjoy his courage, dexterity, etc., and as the robbed—he can stand up to this trick now that he has been told; a secret freedom kept the two from obstructing each other. This fulness in the audience clearly allowed of complex character-building; one need not put hero and villain in black and white; though not everybody in the audience understood such a character they did not object when they only understood partial conflicting interpretations of it. Probably one could make analyses of the possible ways of taking a Shakespeare ' character' like my petty one of the ways of reading Brooke on fish; few people in the audience would get it in only one way, and few in all. And even the man who saw the full interpretation would still use the partial ones; both because he was in contact with the audience the play assumed and because he needed crude as well as delicate means of interpreting it quickly on the stage. This is obvious about surprise effects; the theatregoer has a quite different sequence of emotions in seeing the play a second time, and yet he has not lost the effects due to surprise, even as much as in re-reading a novel, because he can feel some one in the audience still being surprised. But to do this in more serious matters needs a special attitude. What is so impressive about the Elizabethans is that complexity of sympathy was somehow obvious to them; this same power, I think, made them feel at home with dramatic ambiguity and with the vague suggestiveness of the double plot.

The supreme case of dramatic ambiguity is Verrall's interpretation of Euripides; the plays were to dramatise sacred myths for a popular religious festival, yet for some members of the audience they were to suggest criticism of the gods, for others to convey complete disbelief and actually rationalise the myths before their eyes. The whole point was to play off one part of the audience against the other, and yet this made a superb ' complete play ' for the critic who felt what was being felt in the whole audience. This total aesthetic effect would not be ' in the play ' if it was only a clever·secret attack. But the plays are not addressed only to the few; the choruses are straightforward religious poetry; all shades of opinion were to be fused by the infection of the theatre into a unity of experience, under sufficiently different forms to avoid riots. On a smaller scale I think this is usual in the theatre. No doubt, as he said, it was painful to Shakespeare that his audiences were so crude, but any one who has seen Shaw acted in the provinces will know that a dramatist may actually depend on a variety of crudity; on a giggle here, and a clucking of the tongue there, and the power to make them change places. Any ' solid ' play, which can give the individual a rich satisfaction at one time, and therefore different satisfactions at different times from different ' points of view,' is likely to be a play that can satisfy different individuals ; it can face an audience ; the trouble with plays like Maeterlinck's is that they are only good from one ' point of view.' The Elizabethans had anyway to satisfy both groundlings and courtly critics ; there had to be levels of interpretation, each of which made a presentable play. And yet, since the separation of ambiguity into different times for the reader or different persons for an audience is never complete, at each such level you would feel that there were others that made the play ' solid ' ; so far as the audience is an inter-conscious unit they all work on it together.

The mind's ear catches a warning rumble from the psycho-analysts at this point, ' far within, and in their own dimensions like themselves.' Ernest Jones' essay on Hamlet, which may perhaps have caused Mr. Eliot to jettison the play in his later essay, brought out a very far-reaching use of double-plot methods and introduced at least one valuable technical term ; in ' decomposition ' ' one person of complex character is dissolved and replaced by several, each of whom possesses a different aspect of the character which in the simpler form of the myth is combined in one being.' This is supposed always to be due to a regular repression, as by an Œdipus complex producing a tyrant and a loved father, but it obviously has a wider use—wherever a situation, conceived as a myth and repeated with variations, is the root material of the play. The trouble about this approach is its assumption that the only ideas with which an audience can be infected unconsciously are the funda-

mental Freudian ones. Freud's theory of the Group
Mind assumes that once in a crowd the individual loses
all the inhibitions of civilisation, and a theatre audience
satisfies none of M'Dougall's five conditions without
which a group cannot be other than infantile. (I should
say this is less obviously untrue of a cinema audience,
which can't let the actor know what it thinks of him
and therefore makes less delicate exchanges of its
opinions.) One might reply with a Freudian Opposite;
the reason why a mob is the very cauldron of the inner
depths is that an appeal to a circle of a man's equals is
the fundamental escape into the fresh air of the mind.
Mob thought may kill us all before our time, but the
scientist's view of it should not be warped by horror,
and the writer who isolates himself from all feeling for
his audience acquires the faults of romanticism without
its virtues. Probably an audience does to some extent
let loose the hidden traditional ideas common to its
members, which may be a valuable process, but it also
forms a small 'public opinion'; the mutual influence
of its members' judgments, even though expressed by
the most obscure means or only imagined from their
presence, is so strong as to produce a sort of sensibility
held in common, and from their variety it may be
wider, more sensible, than that of any of its members.
It is this fact that the theatre is more really public than
the public of novelists which has made it so fruitful,
and makes its failure or limitation to one class a social
misfortune.

A reviewer of my book on ambiguity rightly said
that I was confusing poetical with dramatic uses of it,
which he said showed that I was treating poems as
phenomena not as things judged by a mind. Certainly

to claim that one can slip from one view to the other is
to assume a disorderly theory of aesthetics, a theory
rather like the version of proletarian aesthetic I was
attacking in the first chapter. It is clear that any theory
has to deal with a puzzle here, and its main business is
so to treat the puzzle as to keep it from doing harm.
This is only Horace *v.* Longinus; a work of art is a
thing judged by the artist and yet a thing inspired which
may mean more than he knew—as may a mathematical
formula for that matter; and a critic's judgment is
only part of the effects of the play, which are what
have to be judged. There is an old argument as to
whether probability is a fundamental notion or one
derived from statistics, and it seems possible that this is
an insoluble puzzle because the two are mutually dependent, like the One and the Many. In the same way a
poetical ambiguity depends on the reader's weighting
the possible meanings according to their probability,
while a dramatic ambiguity depends on the audience's
having the possible reactions in the right proportions,
but the distinction is only a practical one. Once you
break into the godlike unity of the appreciator you find
a microcosm of which the theatre is the macrocosm;
the mind is complex and ill-connected like an audience,
and it is as surprising in the one case as the other that a
sort of unity can be produced by a play.

III

One of my assumptions about double plots was that they invoked certain magical ideas, and I had best give another line of evidence from the thought of the period. Seventeenth-century poets often use a process like this to glorify the loved woman, a trick that seems partly derived from the deification of Elizabeth; to take the deity from her and give it to some one without public importance is like the use of heroic language about the pastoral swain. I should connect this with their occasional hints of pantheism, largely imported from the then popular stoics, since to a pantheist any one may be an example of the universal Nature. The rest of Europe indeed was playing the same tricks.

The deification of Elizabeth can be seen most clearly in the fragment of Ralegh's *Twelfth Book of the Ocean to Cynthia*, written in prison, in her old age, to win back her favour, and apparently abandoned in despair.

> My times that then ran o'er themselves in this
> and now run out in others' happiness
> bring unto those new joys, and new born days,
>
> so could she not, if she were not the sun,
> which sees the birth, and burial, of all else,
> and holds that power, by which she first begun,
>
> leaving each withered body to be torn
> by fortune, and by times tempestuous,
> which by her virtue, once fair fruit had born:
>
> knowing she can renew, and can create
> green from the ground, and flowers, even out of stone,
> by virtue lasting over time and date,

leaving us only woe, which like the muss,
having compassion of unburied bones,
cleaves to mischance, and unrepaired loss

for tender stalks. . . .

The manuscript breaks off, and the ideas were re-hashed
in a painfully flat form for the Queen of James I. It
would seem even more obviously blasphemous when
he re-wrote for Elizabeth the lost ballad about the Virgin
of Walsingham.

> As you came from the holy land
>   of Walsinghame
> Mett you not with my tru loue
>   by the way as you came.
>
>   .   .   .
>
> His [Love's] desire is a dureless content
>   And a trustless joye
> He is wonn with a world of despayre
>   And is lost with a toye :

The poem has been called early and anonymous from the
style of the beginning; Miss Latham's authoritative
text claims it for Ralegh on one manuscript attribution
and the style of the end. There seems clear evidence
that there was an old ballad and that even the first verse
has been re-written. All subsequent authors who quote
it get it wrong in the same way; they all put *Walsingham*
first and the *holy land* in the next line. Merrythought
in the *Burning Pestle* sings the verse like that; a remin-
iscence of the first two lines in *The Weakest goes to the
Wall* (1600) does the same; so does a humorous ballad
in the Pepysian collection, which seems a parody of
Ralegh's original, and would get such a point right to
make this clear. Even the copyist of the surviving

manuscript of the poem, Miss Latham tells us, first
wrote

> As you went to Walsingham,
> to that holy land,

as if this was the way anybody would expect it to start,
and then corrected himself in the margin. The last two
lines of the original first verse are lost, but it seems clear,
since there is a new rhyme, that Ralegh had the impudence to write the exquisitely mediaeval ones of his
version. Apart from this imaginative feat, the clash of
ideas is sufficiently startling.

> I haue loued her all my youth
> butt now ould as you see
> loue likes not the fallyng frute
> nor the wythered tree :

but after all this time she is still

> as the heuens fair
> There is none hath a forme so divine
> in the earth or the ayre.

It is taken for granted that she is immortal. The fundamental idea of the poem is a clash of styles and indeed
of historical periods which sets her up in direct rivalry
to the Queen of Heaven, and in the last verse it is not
clear that true love is to be found in either of them.

The more usual method is to make the thing safely
playful by mixing it both with myth and pastoral, as
when Elizabeth is appropriately the daughter of Pan in
the *Shepherd's Calendar*, or when after those lovely
speeches of pastoral humility by the Shepherd Paris,
swamped among his goddesses in Peele's *Arraignment*,
all the gods in turn, including the Fates, grant that
Elizabeth is above them. They are feigned pagan

gods or mere allegories and she is a real Christian queen, so the thing need not be unchristian; it is put in a fairy-story world which may yet yield profound truths. Yet allegory itself, a comparatively late classical invention, is always liable to return to the deification from which it came, and the more you avoid this by taking a humble example of the quality as its type the more you deify the figure of pastoral.

Something of the kind may, I believe, be felt in the earliest convention of an art based on divine royalty, in the statues of the Pharaohs. This is not such a long jump; the striking thing about Ancient Egypt when you come there from the East is that it is so European, and the noble great head of Amenemhat III in the British Museum (dear good dog—the Prince of Wales always does his best) would be just the thing for a modern War Memorial. But this is very Twelfth Dynasty; the feeling is generally put into the torso, a powerful body so handled as to seem delicate, vulnerable, and touching, in the contrast of the rigid lines. The same clash of the bruiser and the flower (now mainly used in representations of cart-horses) seems at work in one of the statues of the Indus civilisation and is clear in the earliest statues of Buddha at Mathura, based on a clumsier tradition for big earth-gods; then a new idea of spirituality comes in, whether partly Greek or not, and this theme can only dimly be fancied in the normal Buddha. It seems clear in the more satisfying Pharaohs, at any rate, that this conception of the divine king, devoted and unintellectual, doing his best at the work of being a deity, especially in its firm acceptance of the strong man as a touching emblem of nobility, has a double feeling of the same kind as is invoked for pastoral.

DOUBLE PLOTS

At the same time as the unchristian deification of Elizabeth there is in the air a Renaissance desire to make the individual more independent than Christianity allowed; the two ideas are involved for instance in Tamburlane, the scourge of God (subjective or objective genitive) who calls himself master of Jupiter and the Fates and dies as a stoic in face of Necessity. The feeling for independence peeps out in the language about animals. They are envied for not being threatened with heaven or hell, with an external last judgment; this naturally appears as a result of fear of hell, but the wider feeling, that one did not want to submit to the inquisition of a central divine authority even at best, was the necessary background of its appeal. In the last hour of Faustus (who told the devil himself he still didn't believe in Hell) his mind flies to the theories of the soul that do not burden it with a permanent individuality.

> You stars that reigned at my nativity
> Whose influence hath allotted death and hell
> Now draw up Faustus like a foggy mist. . . .
>
> Ah, Pythagoras' metempsychosis, were that true
> This soul should fly from me, and I be changed
> Unto some brutish beast. All beasts are happy,
> For, when they die,
> Their souls are still dissolved in elements;
> But mine must live, still to be plagued in hell.

The first idea is that his soul might melt back into the soul of an impersonal Nature, still remaining soul-stuff; the next idea, of re-birth, does not fit in well with the third, of the mere extinction of the souls of animals at death, and the doubtful word *dissolved* allows pantheism to be still present at the end. Marcus Aurelius keeps just this balance of doubt. You may say that the dissolution

of the individual makes him less responsible, so that
Faustus is trying to be less independent here, but that
was not his intention at the time. Animals turn up in
Donne's Holy Sonnets with the same implication.

> If lecherous goats, if serpents envious
> Cannot be damned, alas, why should I bee ? . . .

> But who am I, that dare dispute with thee
> Oh God ? Oh ! of thy only worthy blood
> And my teares, make a heavenly Lethean flood
> And drown in it my sinnes black memorie ;
> That thou remember them, some claim as debt ;
> I think it mercy, if thou wilt forget.

He has apparently backed away from the idea with
apologies, but it comes back in the last couplet; *them*
must be 'some people' (nobody claims to have their
sins remembered) and the parallel is 'forget me.' This
reflects back some doubt as to how completely he was
to be drowned, and Lethe was where the souls forgot
everything before re-birth. The next example makes a
more interesting use, for the same purpose, of the map
of the world.

> I am a little world made cunningly
> Of Elements, and an Angellike spright,
> But black sinne hath betraid to endlesse night
> My worlds both parts, and (oh) both parts must die.
> You which beyond that heaven which was most high
> Have found new sphears, and of new lands can write,
> Powre new seas in my eyes, that so I might
> Drowne my world with my weeping earnestly,
> Or wash it ; if it must be drowned no more ;
> But oh it must be burnt, alas the fire
> Of lust and envie have burnt it heretofore
> And made it fouler ; Let their flames retire,
> And burne me o Lord, with a fiery zeale
> Of thee and thy house, which doth in eating heale.

The octet, though without indifference to a universal
right and wrong, takes the soul as isolated and independent; it is viewed as the world in the new astronomy,
a small sphere, complete in itself, safe from interference,
in the middle distance. The idea that you can get right
away to America, that human affairs are not organised
round one certainly right authority (*e.g.* the Pope) is
directly compared to the new idea that there are other
worlds like this one, so that the inhabitants of each can
live in their own way. These notions carried a considerable weight of implication, because they lead at once to
a doubt either of the justice or the uniqueness of Christ.
It was bad enough when all the Chinese were certain
of hell because they had not been told of the appearance
of the Messiah, but to damn all inhabitants of other
planets on this count was intolerable. On the other
hand, if Christ went to all the planets his appearances on
each take on a different character; it is a more symbolical
matter, and you can apply the ideas about Christ to
any one who seems worthy of it. This was in fact done,
though with an air of metaphor. *Beyond that heaven
which was most high* adds that heaven, if it is there at
all, is now safely far off; it is difficult to reach across
from either side.

Professor Grierson puts a comma after *or wash it*
in place of the colon of the best manuscript W, which
seems to me better; certainly he is right in putting some
stop, which the 1633 text doesn't. The division between
octet and sestet seems, here and nowhere else in the
sequence, to come a line late; but the thought changes
at the right place. *Drowning* the world *no more* brings
us back to Noah and an entirely pre-Copernican heaven,
and there is a surprise in the first part of the line which

prepares us for it; the distinction between *wash* and *drown* brought out the question as to what was to be drowned. It seems at first that the *sprite* and *elements*, spirit and body, correspond to the day and night of the imagined globe, a fine case of the fusion of soul and body which Donne often attempts. But in that case both are to be drowned; the soul is safe because sure of extinction. The flood pulls us back from this with a reminder of the final fire. 'You, by our eating of you, heal me, and heal your house; your house, in eating you, heals itself; you, by eating with the fires of hell lust and envy, your house, by eating with the fires of Smithfield such heresies as are at the back of my mind, heal me.' Bernard Shaw said that Marlowe was a nasty little boy trying to make our flesh creep over a hell in which he no longer believed. He was in strong danger of a fire undoubtedly material. The symbolism of the use of fire as a punishment for heresy could not but work on a man exposed to it as it was meant to do; it produced a sort of belief. The reader is now safely recalled from the interplanetary spaces, baffled among the cramped, inverted, cannibal, appallingly tangled impulses that are his home upon the world.

The clash here shows what the globe has been used for in Donne's earlier poetry, where it is a continual metaphor; I suppose he had a globe map in his room. To say that his mistress is the whole world is not witty and satisfying merely because the complete hyperbole; if you take *world* not as the universe but as this planet it becomes something one might conceivably get outside but which it would be absurd to try to get outside; there are more than one of them, but each creature is right in giving an absurd importance to his own.

Thou sun art half as happy as we
In that the world's contracted thus;
Thine age asks ease, and since thy duties be
To warm the world, that's done in warming us.
Shine here to us, and thou art everywhere,
This bed thy centre is, these walls thy sphere.

If the world is ending it is only for astronomical reasons that do not involve the last judgment. Since the world has grown small, and the sun near its end, we are set free with a sort of cosiness, an irresponsible concentration, to be happy while we may. The scheme of making the soul of each lover the matter which the soul of the other informs merely carried this process to its conclusion; they are now completely isolated and necessarily die together.

The belief that the world was soon coming to an end, found in Donne, Chapman, and Sir Thomas Browne, seems important to them and is not easily explained. Samuel Butler the elder laughs at it as based on a passage in Copernicus about two determinations of the distance of the sun, of which the second made the sun nearer, so that we seemed to be falling into it; this would provide the last fire. I suspect that there was some astronomical pamphlet which they had all read, but Hakewill's refutation of the belief does not put one on to it. At any rate the belief was respectable but not certain and had proofs from astronomy rather than religion. In a way it strengthened the claims of religion against the hopes of Bacon, but it implied that other worlds would not end when ours did, and this strengthened the feeling that everything was local, even the prophecies in the Bible.

The connection between pantheism and deification is perhaps best approached by a speculative route.

F. M. Cornford developed a theory in *From Religion to Philosophy* that the primitive Greeks invented Nature by throwing out onto the universe the idea of a common life-blood; the living force that made natural events follow reasonable laws, and in particular made the crops grow, was identified with the blood which made the members of the tribe into a unity and which they shared with their totem. So the physicist is well connected by derivation to the physician, the ' leech ' who lets blood. However this may have been in primitive Greece it was a natural fancy for a Christian; the Logos had been formulated as the underlying Reason of the universe and was also the Christ who had saved man by shedding his blood and sharing it in the Communion. It seems to me that there is a trace of the idea in the speech of Faustus.

> The stars move still; time runs; the clock will strike;
> The devil will come, and Faustus must be damned.
> O, I'll leap up to my God, Who pulls me down ?
> See, see where Christ's blood streams in the firmament.

The blood might be the red sunset of the fatal night. It is too far off to help, perhaps, because the firmament had grown further off; what pulls him down is the force that holds him to one world. Clearly the sign is for some reason a portent not a hope; perhaps because the sacrifice of Christ has made his sin more unforgivable. I think there is a feeling that the blood of Christ is what sustains all Nature, therefore it is what makes time run on. And the idea that Christ is somehow diffused through all Nature (into which Faustus himself wishes to be dissolved) makes it the more impossible to escape punishment.

With Donne's *Crosse* we escape the need for conjecture; he makes the pun on *physic* and treats the cross (it is an old fancy) as underlying the natural order.

> All the Globes frame, and spheares, is nothing else,
> But the Meridians crossing Parallels.
> Material crosses, then, good physic be,
> But yet spiritual have chief dignity.

Space itself, the type of explanation, is shown to hold dissolved throughout it, as the differential equation of its structure, the impenetrable tangle of ideas about the sacrifice of the scapegoat and the hero. I am not sure how much Herbert meant by the following example.

> The bloody cross of my dear Lord
> Is both my physic and my sword.

It shows chiefly the naturalness of the metaphor. The notion is more grandly employed by Wordsworth, in one of the crucial passages where he describes the right relation of the individual to Nature.

> . . . Blest the infant Babe,
> (For with my best conjecture I would trace
> The progress of our Being) blest the Babe,
> Nursed in his Mother's arms . . .
> No outcast he, bewildered and depressed:
> Along his infant veins are interfused
> The gravitation and the filial bond
> Of nature, that connect him with the world.

The only flat way to take the metaphors is to say that the common life-blood is interfused along his veins, and that the filial bond at one time came through the placenta. *Gravitation* fits in with the Donne passages because by that Nature holds him to the bosom of one planet, not the other possible ones. Coleridge at least would have felt at home with this line of speculation.

Finally, on such a view might not Christ be the World as revealed to human knowledge—a kind of common sensorium,

79

the idea of the whole that modifies all our thoughts? And might not numerical difference be an exclusive property of phenomena so that he who puts on the likeness of Christ becomes Christ?

Some such deduction had in fact been made.

These last passages are, of course, concerned with the union of the individual to Christ or Nature, not his independence. But once the ideas about Christ have been so far generalised, and those about Nature so far localised, the same trick can be played about any hero you have taken. Donne's poem (*The Crosse*) from which I quoted above implies a considerable independence from the historical Christ.

> . . . But yet spiritual have chief dignity.
> These for extracted chemique medecine serve,
> And cure much better, and as well preserve;
> Then you are your own physic, or need none,
> When stilled, or purged by tribulation.
>
> Who can deny me armes, and liberty
> To stretch mine armes, and my own Crosse to be?
>
> No scandal taken, shall this Crosse withdraw,
> It shall not, for it cannot; for, the losse
> Of this Crosse, were to me another Crosse.

The Cross here seems quite independent of Christianity; it is essential to man's mode of apprehending the world. This of course is a religious poem, and one must not press the words out of their intention; they only show how ready Donne was to go through this process, and how unsuspicious of it. In the early love-poems and the first Anniversary it is used very firmly indeed.

Mr. James Smith, in an excellent essay (*Determinations*, ed. F. R. Leavis), said that the metaphysical conceit was always built out of the immediate realisation of a philosophical problem such as that of the One and the Many. I should agree with this, but I think it was nearly always arrived at in the way I am trying to describe. The supreme example of the problem of the One and the Many was given by the Logos who was an individual man. In all those conceits where the general is given a sort of sacred local habitation in a particular, so that this particular is made much more interesting than all similar particulars (absolutely more interesting, but with a rival suggestion of wit), and the others are all dependent on it, there is an implied comparison to the sacrificial cult-hero, to Christ as the Son of Man. To do this indeed was hardly more than to take personification seriously; it is incarnation already.

> If ever any beauty I did see,
> Which I desir'd, and got, 'twas but a dreame of thee.

> And therefore what thou wert, and who,
>   I bid Love aske, and now
> That it *assume* thy body, I allow,
> And fixe itself in thy lip, eye, and brow.

This at once leads to the dependence of the world upon the person or thing treated as a personification: ' This member of the class is the whole class, or its defining property: this man has a magical importance to all men.' If you choose an important member the result is heroic; if you choose an unimportant one it is pastoral.

> Or if, when thou, the worlds soule, goest,
>   It stay, tis but thy carcase then,
> The fairest woman, but thy ghost,
>   But corrupt wormes, the worthyest men.

> O wrangling schooles, that search what fire
>   Shall burne this world, had none the wit
> Unto this knowledge to aspire,
>   That this her fever might be it?

All Donne's best poems, the Canonization, Twickenham Garden, A Valediction of Weeping, the Nocturnal, the Funeral, the Relique, are built out of this; it is forced into the Exstasie so violently as to make M. Legouis suspect the poem's sincerity:

> To our bodies turne wee then, that so
> Weake men on love reveal'd may looke;
> Loves mysteries in soules do grow,
> But yet the body is his booke.

The idea of arranging that everybody else can look, so as to do them good, ridiculous in itself, follows from the implied comparison to the universal Passion of Christ. This process of thought completed the usefulness of the globe-symbol: 'we can rightly take our world (planet) as the world (universe), because to us it is that one of all the planets which has been made symbolic (in effect simply made real). The others are all like it so need not be examined; the others are all dependent on it so are controlled when it is.'

But indeed this process of uniting particular and general is already involved in the idea of God. God cannot be prior to goodness, so that the good is simply his will, or he is a tyrant without morality; nor can goodness be prior to him, so that he is necessarily good, or he is not free. Though God is a person he and the good must be mutually dependent; it was because Milton refused to play the tricks of the metaphysical and made God merely one of the persons of his story that Satan had so strong a case. It is not an accidental product of a special theology that Christ once made God must be treated in this way. But in the devotional verse of the time the idea is stretched onto other individuals as easily as in the love poetry. Mary Magdalene is treated as a sort of rival Christ in Crashaw's *Weeper*; or perhaps she makes a second atonement, between Christ and the world. It is she now who underlies the order of nature.

> At these thy weeping gates,
> (Watching their watry motion)
> Each winged moment waits,
> Takes his Tear, and gets him gone.
> By thine Ey's tinct ennobled thus
> Time layes him up; he's pretious.

She is not merely a waterclock but *the* waterclock by which Nature measures time; if it were not for her sacrifice time would break up altogether. Since her tears are both the essential stars and the essential dew (and so on) they reconcile earth and heaven, they perform the function of the sacrificed god. 'Portable and compendious oceans' has been thought an absurd phrase merely because it puts specially clearly what such critics would call the absurdity of the whole conception of the poem; her tears are the idea of water, all water, and make water do whatever it does. The Protestants were clearly right in calling this version of the invocation of saints heretical, because it destroys the uniqueness of Christ, but for literary purposes they continued to do it themselves. The idea is stated as clearly and is as central to the poem in a lovesong of Carew which seems to have got into the Oxford Book as an example of 'careless ease.'

> Ask me no more where Jove bestows
> When June is past, the fading rose;
> For in thy beauty's orient deep
> These flowers, as in their causes, sleep.

The trick was common but not as a rule forced on one's attention; there was another way of taking the thing to make it seem sensible, and you could take it that way alone. Queen Elizabeth and the person of importance chosen as a hero of tragedy had an obvious influence on public affairs; to the lover who was speaking the world would seem empty without the loved woman. Indeed if there was no other way of taking it the thing would be pointless. But Donne's use of it in the First Anniversary is peculiar because there is no obvious other way; it is an enormous picture of the complete decay of the universe, and this is caused by the death of a girl of no importance whom Donne had never seen. Ben Jonson said 'if it had been written to the Virgin, it would have been something' but only Christ would be enough; only his removal from the world would explain the destruction foretold by astronomers. The only way to make the poem sensible is to accept Elizabeth Drury as the Logos. Of course this is not necessarily unchristian; those few persons who felt that life was empty after her death were supposed to find in their feelings about her the reality of the doctrines true about Christ. And Donne had very serious feelings about the break-up of the unified world of mediaeval thought with which to fill out his framework. But the frame is itself a symbol of the break-up. He could hardly have used it if he had not felt, with that secret largeness of outlook which is his fascination, that the ideas he handled did not necessarily belong to the one Jesus, that they might just as well, if the sorrowing parents would pay for it, be worked out for Elizabeth Drury.

Evidence as well as probability, then, lets one say that the position of the tragic hero was felt to be like that of Christ, and that elements were exchanged between them. Indeed, to call the Passion tragic, putting the thing

the other way round, was a commonplace; of which
Herrick provides a charming example:

> Not like a Thief, shalt Thou ascend the mount,
> But like a Person of some high Account;
> The Crosse shall be Thy Stage; and Thou shalt there
> The spacious field have for Thy Theater.
>
> And we (Thy Lovers) while we see Thee keep
> The Lawes of Action, will both sigh, and weep.

At the same time the two were very different, and the
tragic idea, having a classical background, was by no
means dependent on the Christian one. The famous
passage in Chapman that uses the globe-metaphor, about
the man that joins himself to the universe and goes on
'round as it,' shows how flatly the idea was derived
from Roman Stoicism; the same metaphor for instance
is in Marcus Aurelius (xi. 2). Mr. Eliot remarked about
this that no man would join himself to the universe if
he had anything better to join himself to, and certainly
there is an element of revolt in the Elizabethan use of
the idea. The reason why Donne's use of the globe is
so much wittier and more solid than Chapman's is that
he shows this; his globe is a way of shutting out the
parsons as well as of completing himself. The idea that
all men have a share in the fundamental and indivisible
Reason was a stoical idea before it became a Christian
one with the Logos, and in these uses is more comfortable
in its pagan form. Indeed, the hero himself stood for a
set of ideas covertly opposed to Christianity; that is why
the mythological ideas about him remain in the background. He stood for 'honour,' pride rather than
humility, self-realisation rather than self-denial, caste
rather than democracy; he can become, as obviously in

the comic hero Macheath, a sort of defence against
Puritanism. The Elizabethans could use the separate
systems of ideas together frankly and fully, but this was
no longer possible after they had been fought over in
the Civil War, and from then on one gets a more underground connection. Probably the most permanent
element was this curious weight put covertly into
metaphor or personification.

I shall list here a few examples which I am sorry to
have let get crowded out. *Piers Plowman* is the most
direct case of the pastoral figure who turns slowly into
Christ and ruler. For device prior to irony, the tragic
ballad with gay irrelevant refrain—'She leaned her
back against a thorn (Fine flowers in the valley).'
For one-in-many business, the *Lyke-Wake Dirge* and
the *Dies Irae* :—

> This *ae* nighte, this ae nighte,
>   *Every* nighte and alle

> Recordare, Jesu pie,
>   Quod *sum* causa tuae viae,
> Ne *me* perdas illa die.

And *Wuthering Heights* is a good case of double plot in
the novel, both for covert deification and telling the
same story twice with the two possible endings.

They That Have Power

*Twist of Heroic-Pastoral Ideas into an Ironical
Acceptance of Aristocracy*

I

IT is agreed that *They that have power to hurt and will do none* is a piece of grave irony, but there the matter is generally left; you can work through all the notes in the Variorum without finding out whether flower, lily, 'owner,' and person addressed are alike or opposed. One would like to say that the poem has all possible such meanings, digested into some order, and then try to show how this is done, but the mere number of possible interpretations is amusingly too great. Taking the simplest view (that any two may be alike in some one property) any one of the four either is or is not and either should or should not be like each of the others; this yields 4096 possible movements of thought, with other possibilities. The niggler is routed here; one has honestly to consider what seems important.

'The best people are indifferent to temptation and detached from the world; nor is this state selfish, because they do good by unconscious influence, like the flower. You must be like them; you are quite like them already. But even the best people must be continually on their guard, because they become the worst, just as the pure and detached lily smells worst, once they fall from their perfection '—(' one's prejudice against them is only one's consciousness of this fact '—the hint of irony in the poem might be covered by this). It is a coherent enough Confucian sentiment, and there is no very clear hint as to irony in the words. No doubt *as stone* goes intentionally too far for sympathy, and there is a suggestive gap in the argument between octet and sestet, but one would not feel this if it was Shakespeare's only surviving work.

There is no reason why the subtlety of the irony in so complex a material must be capable of being pegged out into verbal explanations. The vague and generalised language of the descriptions, which might be talking about so many sorts of people as well as feeling so many things about them, somehow makes a unity like a cross-roads, which analysis does not deal with by exploring down the roads; makes a solid flute on which you can play a multitude of tunes, whose solidity no list of all possible tunes would go far to explain. The balance of feeling is both very complex and very fertile; experiences are recorded, and metaphors invented, in the Sonnets, which he went on 'applying' as a dramatist, taking particular cases of them as if they were wide generalisations, for the rest of his life. One can't expect, in writing about such a process, to say anything very tidy and complete.

But one does not start interpreting out of the void, even though the poem once partly interpreted seems to stand on its own. If this was Shakespeare's only surviving work it would still be clear, supposing one knew about the other Elizabethans, that it involves somehow their feelings about the Machiavellian, the wicked plotter who is exciting and civilised and in some way right about life; which seems an important though rather secret element in the romance that Shakespeare extracted from his patron. In any case one has only to look at the sonnets before and after it to be sure that it has some kind of irony. The one before is full of fear and horror at the hypocrisy he is so soon to recommend; and yet it is

already somehow cuddled, as if in fascination or out of
a refusal to admit that it was there.

> So shall I liue, supposing thou art true,
> Like a deceiued husband, . . .
> For ther can liue no hatred in thine eye
> Therefore in that I cannot know thy change, . . .
> How like *Eaues* apple doth thy beauty grow,
> If thy sweet vertue answere not thy show.

So the *summer's flower* may be its apple-blossom.
His virtue is still sweet, whether he has any or not; the
clash of fact with platonic idealism is too fearful to be
faced directly. In the sonnet after, with a blank and
exhausted humility, it has been faced; there remains
for the expression of his love, in the least flaunting of
poetry, the voice of caution.

> How sweet and louely dost thou make the shame, . . .
> Take heed (deare heart) of this large priuilege.

The praise of hypocrisy is in a crucial and precarious
condition of balance between these two states of mind.

The root of the ambivalence, I think, is that W. H. is
loved as an arriviste, for an impudent worldliness that
Shakespeare finds shocking and delightful. The reasons
why he treated his poet badly are the same as the reasons
why he was fascinating, which gives its immediate point
to the profound ambivalence about the selfishness of the
flower. Perhaps he is like the cold person in his hardness
and worldly judgment, not in his sensuality and generosity of occasional impulse; like the flower in its beauty,
vulnerability, tendency to excite thoughts about the
shortness of life, self-centredness, and power in spite of
it to give pleasure, not in its innocence and fertility;
but the irony may make any of these change over.
Both owner and flower seem self-centred and inscrutable,

and the cold person is at least like the lily in that it is symbolically chaste, but the summer's flower, unlike the lily, seems to stand for the full life of instinct. It is not certain that the owner is liable to fester as the lily is— Angelo did, but W. H. is usually urged to acquire the virtues of Angelo. Clearly there is a jump from octet to sestet; the flower is not like the owner in its solitude and its incapacity to hurt or simulate; it might be because of this that it is of a summer only and may fester; yet we seem chiefly meant to hold W. H. in mind and take .them as parallel. As for punctuation, the only full stop is at the end; all lines have commas after them except the fourth, eighth, and twelfth, which have colons.

> They that haue powre to hurt, and will doe none,
> That doe not do the thing, they most do showe,
> Who mouing others, are themselves as stone,
> Vnmoued, could, and to temptation slow :

They may *show*, while hiding the alternative, for the first couplet, the power to hurt or the determination not to hurt—cruelty or mercy, for the second, the strength due to chastity or to sensual experience, for either, a reckless or cautious will, and the desire for love or for control; all whether they are stealers of hearts or of public power. They are a very widespread group; we are only sure at the end that some kind of hypocrisy has been advised and threatened.

> They rightly do inherit heavens graces,
> And husband natures ritches from expence,

Either ' inherit, they alone, by right ' or ' inherit what all men inherit and use it rightly '; these correspond to the opposed views of W. H. as aristocrat and vulgar careerist. There is a similar range of idea, half hidden by the pretence of easy filling of the form, in the pun on *graces* and shift to *riches*. *Heaven's graces* may be prevenient grace (strength from God to do well), personal graces which seem to imply heavenly virtues (the charm by which you deceive people), or merely God's gracious gift of *nature's riches*; which again may be the personal graces, or the strength and taste which make him capable either of ' upholding his house ' or of taking his pleasure, or merely the actual wealth of which he is an *owner*. Clearly this gives plenty of room for irony in the statement that the cold people, with their fine claims, do well all round; it also conveys ' I am seeing you as a whole; I am seeing these things as necessary rather than as your fault.'

> They are the Lords and owners of their faces,
> Others, but stewards of their excellence:

It may be their beauty they put to their own uses, high or low, or they may just have poker-faces; this gives the same range of statement. The capital which tends to isolate *lords* from its phrase suggests ' they are the only true aristocrats; if you are not like them you should not pretend to be one.' *Others* may be stewards of their own excellence (in contrast with *faces*—' though they are enslaved they may be better and less superficial than the cold people ') or of the cold people's excellence (with a suggestion of ' Their Excellencies ') ; the less plausible sense is insisted on by the comma after *others*. This repeats the doubt about how far the cold people are really excellent, and there may be a hint of a doubt about how far the individual is isolated, which anticipates the metaphor of the flower. And ' stewards of their own excellence ' may be like ' stewards of the buttery ' or like ' stewards of a certain lord '; either ' the good things they have do good to others, not to them ' (they are too generous; I cannot ask you to aim so high in virtue, because I desire your welfare, not other people's, and indeed because you wouldn't do it anyway) or ' they are under the power of their own impulses, which are good things so long as they are not in power ' (they are deceived; acts caused by weakness are not really generous at all). Yet this may be the condition of the flower and the condition for fullness of life; you cannot know beforehand what life will bring you if you open yourself to it, and certainly the flower does not; it is because they are unnatural and unlike flowers that the cold people rule nature, and the cost may be too great. Or the flower and the cold person may be two unlike examples of the limitation necessary to success, one experienced in its own nature, the other in the world; both, the irony would imply, are in fact *stewards*.

There is a Christian parable at work in both octet and sestet; in the octet that of the talents. You will not be forgiven for hoarding your talents; some sort of success is demanded; you must at least use your powers to the full even if for your own squalid purpose. The pain and wit and solemnity of *rightly*, its air of summing up a long argument, depend on the fact that these metaphors have been used to recommend things to W. H. before.

> Natures bequest giues nothing but doth lend,
> And being franck she lends to those are free :
>
> Who lets so faire a house fall to decay,
> Which husbandry in honour might uphold,

Rightly to be free with yourself, in the first simple

paradox, was the best saving of yourself (you should put
your money into marriage and a son); it is too late now
to advise that, or to say it without being sure to be
understood wrongly (this is 94; the first sonnet about his
taking Shakespeare's mistress is 40); the advice to be
generous as natural has become the richer but more
contorted advice to be like the flower. Rightly to
husband nature's riches, earlier in the sequence, was to
accept the fact that one is only steward of them;

> Thou that art now the worlds fresh ornament,
> And only herauld to the gaudy spring,
> Within thine owne bud buriest thy content,
> And tender chorle makst waste in niggarding:

the flower was wrong to live to itself alone, and would
become a tottered weed (2) whether it met with infection
or not.

Though indeed *husbandry* is still recommended; it is
not the change of opinion that has so much effect but
the use of the same metaphors with a shift of feeling in
them. The legal metaphors (debts to nature and so forth)
used for the loving complaint that the man's chastity
was selfish are still used when he becomes selfish in his
debauchery; Shakespeare's own notation here seems to
teach him; the more curiously because the metaphors
were used so flatly in the earliest sonnets (1, 2, 4, 6, then
13; not again till now), only formally urging marriage,
and perhaps written to order. It is like using a mathematical identity which implies a proof about a particular
curve and then finding that it has a quite new meaning
if you take the old constants as variables. It is these
metaphors that have grown, till they involve relations
between a man's powers and their use, his nature and his

will, the individual and the society, which could be applied afterwards to all human circumstances.

> The sommers flowre is to the sommer sweet,
> Though to it selfe, it onely liue and die,

The use of *the* summer's flower about a human being is enough to put it at us that the flower will die by the end of summer, that the man's life is not much longer, and that the pleasures of the creature therefore cannot be despised for what they are. *Sweet to the summer* (said of the flower), since the summer is omnipresent and in a way Nature herself, may mean ' sweet to God ' (said of the man) ; or may mean ' adding to the general sweetness ; sweet to everybody that comes across it in its time.' It may do good to others though not by effort or may simply be a good end in itself (or combining these, may only be able to do good by concentrating on itself as an end) ; a preparatory evasion of the central issue about egotism.

Either ' though it lives only for itself ' or ' though, in its own opinion, so far as it can see, it does no more than live and die.' In the first it is a rose, extravagant and doing good because the public likes to see it flaunting ; in the second a violet, humble and doing good in private through an odour of sanctity. It is the less plausible sense which is insisted on by the comma after *itself*. Or you may well say that the flower is neither, but the final lily ; the whole passage is hinting at the lilies of the field like whom Solomon was not arrayed.

This parable itself combines what the poem so ingeniously keeps on combining ; the personal power of beauty and the political power of wisdom ; so as to imply that the political power has in itself a sort of beauty and the personal beauty, however hollow it may be, a sort of moral grandeur through power. But in England 'consider the lilies of the field,' were we not at once told of their glory, would suggest lilies-of-the-valley; that name indeed occurs in the Song of Solomon, in surprising correspondence to the obviously grandiose Rose of Sharon. Shakespeare. I think, had done what the inventor of the name must have done, had read into the random flower-names of the Bible the same rich clash of suggestion—an implied mutual comparison that elevates both parties—as he makes here between the garden flower and the wild flower. The first sense (the rose) gives the root idea—'a brilliant aristocrat like you gives great pleasure by living as he likes; for such a person the issue of selfishness does not arise'; this makes W. H. a Renaissance Magnificent Man, combining all the virtues with a manysidedness like that of these phrases about him. The unlikeness of the cold people and the flowers, if you accept them as like, then implies : man is not placed like flowers and though he had best imitate them may be misled in doing so; the Machiavellian is much more really like the flower than the Swain is." And yet there is a suggestion in the comparison to the flower (since only beauty is demanded of it—Sonnet 54 made an odd and impermanent attempt at quelling this doubt by equating truth with scent) that W. H. has only power to keep up an air of reconciling in himself the inconsistent virtues, or even of being a Machiavellian about the matter, and that it is this that puts him in danger like the flower. Or however genuine he may be he is pathetic; such a man is all too 'natural'; there is no need to prop up our ideas about him with an aristocratic 'artificial' flower. So this class-centred praise is then careful half to hide itself by adding the second sense and the humble flower, and this leads it to a generalisation: ' all men do most good to others by fulfilling their own natures.' Full as they are of Christian echoes, the Sonnets are concerned with an idea strong enough to be balanced against Christianity; they state the opposite to the idea of self-sacrifice.

But the machinery of the statement is peculiar; its clash of admiration and contempt seems dependent on a clash of feeling about the classes. One might connect it with that curious trick of pastoral which for extreme courtly flattery—perhaps to give self-respect to both poet and patron, to show that the poet is not ignorantly easy to impress, nor the patron to flatter—writes about the poorest people; and with those jazz songs which give an intense effect of luxury and silk underwear by pretending to be about slaves naked in the fields. To those who care chiefly about biography this trick must seem monstrously tantalising; Wilde built the paradox of his essay on it, and it is true that Shakespeare might have set the whole thing to work from the other end about a highly trained mudlark brought in to act his princesses. But it is the very queerness of the trick that makes it so often useful in building models of the human mind; and yet the power no less than the universality of this poem depends on generalising the trick so completely as to seem independent of it.

> But if that flowre with base infection meete,
> The basest weed out-braues his dignity:
>> For sweetest things turn sowrest by their deedes,
>> Lilies that fester, smell far worse than weeds.

It is not clear how the metaphor from ' meet ' acts; it may be like ' meet with disaster '—' if it catches infection, which would be bad luck,' or like meeting someone

in the street, as most men do safely—'*any* contact
with infection is fatal to so peculiarly placed a creature.'
The first applies to the natural and unprotected flower,
the second to the lily that has the hubris and fate of
greatness. They are not of course firmly separated,
but *lilies* are separated from the *flower* by a colon and
an intervening generalisation, whereas the flower is
only separated from the cold people (not all of whom
need be lilies) by a colon; certainly the flower as well
as the lily is in danger, but this does not make them
identical and equal to W. H. The neighbouring sonnets
continually say that his deeds can do nothing to destroy
his sweetness, and this seems to make the terrible last
line point at him somewhat less directly. One may
indeed take it as 'Though so debauched, you keep
your looks. Only mean people who never give themselves heartily to anything can do that. But the best
hypocrite is found out in the end, and shown as the
worst.' But Shakespeare may also be congratulating
W. H. on an imperfection which acts as a preservative;
he is a son of the world and can protect himself, like
the cold people, or a spontaneous and therefore fresh
sinner, like the flower; he may safely stain, as heaven's
sun, the kisser of carrion, staineth. At any rate it is
not of virginity, at this stage, that he can be accused.
The smell of a big lily is so lush and insolent, suggests
so powerfully both incense and pampered flesh—the
traditional metaphor about it is so perfect—that its
festering can only be that due to the hubris of spirituality; it is ironically generous to apply it to the
careerist to whom hypocrisy is recommended; and
yet in the fact that we seem meant to apply it to him
there is a glance backwards, as if to justify him, at the

ambition involved in even the most genuine attempt on
heaven. You may say that Shakespeare dragged in the
last line as a quotation from *Edward III* that doesn't
quite fit; it is also possible that (as often happens to
poets, who tend to make in their lives a situation they
have already written about) he did not till now see the
full width of its application.

In a sense the total effect is an evasion of Shakespeare's
problem; it gives him a way of praising W. H. in
spite of anything. In the flower the oppositions are
transcended; it is because it is self-concentrated that it
has so much to give and because it is undesigning that
it is more grandiose in beauty than Solomon. But it
is held in mind chiefly for comfort; none of the people
suggested to us are able to imitate it very successfully;
nor if they could would they be safe. Yet if W. H.
has festered, that at least makes him a lily, and at least
not a stone; if he is not a lily, he is in the less danger
of festering.

I must try to sum up the effect of so complex an irony,
half by trying to follow it through a gradation. ' I am
praising to you the contemptible things you admire,
you little plotter; this is how the others try to betray
you through flattery; yet it is your little generosity,
though it show only as lewdness, which will betray
you; for it is wise to be cold, both because you are too
inflammable and because I have been so much hurt by
you who are heartless; yet I can the better forgive you
through that argument from our common isolation;
I must praise to you your very faults, especially your
selfishness, because you can only now be safe by culti-
vating them further; yet this is the most dangerous of
necessities; people are greedy for your fall as for that

of any of the great; indeed no one can rise above common life, as you have done so fully, without in the same degree sinking below it; you have made this advice real to me, because I cannot despise it for your sake; I am only sure that you are valuable and in danger.'

II

One may point out that the reason so little can be deduced about W. H., the reason why Butler and Wilde (though he had so much sympathy for snobbery) could make a plausible case for his being not a patron but an actor, is that this process of interaction between metaphors, which acts like a generalisation, is always carried so far; the contradictory elements in the relation are brought out and opposed absolutely, so that we cannot know their proportions in real life. It is hard not to go off down one of the roads at the crossing, and get one plain meaning for the poem from that, because Shakespeare himself did that so very effectively afterwards; a part of the situation of the Sonnets, the actual phrases designed for it, are given to Prince Henry, to Angelo, to Troilus, to the Greek army; getting further from the original as time went on. I shall look at the first two. It is only partly true that this untidy process, if successful, might tell one more about the original situation; discoveries of language and feeling made from a personal situation may develop themselves so that they can be applied to quite different dramatic situations; but to know about these might tell one more about the original discoveries. The fact that the feelings in this sonnet could be used for such different people as Angelo and Prince Henry, different both in their power and their coldness, is an essential part of its breadth.

The crucial first soliloquy of Prince Henry was put in to save his reputation with the audience; it is a wilful destruction of his claims to generosity, indeed to honesty, if only in Falstaff's sense; but this is not to say that it was a mere job with no feeling behind it. It was a concession to normal and decent opinion rather than to the groundlings; the man who was to write *Henry V* could feel the force of that as well as take care of his plot; on the other hand, it cannot have been written without bitterness against the prince. It was probably written about two years after the second, more intimate dedication to Southampton, and is almost a cento from the Sonnets.

We would probably find the prince less puzzling if Shakespeare had re-written *Henry VI* in his prime. The theme at the back of the series, after all, is that the Henries are usurpers; however great the virtues of Henry V may be, however rightly the nation may glory in his deeds, there is something fishy about him and the justice of Heaven will overtake his son. In having some sort of double attitude to the prince Shakespeare was merely doing his work as a history-writer. For the critic to drag in a personal situation from the Sonnets is neither an attack nor a justification; it claims only to show where the feelings the play needed were obtained.

Sir Walter Raleigh said that the play was written when Shakespeare was becoming successful and buying New Place, so that he became interested in the problems of successful people like Henries IV and V rather than in poetical failures like Richard II. On this view we are to see in Prince Henry the Swan himself; he has made low friends only to get local colour out of them, and now drops them with a bang because he has made money and grand friends. It is possible enough, though I don't know why it was thought pleasant; anyway such a personal association is far at the back of the mind and one would expect several to be at work together. Henry might carry a grim externalisation of self-contempt as well as a still half-delighted reverberation of Southampton; Falstaff an attack on some rival playwright or on Florio as tutor of Southampton as well as a savage and joyous externalisation of self-contempt. But I think only the second of these alternatives fits in with the language and echoes a serious personal situation. Henry's soliloquy demands from us just the sonnets' mood of bitter complaisance; the young man must still be praised and loved, however he betrays his intimates, because we see him all shining with the virtues of success. So I shall now fancy Falstaff as Shakespeare (he has obviously some great forces behind him) and Henry as the patron who has recently betrayed him.

> I know you all, and will a-while vphold
> The vnyoak'd humor of your idlenesse:
> Yet heerein will I imitate the Sunne,
> Who doth permit the base contagious cloudes
> To smother vp his Beauty from the world,
> That when he please again to be himselfe,
> Being wanted, he may be more wondred at,
> By breaking through the foule and vgly mists
> Of vapours, that did seeme to strangle him.

This seems quite certainly drawn from the earliest and most pathetic of the attempts to justify W. H.

> Fvll many a glorious morning haue I scene, . . .
> Anon permit the *basest cloudes* to ride, . . .
> With *ougly* rack on his celestiall face, . . .
>   *Suns* of the world may staine, when heauens sun staineth.

But it is turned backwards; the sun is now to free itself from the clouds by the very act of betrayal. 'Oh that you were yourself' (13) and 'have eyes to wonder'

(106) are given the same twist into humility; Shakespeare admits, with Falstaff in front of him, that the patron would be better off without friends in low life. The next four lines, developing the idea that you make the best impression on people by only treating them well at rare intervals, are a prosaic re-hash of 'Therefore are feasts so solemn and so rare,' etc. (52); what was said of the policy of the friend is now used for the policy of the politician, though in both play and sonnet they are opposed. The connection in the next lines is more doubtful.

> So when this loose behaviour I throw off
> And pay the debt I never promised
> By so much better than my word I am
> By so much shall I falsify men's hopes

(He does indeed, by just so much.) This *debt* looks like an echo of the debt to nature there was so much doubt about W. H.'s method of paying; it has turned into a debt to society. At any rate in the sonnet-like final couplet

> I'll so offend, to make offence a skill

(' The tongue that tells the story of thy days . . . Cannot dispraise but in a kind of praise ') we have the central theme of all the sonnets of apology; the only difference, though it is a big one, is that this man says it about himself.

One element at least in this seems to reflect a further doubt on to the sonnet I have considered; the prince may be showing by this soliloquy that he can avoid infection, or may be an example of how sour a lord and owner can turn in his deeds on Coronation Day. The last irony and most contorted generosity one can extract from the sonnet is in the view that Shakespeare himself is the basest weed, that to meet him is to meet infection, that the result of being faithful to his friendship would be to be outbraved even by him, that the advice to be a cold person and avoid the fate of the lily is advice to abandon Shakespeare once for all.

This interpretation is more than once as firmly contradicted by Falstaff as it will be by my readers. He first comes on in a great fuss about his good name; he has been rated in the streets for leading astray Harry. At the end of the scene we find that this was unfair to him; the prince makes clear by the soliloquy that he is well able to look after himself. Meanwhile Falstaff amuses himself by turning the accusation the other way round.

> O, thou hast damnable iteration, and art indeede able to corrupt a Saint. Thou hast done much harme unto me *Hal,* God forgiue thee for it. Before I knew thee *Hal,* I knew nothing: and now I am (if a man shold speake truly) little better than one of the wicked. I must giue ouer this life, and I will giue it over: and I do not, I am a Villaine. Ile be damn'd for never a Kings sonne in Christendome.
>
> PRIN. Where shall we take a purse to morrow, Iacke?

The audience were not expected to believe this aspect of the matter, but there may well be some truth in it if applied to the situation Shakespeare had at the back of his mind. The other aspect is also preserved for us in the Sonnets.

> I may not euer-more acknowledge thee,
> Least my bewailed guilt should do thee shame,
> Nor thou with publike kindnesse honour me,
> Unlesse thou take that honour from thy name:

' I not only warn you against bad company; I admit I

am part of it.' One could throw in here that letter about Southampton wasting his time at the playhouse and out of favour with the Queen.

There are two sums of a thousand pounds concerned, so that the phrase is kept echoing through both parts of the history; it seems to become a symbol of Falstaff's hopes and his betrayal. The first he got by the robbery at Gadshill, and the prince at once robbed him of it; supposedly to give back to its owner, if you take his reluctance to steal seriously (he does give it back later, but one is free to suspect only under threat of exposure). He says he will give it to Francis the drawer, and Falstaff pacifies the hostess by saying he will get it back.

> HOSTESS. . . . and sayde this other day, You ought him a thousand pound.
> PRINCE. Sirrah, do I owe you a thousand pound?
> FALSTAFF. A thousand pound *Hal*? A Million. Thy loue is worth a Million: thou ow'st me thy loue. Part I, III. iii.

He will pay neither. But Falstaff gets another thousand pounds from Shallow, and the phrase is all he clings to in the riddling sentence at his final discomfiture: 'Master Shallow, I owe you a thousand pound.' This is necessary, to seem calm and reassure Shallow; it is either a sweeping gesture of renunciation (' What use to me now is the money I need never have repaid to this fool?') or a comfort since it reminds him that he has got the money and certainly won't repay it; but it is meant also for the king to hear and remember ('I class you with Shallow and the rest of my friends'). I cannot help fancying an obscure connection between this sum and the thousand pounds which, we are told, Southampton once gave Shakespeare, to go through with a purchase that he had a mind to.

It is as well to look at Falstaff in general for a moment, to show what this tender attitude to him has to fit in with. The plot treats him as a simple Punch, whom you laugh at with good-humour, though he is wicked, because he is always knocked down and always bobs up again. (Our attitude to him as a Character entirely depends on the Plot, and yet he is a Character who very nearly destroyed the Plot as a whole.) People sometimes take advantage of this to view him as a lovable old dear; a notion which one can best refute by considering him as an officer.

Part I. v. iii.

> I haue led my rag of Muffins where they are pepper'd: there's not three of my 150 left alive, and they for the Townes end, to beg during life.

We saw him levy a tax in bribes on the men he left; he now kills all the weaklings he conscripted, in order to keep their pay. A large proportion of the groundlings consisted of disbanded soldiers who had suffered under such a system; the laughter was a roar of hatred here; he is 'comic' like a Miracle Play Herod. (Whereas Harry has no qualities that are obviously not 'V. H.'s.) And yet it is out of his defence against this, the least popularisable charge against him, that he makes his most unanswerable retort to the prince.

> PRINCE. Tell me, Jack, whose fellows are these that come after?
> FAL. Mine, Hal, mine.
> PRINCE. I never did see such pitiful rascals.
> FAL. Tut, tut; good enough to toss; food for powder, food for powder; they'll fill a pit as well as better; tush, man, mortal men, mortal men.

Mortal conveys both ' all men are in the same boat, all

equal before God' and 'all you want is slaughter.'
No one in the audience was tempted to think Harry as
wicked as his enemy Hotspur, who deserved death as
much as Lear for wanting to divide England. But this
remark needed to be an impudent cover for villainy
if the strength of mind and heart in it were not to be
too strong, to make the squabbles of ambitious and
usurping persons too contemptible.

On the other hand, Falstaff's love for the prince is
certainly meant as a gap in his armour; one statement
(out of so many) of this comes where the prince[1] is
putting his life in danger and robbing him of the (stolen)
thousand pounds.

> I haue forsworne his company hourely any time this two and
> twenty yeares, and yet I am bewitcht with the Rogues company.
> If the Rascal haue not giuen me medecines to make me loue him,
> Ile be hang'd; it could not be else; I haue drunke Medecines.

He could continually be made to say such things without
stopping the laugh at him, partly because one thinks he
is pretending love to the prince for his own interest;
'never any man's thought keeps the roadway' as well
as those of the groundlings who think him a hypocrite
about it, but this phrase of mockery at them is used
only to dignify the prince; the more serious Falstaff's
expression of love becomes the more comic it is, whether
as hopeless or as hypocrisy. But to stretch one's mind
round the whole character (as is generally admitted)
one must take him, though as the supreme expression
of the cult of mockery as strength and the comic idealisa-

[1] This is a mistake; it must be Poins whom Falstaff accuses of
administering the love-philtre. But I think Falstaff is drawn as
regularly expressing love for young men who rob for him, without
complete insincerity, and as being unusually sincere in the case of the
prince.

tion of freedom, yet as both villainous and tragically ill-used.

Angelo is further from the sonnets than Henry both in date and situation; he is merely an extreme, perhaps not very credible, example of the cold person and the lily; both simply as chaste and as claiming to be more than human, which involves being at least liable to be as much less. He has odd connections with this sonnet through *Edward III*, which may help to show that there is a real connection of ideas. In the following lines he is recoiling with horror from the idea that Isabella has been using her virtue as a temptation for him, which was just what her brother expected her to do (I. ii. 185— she is a cold person but can ' move men ').

II. ii. 165-8.

> Not she : nor doth she tempt ; but it is I,
> That, lying by the Violet in the Sunne,
> Doe as the Carrion do's, not as the flowre,
> Corrupt with vertuous season :

Edward III is also a man in authority tempting a chaste woman, and he too uses the notion that her qualities are a temptation, so that it is half her fault.

II. i. 58.

> the queen of beauty's queens shall see
> Herself the ground of my infirmity.

Both Angelo's metaphor and the chief line of this sonnet come from a speech by the lady's father, which contains the germ of most of the ideas we are dealing with.

II. i. 430-457.

> The greater man, the greater is the thing,
> Be it good or bad, that he shall undertake . . .
> The freshest summer's day doth soonest taint
> The loathed carrion that it seems to kiss . . .

Lilies that fester smell far worse than weeds;
And every glory that inclines to sin,
The shame is treble by the opposite.

The freshest summer's day is always likely to kiss carrion, and the suggestion from this is that the great man is always likely to do great harm as well as great good. The sun kissing carrion is brought out again both for Falstaff and by Hamlet (1 *Henry IV*, II. iv. 113; *Hamlet*, II. ii. 158); it is clear that the complex of metaphor in this speech, whether Shakespeare wrote it or not, developed afterwards as a whole in his mind.

The obvious uses of the language of the Sonnets about Angelo all come in the first definition of his character by the Duke; once started like this he goes off on his own. The fascination of the irony of the passage is that it applies to Angelo's incorruptible virtues, associated with his chastity, the arguments and metaphors which had been used to urge abrogation of chastity on W. H.; nor is this irrelevant to the play. As in *virtues, torches,* and *fine touches,* its language, here and throughout, is always perversely on the edge of a bawdy meaning; even *belongings* may have a suggestion, helped out by ' longings,' of nature's gift of desire. It seems impossible even to praise the good qualities of Angelo without bringing into the hearer's mind those other good qualities that Angelo refuses to recognise. The most brilliant example of this trick in the play is the continual pun on *sense,* for sensuality, sensibleness (which implies the claim of Lucio) and sensibility (which implies a further claim of the poet). The first use may be unequivocal, as if to force the sexual meaning on our notice.

I. iv. 59.   The wanton stings, and motions of the sence.

II. ii. 141. ANGELO. Shee speakes, and 'tis such sence
                    That my sence breeds with it; fare you well.
II. ii. 168.   Can it be
                    That Modesty may more betray our Sence
                    Than womans lightnesse?
II. iv. 73.   Nay, but heare me,
                    Your sence pursues not mine: either you are
                       ignorant,
                    Or seeme so craft(il)y; and that's not good.
IV. iv. 27.   He should haue liu'd,
                    Save that his riotous youth with dangerous
                       sence,
                    Might in ſie times to come have ta'en revenge.
V. i. 225. MARIANA. As there ſ; sence in truth, and truth in vertue,
                    I am affianced this man's wife, as strongly
                    As words could make vp vowes:

But this sort of thing does not depend on echoes from
the Sonnets, and I think those that occur have a further
effect.

                    Thy selfe, and thy belongings
               Are not thine owne so proper, as to waste
               Thy selfe upon thy vertues; they on thee:
               Heauen doth with us, as we, with Torches doe,
               Not light them for themselves: For if our vertues
               Did not goe forth of us, 'twere all alike
               As if we had them not: Spirits are not finely touch'd,
               But to fine issues: nor nature never lends
               The smallest scruple of her excellence,
               But like a thrifty goddesse, she determines
               Her selfe the glory of a creditour,
               Both thanks, and vse;

'All are but stewards of her excellence '—indeed *their*
in the sonnet might refer back to *nature's riches.* Even
Angelo is wrong to think he can be a lord and owner,
though he seems the extreme case of those capable of
reserve and power. He is a *torch* whom nature tricks

because she destroys it by making it brilliant; it was because he accepted office and prepared to use his virtues that she could trick him all but disastrously into using more of them than he intended. For 'virtues' mean both 'good qualities' and 'capacities' ('a dormitive virtue') whether for good or ill; the same ambivalent attitude both towards worldly goods and towards what claim to be spiritual goods is conveyed by this as by the clash between *heaven's graces* and *nature's riches*. The same pun and irony on it, with a hint of a similar movement of thought about *honour*, are used when Isabella takes leave of Angelo after her first interviews.

II. ii. 162-4. ISAB. Saue your Honour.
            ANG. From thee: euen from thy vertue.
                    What's this? what's this? is this her fault, or
                    mine?
                    The Tempter, or the Tempted, who sins most?

It is his virtues and Isabella's between them that both trick him and nearly destroy Claudio. Not of course that this is straightforward satire against virtue in the sense of chastity; the first great speech of Claudio about 'too much liberty' has all the weight and horror of the lust sonnet (129) from which it is drawn; only the still greater mockery of Claudio could so drag the play back to its attack on Puritanism.

The issue indeed is more general than the sexual one; it is 'liberty, my Lucio, liberty,' as Claudio makes clear at once; which runs through pastoral and is at the heart of the clowns. (Lawrence too seems to make sex the type of liberty; Shaw's Don Juan liberty the type of sex.) 'Nature in general is a cheat, and all those who think themselves owners are pathetic.' Yet we seem here to transfer to Nature the tone of bitter complaisance taken up towards W. H. when he seemed an owner; she now, as he was, must be given the benefit of the doubt inseparable from these shifting phrases; she too must be let rob you by tricks and still be worshipped. There is the same suggestion with the same metaphors in that splendid lecture to Achilles to make him use his virtues as a fighter further; whether rightly to *thank* her is to view yourself as an owner or a steward, you must still in the end pay her the compound interest on her gifts, and still keep up the pretence that they are free. This tone of generous distaste for the conditions of life, which gives the play one of its few suggestions of sympathy for Angelo, I think usually goes with a suggestion of the Sonnets. For instance, it is the whole point about Bassanio; more than any other suitor he is an arriviste loved only for success and seeming; his one merit, and it is enough, is to recognise this truth with Christian humility. His speech before the caskets about the falsity of seeming is full of phrases from the Sonnets (*e.g.* 68, about hair) and may even have a dim reference to the Dark Lady. It is not surprising that this sentiment should make Shakespeare's mind hark back to the Sonnets, because it was there so essential; these poems of idealisation of a patron and careerist depend upon it for their strength and dignity. ' Man is so placed that the sort of thing you do is in degree all that any one can do; success does not come from mere virtue, and without some external success a virtue is not real even to itself. One must not look elsewhere; success of the same nature as yours is all that the dignity, whether of life or poetry, can be based upon.' This queer sort of realism, indeed, is one of the main things he had to say.

The feeling that life is essentially inadequate to the

human spirit, and yet that a good life must avoid saying so, is naturally at home with most versions of pastoral; in pastoral you take a limited life and pretend it is the full and normal one, and a suggestion that one must do this with all life, because the normal is itself limited, is easily put into the trick though not necessary to its power. Conversely any expression of the idea that all life is limited may be regarded as only a trick of pastoral, perhaps chiefly intended to hold all our attention and sympathy for some limited life, though again this is not necessary to it either on grounds of truth or beauty; in fact the suggestion of pastoral may be only a protection for the idea which must at last be taken alone. The business of interpretation is obviously very complicated. Literary uses of the problem of free-will and necessity, for example, may be noticed to give curiously bad arguments and I should think get their strength from keeping you in doubt between the two methods. Thus Hardy is fond of showing us an unusually stupid person subjected to very unusually bad luck, and then a moral is drawn, not merely by inference but by solemn assertion, that we are all in the same boat as this person whose story is striking precisely because it is unusual. The effect may be very grand, but to make an otherwise logical reader accept the process must depend on giving him obscure reasons for wishing it so. It is clear at any rate that this grand notion of the inadequacy of life, so various in its means of expression, so reliable a bass note in the arts, needs to be counted as a possible territory of pastoral.

Marvell's Garden

The Ideal Simplicity Approached by Resolving Contradictions

THE chief point of the poem is to contrast and reconcile conscious and unconscious states, intuitive and intellectual modes of apprehension; and yet that distinction is never made, perhaps could not have been made; his thought is implied by his metaphors. There is something very Far-Eastern about this; I was set to work on the poem by Dr. Richards' recent discussion of a philosophical argument in Mencius. The Oxford edition notes bring out a crucial double meaning (so that this at least is not my own fancy) in the most analytical statement of the poem, about the Mind—

> Annihilating all that's made
> To a green thought in a green shade.

'Either "reducing the whole material world to nothing material, *i.e.* to a green thought," or "considering the material world as of no value compared to a green thought"'; either contemplating everything or shutting everything out. This combines the idea of the conscious mind, including everything because understanding it, and that of the unconscious animal nature, including everything because in harmony with it. Evidently the object of such a fundamental contradiction (seen in the etymology: turning all *ad nihil*, *to* nothing, and *to* a thought) is to deny its reality; the point is not that these two are essentially different but that they must cease to be different so far as either is to be known. So far as he has achieved his state of ecstasy he combines them, he is 'neither conscious nor not conscious,' like the seventh

Buddhist state of enlightenment. This gives its point, I think, to the other ambiguity, clear from the context, as to whether the *all* considered was *made* in the mind of the author or the Creator; to so peculiarly 'creative' a knower there is little difference between the two. Here as usual with 'profound' remarks the strength of the thing is to combine unusually intellectual with unusually primitive ideas; thought about the conditions of knowledge with a magical idea that the adept controls the external world by thought.

The vehemence of the couplet, and this hint of physical power in thought itself (in the same way as the next line gives it colour), may hint at an idea that one would like to feel was present, as otherwise it is the only main idea about Nature that the poem leaves out; that of the *Hymn to David* and *The Ancient Mariner*, the Orpheus idea, that by delight in Nature when terrible man gains strength to control it. This grand theme too has a root in magic; it is an important version of the idea of the man powerful because he has included everything in himself, is still strong, one would think, among the mountain climbers and often the scientists, and deserves a few examples here. I call it the idea of the *Hymn to David*, though being hidden behind the religious one it is nowhere overtly stated, except perhaps in the line

> Praise above all, for praise prevails.

David is a case of Orpheus-like behaviour because his music restrained the madness of Saul.

> His furious foes no more maligned
> When he such melody divined,
> And sense and soul detained;

By *divining*—intuiting—the harmony behind the universe

he ' makes it divine,' rather as to discover a law of nature is to ' give nature laws,' and this restrains the madman who embodies the unruled forces of nature from killing him. The main argument of the verses describing nature (or nature as described by David) is that the violence of Nature is an expression of her adoration of God, and therefore that the man of prayer who also adores God delights in it and can control it.

> Strong the gier eagle on his sail
> Strong against tide, th' enormous whale
> Emerges, as he goes.
>
> But stronger still, in earth or air
> Or in the sea, the man of prayer,
> And far beneath the tide.

The feeling is chiefly carried by the sound; long Latin words are packed into the short lines against a short one-syllable rhyming word full of consonants; it is like dancing in heavy skirts; he juggles with the whole cumbrous complexity of the world. The *Mariner* makes a more conscious and direct use of the theme, but in some degree runs away from it at the end. The reason it was a magical crime for a sailor to kill the albatross is that it both occurs among terrible scenes of Nature and symbolises man's power to extract life from them, so ought doubly to be delighted in. So long as the Mariner is horrified by the creatures of the calm he is their slave; he is set free to act, in the supreme verses of the poem, as soon as he delights in them. The final moral is

> He prayeth best, that loveth best
> All things both great and small.

But that copybook maxim is fine only if you can hold

it firmly together with such verses as this, which Coleridge later omitted :

> The very deeps did rot ; oh Christ
> That such a thing could be ;
> Yea, slimy things did crawl with legs
> Upon the slimy sea.

And it was these creatures, as he insisted in the margin by giving the same name to both, that the Mariner blessed unaware when he discovered their beauty. This is what Coleridge meant by alternately saying that the poem has too much of the moral and too little ; knowing what the conventional phrases of modern Christianity ought to mean he thought he could shift to a conventional moral that needs to be based upon the real one. Byron's nature-poetry gives more obvious examples of the theme ; he likes to compare a storm on the Jura or what not to a woman whom, we are to feel, only Byron could dominate. Poe was startled and liberated by it into a symbol of his own achievement ; the sailor in *The Maelstrom* is so horrified as to be frozen, through a trick of neurosis, into idle curiosity, and this becomes a scientific interest in the portent which shows him the way to escape from it.

Nature when terrible is no theme of Marvell's, and he gets this note of triumph rather from using nature when peaceful to control the world of man.

> How safe, methinks, and strong, behind
> These Trees have I encamp'd my Mind ;
> Where Beauty, aiming at the Heart,
> Bends in some Tree its useless Dart ;
> And where the World no certain Shot
> Can make, or me it toucheth not.
> But I on it securely play,
> And gaul its Horsemen all the Day.

MARVELL'S GARDEN

The masculine energy of the last couplet is balanced immediately by an acceptance of Nature more masochist than passive, in which he becomes Christ with both the nails and the thorns. (*Appleton House*, lxxvi.)

> Bind me ye *Woodbines* in your 'twines,
> Curle me about ye gadding *Vines*,
> And Oh so close your Circles lace,
> That I may never leave this Place :
> But, lest your Fetters prove too weak,
> Ere I your Silken Bondage break,
> Do you, *O Brambles*, chain me too,
> And courteous *Briars* nail me through.

He does not deify himself more actively, and in any case the theme of the *Garden* is a repose.

> How vainly men themselves amaze
> To win the Palm, or Oke, or Bayes ;
> And their uncessant Labours see
> Crown'd from some single Herb or Tree.
> Whose short and narrow verged Shade
> Does prudently their Toyles upbraid ;
> While all Flow'rs and all Trees do close
> To weave the Garlands of repose.

This first verse comes nearest to stating what seems the essential distinction, with that between powers inherent and powers worked out in practice, being a general and feeling one could be ; in this ideal case, so the wit of the thing claims, the power to have been a general is already satisfied in the garden. ' Unemployment ' is too painful and normal even in the fullest life for such a theme to be trivial. But self-knowledge is possible in such a state so far as the unruly impulses are digested, ordered, made transparent, not by their being known, at the time, as unruly. Consciousness no longer makes an important distinction; the impulses, since they must be balanced already, neither need it to put them right nor are put wrong by the way it forces across their boundaries. They let themselves be known because they are not altered by being known, because their principle of indeterminacy no longer acts. This idea is important for all the versions of pastoral, for the pastoral figure is always ready to be the critic; he not only includes everything but may in some unexpected way know it.

Another range of his knowledge might be mentioned here. I am not sure what arrangement of flower-beds is described in the last verse, but it seems clear that the sun goes through the 'zodiac' of flowers in one day, and that the bees too, in going from one bed to another, reminding us of the labours of the first verse, pass all summer in a day. They compute their time as well as we in that though their lives are shorter they too contract all experience into it, and this makes the poet watch over large periods of time as well as space. So far he becomes Nature, he becomes permanent. It is a graceful finale to the all-in-one theme, but not, I think, very important; the crisis of the poem is in the middle.

Once you accept the Oxford edition's note you may as well apply it to the whole verse.

> Meanwhile the Mind, from pleasure less,
> Withdraws into its happiness;
> The Mind, that Ocean where each kind
> Does streight its own resemblance find;
> Yet it creates, transcending these,
> Far other worlds, and other Seas,
> Annihilating . . .

From pleasure less. Either 'from the lessening of pleasure'—'we are quiet in the country, but our dullness

gives a sober and self-knowing happiness, more intellectual than that of the over-stimulated pleasures of the
town' or 'made less by this pleasure'—'The pleasures
of the country give a repose and intellectual release which
make me less intellectual, make my mind less worrying
and introspective.' This is the same puzzle as to the
consciousness of the thought; the ambiguity gives two
meanings to pleasure, corresponding to his Puritan
ambivalence about it, and to the opposition between
pleasure and happiness. *Happiness*, again, names a
conscious state, and yet involves the idea of things falling
right, happening so, no being ordered by an anxiety of
the conscious reason. (So that as a rule it is a weak word;
it is by seeming to look at it hard and bring out its implications that the verse here makes it act as a strong one.)

The same doubt gives all their grandeur to the next
lines. The sea if calm reflects everything near it; the
mind as knower is a conscious mirror. Somewhere in
the sea are sea-lions and -horses and everything else,
though they are different from land ones; the uncon-
sciousness is unplumbed and pathless, and there is no
instinct so strange among the beasts that it lacks its
fantastic echo in the mind. In the first version thoughts
are shadows, in the second (like the *green thought*) they
are as solid as what they image; and yet they still
correspond to something in the outer world, so that the
poet's intuition is comparable to pure knowledge. This
metaphor may reflect back so that *withdraws* means the
tide going down; the *mind* is *less* now, but will return,
and it is now that one can see the rock-pools. On the
Freudian view of an Ocean, *withdraws* would make this
repose in Nature a return to the womb; anyway it may
mean either 'withdraws into self-contemplation' or

'withdraws altogether, into its mysterious processes of digestion.' *Streight* may mean 'packed together,' in the microcosm, or 'at once'; the beasts see their reflection (perhaps the root idea of the metaphor) as soon as they look for it; the calm of Nature gives the poet an immediate self-knowledge. But we have already had two entrancingly witty verses about the sublimation of sexual desire into a taste for Nature (I should not say that this theme was the main emotional drive behind the poem, but it takes up a large part of its overt thought), and the *kinds* look for their *resemblance*, in practice, out of a desire for *creation*; in the mind, at this fertile time for the poet, they can *find* it 'at once,' being 'packed together.' The transition from the beast and its reflection to the two pairing beasts implies a transition from the correspondences of thought with fact to those of thought with thought, to find which is to be creative; there is necessarily here a suggestion of rising from one 'level' of thought to another; and in the next couplet not only does the mind transcend the world it mirrors, but a sea, to which it is parallel, transcends both land and sea too, which implies self-consciousness and all the antinomies of philosophy. Whether or not you give *transcendent* the technical sense 'predicable of all categories' makes no great difference; in including everything in itself the mind includes as a detail itself and all its inclusions. And it is true that the sea reflects the *other worlds* of the stars; Donne's metaphor of the globe is in the background. Yet even here the double meaning is not lost; all land-beasts have their sea-beasts, but the sea also has the kraken; in the depths as well as the transcendence of the mind are things stranger than all the kinds of the world.

Miss M. C. Bradbrook has pointed out to me that the next verse, while less triumphant, gives the process a more firmly religious interpretation.

> Here at the Fountains sliding foot,
> Or by some Fruit-trees mossy root,
> Casting the Bodies Vest aside,
> My Soul into the boughs does glide;
> There like a Bird it sits, and sings,
> Then whets, and combs its silver Wings;
> And, till prepar'd for longer flight,
> Waves in its Plumes the various Light.

The bird is the dove of the Holy Spirit and carries a suggestion of the rainbow of the covenant. By becoming inherent in everything he becomes a soul not pantheist but clearly above and apart from the world even while still living in it. Yet the paradoxes are still firmly maintained here, and the soul is as solid as the green thought. The next verse returns naturally and still with exultation to the jokes in favour of solitude against women.

Green takes on great weight here, as Miss Sackville West pointed out, because it has been a pet word of Marvell's before. To list the uses before the satires may seem an affectation of pedantry, but shows how often the word was used; and they are pleasant things to look up. In the Oxford text: pages 12, l. 23; 17, l. 18; 25, l. 11; 27, l. 4; 38, l. 3; 45, l. 3; 46, l. 25; 48, l. 18; 49, l. 48; 70, l. 376; 71, l. 390; 74, l. 510; 122, l. 2. Less rich uses: 15, l. 18; 21, l. 44; 30, l. 55; 42, l. 14; 69, l. 339; 74, ll. 484, 496; 78, l. 628; 85, l. 82; 89, l. 94; 108, l. 196. It is connected here with grass, buds, children, an as yet virginal prospect of sexuality, and the peasant stock from which the great families emerge. The 'unfathomable' grass makes the soil fertile and shows it to be so; it is the humble, permanent, undeveloped nature which sustains everything, and to which everything must return. No doubt D. H. Lawrence was right when he spoke up for Leaves of Grass against Whitman and said they felt themselves to be very aristocratic, but that too is eminently a pastoral fancy. Children are connected with this both as buds, and because of their contact with Nature (as in Wordsworth), and unique fitness for Heaven (as in the Gospels).

> The tawny mowers enter next,
> Who seem like Israelites to be,
> Walking on foot through a green sea.

connects greenness with oceans and gives it a magical security;

> And in the greenness of the grass
> Did see my hopes as in a glass

connects greenness with mirrors and the partial knowledge of the mind. The complex of ideas he concentrates into this passage, in fact, had been worked out already, and in a context that shows how firmly these ideas about Nature were connected with direct pastoral. The poem indeed comes immediately after a pastoral series about the mower of grass.

> I am the Mower Damon, known
> Through all the Meadows I have mown;
> On me the Morn her dew distills
> Before her darling Daffodils.

In these meadows he feels he has left his mark on a great territory, if not on everything, and as a typical figure he has mown all the meadows of the world; in either case

Nature gives him regal and magical honours, and I
suppose he is not only the ruler but the executioner of the
daffodils—the Clown as Death.

> Only for him no Cure is found,
> Whom Juliana's Eyes do wound.
> 'Tis death alone that this must do:
> For Death thou art a Mower too.

He provides indeed more conscious and comic mixtures
of heroic and pastoral:

> every Mower's wholesome heat
> Smelled like an Alexander's sweat.

It is his grand attack on gardens which introduces both
the connection through wit between the love of woman
and of nature, which is handled so firmly in the *Garden*:

> No white nor red was ever seen
> So am'rous as this lovely green:

—and the belief that the fruitful attitude to Nature is the
passive one:

> His [the gardener's] green *Seraglio* has its Eunuchs too;
> Lest any Tyrant him outdoe.
> And in the Cherry he does Nature vex,
> To procreate without a Sex.
> 'Tis all enforced; the Fountain and the Grot;
> While the sweet Fields do lye forgot;
> Where willing Nature does to all dispence
> A wild and fragrant Innocence:
> And *Fauns* and *Faryes* do the Meadows till,
> More by their presence than their skill.

It is Marvell himself who tills the Garden by these
magical and contemplative powers.

Grass indeed comes to be taken for granted as the symbol of pastoral humility:

> Unhappy Birds! what does it boot
> To build below the Grasses' Root;
> When Lowness is unsafe as Hight,
> And Chance o'ertakes what scapeth Spight?

It is a humility of Nature from which she is still higher than man, so that the grasshoppers preach to him from their pinnacles:

> And now to the Abyss I pass
> Of that unfathomable Grass,
> Where men like Grashoppers appear,
> But Grashoppers are Gyants there;
> They, in there squeking Laugh, contemn
> Us as we walk more low than them:
> And, from the Precipices tall
> Of the green spire's, to us do call.

It seems also to be an obscure merit of grass that it produces ' hay,' which was the name of a country dance, so that the humility is gaiety.

> With this the golden fleece I shear
> Of all these Closes ev'ry Year,
> And though in Wool more poor than they,
> Yet I am richer far in Hay.

To nineteenth-century taste the only really poetical verse of the poem is the central fifth of the nine; I have been discussing the sixth, whose dramatic position is an illustration of its very penetrating theory. The first four are a crescendo of wit, on the themes ' success or failure is not important, only the repose that follows the exercise of one's powers ' and ' women, I am pleased to say, are no longer interesting to me, because nature is more

beautiful.' One effect of the wit is to admit, and so make
charming, the impertinence of the second of these, which
indeed the first puts in its place; it is only for a time, and
after effort among human beings, that he can enjoy
solitude. The value of these moments made it fitting
to pretend they were eternal; and yet the lightness of
his expression of their sense of power is more intelligent,
and so more convincing, than Wordsworth's solemnity
on the same theme, because it does not forget the
opposing forces.

> When we have run our Passions heat,
> Love hither makes his best retreat.
> The *Gods*, that mortal beauty chase,
> Still in a Tree did end their race.
> *Apollo* hunted *Daphne* so,
> Only that she might Laurel grow,
> And *Pan* did after *Syrinx* speed,
> Not as a Nymph, but for a Reed.

The energy and delight of the conceit has been sharp-
ened or keyed up here till it seems to burst and transform
itself; it dissolves in the next verse into the style of
Keats. So his observation of the garden might mount
to an ecstasy which disregarded it; he seems in this next
verse to imitate the process he has described, to enjoy
in a receptive state the exhilaration which an exercise
of wit has achieved. But striking as the change of style
is, it is unfair to empty the verse of thought and treat
it as random description; what happens is that he steps
back from overt classical conceits to a rich and intuitive
use of Christian imagery. When people treat it as the
one good ' bit ' of the poem one does not know whether
they have recognised that the Alpha and Omega of the
verse are the Apple and the Fall.

What wond'rous Life in this I lead!
Ripe Apples drop about my head;
The Luscious Clusters of the Vine
Upon my Mouth do crush their Wine;
The Nectaren, and curious Peach,
Into my hands themselves do reach;
Stumbling on Melons, as I pass,
Insnar'd with Flow'rs, I fall on Grass.

Melon, again, is the Greek for apple; 'all flesh is *grass*,' and its own *flowers* here are the snakes in it that stopped Eurydice. Mere grapes are at once the primitive and the innocent wine; the *nectar* of Eden, and yet the blood of sacrifice. *Curious* could mean 'rich and strange' (nature), 'improved by care' (art) or 'inquisitive' (feeling towards me, since nature is a mirror, as I do towards her). All these eatable beauties give themselves so as to lose themselves, like a lover, with a forceful generosity; like a lover they *ensnare* him. It is the triumph of the attempt to impose a sexual interest upon nature; there need be no more Puritanism in this use of sacrificial ideas than is already inherent in the praise of solitude; and it is because his repose in the orchard hints at such a variety of emotions that he is contemplating *all that's made*. Sensibility here repeats what wit said in the verse before; he tosses into the fantastic treasure-chest of the poem's thought all the pathos and dignity that Milton was to feel in his more celebrated Garden; and it is while this is going on, we are told in the next verse, that the mind performs its ambiguous and memorable *withdrawal*. For each of the three central verses he gives a twist to the screw of the microscope and is living in another world.

I must go back to the *annihilating* lines, whose method is less uncommon. Similar ideas and tricks of language are used in Donne's *Exstasie*, where various puns impose on us the idea that an adequate success in love is a kind of knowledge which transcends the barriers of the ordinary kind. There is again some doubt how far the author knew what he was doing.

> As our blood labours to beget
>   Spirits, as like souls as it can, . . .
> So must pure louers' soules descend. . . .

To the modern reader this is a pun on the senses 'subtle material essence' (*e.g.* 'spirits of salt') and 'non-material unit of life'; it seems used with as much 'wit' as the other puns, to trick us into feeling that soul and body may be interfused. The Oxford edition notes make clear that to Donne this was neither a pun nor a sophistry; 'The spirits . . . are the thin and active part of the blood, and are of a kind of middle nature, between soul and body' (Sermons); one view of them was that there was a hierarchy of more and more spiritual ones. It is curious how the change in the word leaves the poetry unaffected; by Swift's time the two senses were an absurd accident from which one could get ironies against materialism. No doubt in some important senses Donne was right, but however supported by Cambridge Platonism it is a genuine primitive use of the word. Whereas he would certainly have known there was a pun on 'sense' even if he took it for granted. 'Our bodies why do we forbeare?' . . .

> We owe them thankes, because they thus,
>   Did us, to us, at first convey,
> Yielded their forces, sense, to us,
>   Nor are dross to us, but allay.

The antithesis for *allay* makes it mean 'alloy,' a less

valuable substance put into their gold to strengthen it for practical use; *allay* could mean 'keeping the spiritual pleasure from being too great, more than our strength could bear,' which goes with 'alloy,' then, behind that, 'relief to the pain of desire,' which makes the flesh less unimportant. This is reinforced by the special meaning of sense ('the wanton stings and motions of the s'). That rich word confuses the pleasure and the knowledge given by the senses (Donne wants to imply they are mutually dependent) and suggests that soul and body are in a healthy intuitive relation—'plenty of sense.' The use of *sense* for sensibleness became stronger later in the century, but it is already clearly an element in the word—for example in saying 'there is no sense' in a statement when it has meaning but is not sensible. 'We could not know each other at all without sensations, therefore cannot know each other fully without sensuality, nor would it be sensible to try to do so.'

The poem uses the word again later, and there the sexual meaning is clear.

> So must pure louers soules descend
>   To affections, and to faculties,
> Which sense may reach and apprehend,
>   Else a great Prince in prison lies.
> To our bodies turn we then. . . .

Affections are 'loves,' 'weaknesses,' and in the philosophical sense 'physical effects.' *Apprehend* means 'know' and by derivation 'clutch,' and *reach* would go with either, which gives *sense* a sort of bridge between its meanings.

It is possible that Donne means to throw in a pun on 'know,' as in 'Adam knew his wife.'

> Wee then, who are this new soule, know,
> Of what we are compos'd, and made,
> For, the Atomies of which we grow,
> Are soules, which no change can invade.

Know is isolated by the comma (' know each other '),
and *of* may then take a step towards ' by means of.'
Then, with Donne's usual leap in pretending to give a
reason, he makes each soul entirely immaterial; ' the
intellectual knowledge has, for us, all the advantages of
the physical one, even granted that they are distinguish-
able.' If he did this it would have to be done consciously
and wilfully.

One should not of course take such poetry as only a
clever game. This truth-seeking idea seems fundamental
to the European convention of love-poetry; love is
always idealised as a source of knowledge not only of
the other party but of oneself and of the world:

> This Exstasie doth unperplex

because it makes the disparate impulses of the human
creature not merely open to the prying of the mind but
prepared for its intrusion. It is along these lines, I think,
that D. H. Lawrence's hatred of the whole conception
might be answered, or rather that he answered it himself.
On the other hand, I think Donne felt quite casual about
these particular tricks; the juggle with *sense* has the same
graceful impudence as his frankly absurd arguments.
M. Legouis may be right in saying that he set out merely
to dramatise the process of seduction; it is only clear
that he found the argument fascinating and believed that
it had some truth in some cases. He did not think it
so false as to depend on his puns, even where he recognised them; he may well have understood what the

puns themselves depend upon. They insist on relics of
primitive thought in civilised language, and thereby
force the language to break down its later distinctions
and return to ideas natural to the human mind.   Dr.
Richards' account of romantic nature poetry in *Coleridge
on Imagination* is a very good example; the personalised
Nature is treated both as external to man and as created
by an instinct of the mind, and by tricks of language
these are made to seem the same.   But if they were
simply called the same we would not so easily be satisfied
by the tricks.   What we feel is that though they are
essentially unlike they are practically unlike in different
degrees at different times; a supreme condition can
therefore be imagined, though not attained, in which
they are essentially like.   (To put it like this is no doubt
to evade a philosophic issue.)   A hint of the supreme
condition is thus found in the actual one (this makes
the actual one include everything in itself), but this
apparently exalted claim is essentially joined to humility;
it is effective only through the admission that it is only
a hint.   Something of the tone of pastoral is therefore
inherent in the claim; the fault of the Wordsworthian
method seems to be that it does not show this.

I shall add here a pun from *As You Like It*, which shows
how the same issue may be raised by a casual joke.   The
pun in its context makes a contradiction, and this is felt
to show an intuitive grasp of some of the puzzles of the
context.   Fortunately there is no doubt that a pun is
meant because the text insists upon it; the *N.E.D.*
shows that the modern spellings, though used loosely,
already made the distinction.   Apart from facsimiles
no edition that I have seen has yet printed the text.
The point of the two spellings is to show that the two

senses are at work; it is none the less fair to take the senses the other way round. (This is from the Folio; there is no Quarto.)

> CLOWN. ... truly, I would the Gods hadde made thee poeticall.
> AUDREY. I do not know what Poetical is: is it honest in word and deed: is it a true thing?
> CLOWN. No trulie: for the truest poetrie is the most faining, and Louers are given to Poetrie: and what they sweare in Poetrie, may be said as Louers, they do feigne.
> AUDREY. Do you wish then that the Gods had made me Poetical?
> CLOWN. I do truly: for thou swear'st to me thou art honest: Now if thou wert a Poet, I might haue some hope thou didst feigne.

'A material fool' is the pleased judgment of the listening Jaques; he feels that there is a complete copy of the human world among fools, as of beasts among sea-beasts. This indeed is one of the assumptions of pastoral, that you can say everything about complex people by a complete consideration of simple people. The jokes are mainly carried on by puns on 'honest'— chastity in women, truth in speech, simplicity in clowns, and the hearty sense 'generous because free from hypocrisy'; my point is the pun on 'fain' (*desiring*) and 'feign' (*pretend*; in lovers *pretend honest desire*). The doubt of the poet's honesty is referred to the broader doubt of his self-knowledge, just as *honest* itself shifts from 'truth-telling' to 'sincere in his own mind.' The pun itself is common, though I think it is only here, where it enriches the thought so much, that Shakespeare spelt it out for the reader.

> EGEUS. Thou hast by moonlight at her window sang
> With faining voice, verses of faining love,
> And stolne the impression of her fantasie.

He feigns true love because he would fain possess her;
the word *love* itself may be used of a desire not permanent
or generous; Egeus would call that a feigning love even
if Nature deceives both of them, and the man thinks
himself sincere. The easy but capacious mind of Spenser
takes this for granted (F.Q., V. xii. 36; Hymn to Love,
216); nobody pretends without purpose, so it is a
useful trick of language. Touchstone's use of it about
poetry is more searching.

The root of the joke is that a physical desire drives
the human creature to a spiritual one. The best poetry
is the most genuinely passionate (fain) but there may be
two pretences (feign), that the desire felt for this woman
is spiritual and that any woman is the object of so spiritual
a desire. 'To write poetry is not the quickest way to
satisfy desire; there must be some other impulse behind
the convention of love-poetry; something feigned in the
choice of topic; some other thing of which they are
fain.' As for the distinction between their rôles as poets
and lovers, both senses may apply to them in both, also
to *swearing*, since ' go to hell ' is spontaneous, not meant,
not meant to deceive, and a sort of feigning in which
you are fain of what you feign. For that matter they are
wooing the reader even if they are not trying to seduce
a mistress; the process at its simplest involves desire
and detachment, nature and sophistication; levels
mysteriously inter-related which a sane man separates
only for a joke. Touchstone's pretence of acidity allows
of a real plea for his own case because it implies that the
most refined desires are inherent in the plainest, and
would be false if they weren't; he shows a staircase by
giving the two lowest steps, lust and cheating. In the
Marvell and Donne examples it is the top of a staircase

that is in question, but the same method is used to define
it. Two ideas are united which in normal use are contradictory, and our machinery of interpretation so acts
that we feel there is a series of senses in which they
could be more and more truly combined. This is clearest
in what Mr. James Smith defined as metaphysical conceits, those that genuinely sum up a metaphysical
problem. The top and next steps in the Aristotelian
staircase about form and matter, for example, would
be pure form and the material, already form, which it
informs. Donne is using this when he calls each lover's
soul the body of the other's; the fact that we do not
believe that the lovers are in this condition does not keep
us from a feeling of belief in the conceit, because we
believe in the staircase which it defines; the lovers appear
as conscious of the staircase and higher up on it than
most. Nor for that matter do we believe that the
clown is at the bottom of his staircase; his understanding
of it acts as a proof that he isn't. A good case of a poem
with some doubt about the staircase it requires is provided by Shakespeare's *Phoenix and Turtle*; it depends
on the same ideas as Donne's *First Anniversary*, but gets
very different feelings out of them. The entire flatness
of the use of the convention makes it seem first an
engagingly simpleminded piece of 'idealism' and then,
since the union of the birds is likely after all to be of a
simple kind, an expression of cultivated and good-
humoured sensuality; this does not by any means
destroy the pathetic dignity of the close. There is a
suggestion that the author finds the convention fascinating but absurd, which he shows mainly by his sound-
effects. This seems to me intentional, very delightful,
and not a thing that Chapman (who has been suggested

as the author) could possibly have done. It is clear here that once you cease to impose a staircase the thing shifts from heroic to mock-pastoral. Some such idea needs to be added to Mr. James Smith's account (perhaps he would call it obvious) because otherwise there seems no way of putting in a judgment of value; on his account a metaphysical conceit is essentially a vivid statement of a puzzle, and in practice it is more.

I should say that this process is at work in much poetry that does not seem ambiguous at all, and shall pursue the question into Homer as the fountainhead of simplicity. This may also throw some light on the obscure connection between heroic and pastoral; the fact seems to be that both rely on a ' complex in simple ' formula.

One idea essential to a primitive epic style is that the good is not separable (anyway at first level judgments) from a life of straightforward worldly success in which you keep certain rules; the plain satisfactions are good in themselves and make great the men who enjoy them. From this comes the ' sense of glory ' and of controlling nature by delight in it. It is absurd to call this a ' pre-moralistic ' view, since the rules may demand great sacrifices and it is shameful not to keep them; there is merely a naïve view of the nature of good. (Both a limitation of the things that are good and a partial failure to separate the idea of good from the idea of those things.) The naïve view is so often more true than the sophisticated ones that this comes in later ages to take on an air of massive grandeur; it gives a feeling of freedom from humbug which is undoubtedly noble, and the Homeric heroes support this by the far from savage trait of questioning the beliefs they still die for. Stock epithets about ' the good wine ' or ' the well-built

gates' imply 'so one always rightly feels'; such a thing
essentially has virtue in it, *is* a piece of virtue; a later
reader feels this to be symbolic, a process of packing all
the sorts of good into a simple one. Material things are
taken as part of a moral admiration, and to a later reader
(with less pride, for example, in the fact that his culture
uses iron) this seems an inspiriting moral paradox like
those of pastoral—' to one who knows how to live the
ideal is easily reached.' It is assumed that Ajax is still
enormously grand when he cooks his dinner; the later
reader feels he must really be very grand not to lose his
dignity, whereas at the time it was a thing of some
splendour to have so much dinner to cook or such
implements to do it with. This comes to have the same
effect as a pretence of pastoral humility in the author.
Also the heroic individual has an enormous effect on
everything in sight, gods and men, and yet finds everything of manageable dimensions; the later reader feels
that this belongs to a village society rather than a large-
town one. Certainly the heroes are not grand merely
because they are brave; they can run away like other
people, and say so more frankly. Indeed a great part
of their dignity comes from the naïve freshness with
which they can jump from one level of argument to
another, and this leaves room for the effects I am considering.

Thus the puzzles become more obvious later, but this
is not to say they were not used at the start. The heroes
are given a directly moral grandeur by the perpetual
clashes between free-will and necessity, symbolised by
their relations with the gods, out of which they construct
their speeches; they fight on when certain of failure
and kill each other with the apology that they too are

fated, and such fore-knowledge as they have makes them
half divine. It is very curious that what is supposed to
be another branch of the same race, when it arrived in
India, had none of this interest in the problems of free-
will; the dignity of the heroes in the Mahabarata is based
on puzzles about the One and the Many. Nor did it
develop later; the Buddha was once actually faced
with the problem of freewill raised so starkly by his
system, and brushed it aside on grounds of morality;
I understand that all Buddhist theologians have ignored
the issue. Whereas all new ideas in Europe, Christianity
and the sciences in turn, have been taken as new problems
about necessity and free-will. Thus the reason why the
Homeric *but* where one expects ' and ' has so much poetic
force is that it implies some argument, such as all the
characters are happy with, and the argument would
lead you to other levels of thought. (This acts as a
feeling that the two things put together are vividly
different in themselves.) 'He spoke, and held still his
hand upon the silvery hilt, and thrust back the great
sword into the scabbard, nor did he disobey the order
of Minerva; but she had gone to Olympus, to the
mansions of aegis-bearing Jove, amongst the other
deities.' *But* makes her already indifferent; the puzzle
about how far men are free and how far the gods are
only forces in their minds is thrust upon your attention.
Also there is a strong feeling in the epic that the heroes
are too great to kill each other for detested Helen and
the unnecessary recovery of corpses (' Nor do I fear so
much about the dead body of Patroclus, which will
quickly satiate the dogs and birds of the Trojans, as much
as I fear for my own head, lest it suffer anything, and
for thine ') and yet that only this would display their

greatness; a rich contradiction on which to build a hierarchy of value. I began by saying that such writing was based on a naïve idea of the nature of good, but in fact other ideas of good are implicit in it; Shakespeare's *Troilus and Cressida* is often taken as a sort of parody of the *Iliad*, but there is little in it that Homer did not imply. What becomes strange to a more sophisticated society is the order in which the ideas can be built up; in such a society everybody has been told some refined ideas about good (or what not) and wants them put in at once; to take a simple thing and imply a hierarchy in it can then only be done in a strange world like that of Milton's Adam or a convention like that of pastoral. To say this is to echo what many of Homer's critics, including Milton himself, have said about the peculiar advantage he got from his date, and I am only trying to show that it fits in with my theory.

I have not been able to say what machinery erects a staircase on a contradiction, but then the only essential for the poet is to give the reader a chance to build an interesting one; there are continual opportunities in the most normal uses of language. Any statement of identity between terms already defined (' God is love ') is a contradiction because you already know they are not identical; you have to ignore senses that would be unimportant (' the first cause was a creative impulse ') and there are likely to be degrees in which the two may be called identical which lead to different important senses. That the process is not simple is obvious when you turn them round; ' love is God ' would be quite different. ' Might is Right ' and ' Right is Might ' were felt to be clear and opposite statements of ethical theory, and it is not clear how this was possible. It is no good to read them as 'if a man has might, then he has right,' etc.; a supporter of this opinion would say that if a man has no might he has no right, and the two sentences are still identical. The same applies to the similar interpretations 'Might is a member of the class Right,' etc.; it would be the only member of its class. I think these are at work; the analogy of the second word to an adjective in this version shows how the first is felt to be the more solid and unchangeable. But the second word is in fact belittled rather than made inclusive. Yet you cannot read them simply as substitutions; 'always say might instead of right; there is no reason for not making a full use of power' and 'never calculate chances; to be in the right is the only thing to be considered.' These are present and seem to control the senses from the back, but the subdued word is still there and is not negated. *Right* in the first is some sort of justification and *might* in the second some sort of hope or claim. 'A great and crowded nation has the right to expand'; 'because we have right on our side we are certain to win.' A vague sense that 'is' has other uses than the expression of identity makes us ready to find meanings in such sentences; this may well have been the historical reason why it was too convenient to be simplified. But the principle of language that makes the two different is simply a traffic rule; the two words are felt to cover some of the same ground and in some cases of conflict the first has the right of way.

It might I think also be argued that any contradiction implies a regress, though not one definite one. To say that it is always an example of the supreme process of seeing the Many as One is to ignore the differences in the feelings aroused by different examples; but there may always be a less ambitious process at work that uses similar machinery. The pretence that two words are identical acts as a hint that they have been fitted into some system, in which each key word is dependent on the others, like the parts of an organism; admittedly the words are not the same but they have been ' unified.' One characteristic of an organism is that you can only change it (as a whole and without killing it) by a process like edging up a chimney in rock-climbing; one element must be changed to the small extent that the elasticity of the system allows and then the others must be changed to fit it. So to find your way into the interpretation seems essentially a process of shifting the words again and again. This at least describes the sense of richness (readiness for argument not pursued) in such language and the fact that one ambiguity, even though obtained in several parallel words, is not enough for it.

That this talk about a hierarchy of ' levels ' is vague I can cheerfully admit; the idea is generally vague in the authors who use it, and none the less powerful for being left in a suggestive form. But the three central verses of the Marvell poem are at least a definite example; in the course of suggesting various interlocking hierarchies (knowing that you know that you know, reconciling the remaining unconscious with the increasing consciousness, uniting in various degrees perception and creation, the one and the many), it does in fact rise through a hierarchy of three sharply contrasted styles and with them give a more and more inclusive account of the mind's relation to Nature. Only a metaphysical poet with so perfect a sense of form and so complete a control over the tricks of the style, at the end of its development, could actually dramatise these hints as he gave them.

Milton and Bentley

The Pastoral of the Innocence of
Man and Nature

BENTLEY'S escapade has remained something of a scandal; if he was really incapable of understanding Milton, said Mrs. Woolf, how far can we credit these eminent classicists on their own ground? Or is it Milton, after all, whose language must not be taken seriously, as if he was a real classic? English critics adopt a curious air of social superiority to Bentley; he is the Man who said the Tactless Thing. There seems no doubt that he raised several important questions about Milton's use of language, that no one could answer them at the time, and that it is still worth while to look for the answer.

So far as I know, Zachary Pearce, later a bishop, only, of the many contemporary opponents of Bentley (his first notes on the edition were rushed out the same year), did not take refuge in being rude. The result is that they seem very alike, both in their merits and their limitations; Pearce often gave in to Bentley, or gave more plausible emendations (as by altering punctuation) so as to accept Bentley's objections, when nowadays the original text seems normal and beautiful. Pearce often gives valuable help, but for a serious answer he counts as on Bentley's side; he is even more 'rational'; which may help to make Bentley seem less stupid.

The anonymous rudeness (some of which was Pearce's own) is as charming as the rest of the controversy. For Bentley's inquiry about 'darkness visible':

> Ah, these Poets, these Poets, with their bold Figures and Flights, and all that, I'gad, do often leave us in the Dark: Hey,

Doctor . . . No, no, my Friend, this Note is none of ours; It has indisputably been foisted in by some Dunce of an Editor.

Lay vanquished, rolling in the fiery flood.

> *vanquished*. This is too low a Word, you desire it may be—Lay *stonied, stounded, stunn'd*. With all my Heart, they are words which are astoundingly Sublime and Poetical.

Four speedy cherubim
Put to their mouths the sounding alchemy

> sturdy, stout, robust, able to blow a strong Blast—Um, this is like `stonied, stounded, stunn'd, i. 52.

They are alike, I think, because the alliteration makes one feel that Bentley is trying to write his own poetry, but this man has not yet thought why they are alike; we are given his ' reactions '; it would be good talk if he had just picked the book up at a coffee-house.

v. 602. All but the wakeful Nightingale.

> You read *not all*, instead of *all but*; for the *Owls*, you say, did not Strike off at the Approach of Darkness any more than the Nightingale. Why, truly, Doctor, it was a little careless of the Poet, not to take any notice at all of the poor Owl. But you see what the world was come to even in Milton's time; everything that was solemn and grave neglected.

This was the only safe method; continually Pearce's detailed replies offer the pathetic spectacle of a man knowing that the original text was somehow more beautiful, but bound to confess that it could not be defended. Thus he never takes refuge in the ' sound ' of a passage, even under the most shocking provocation, whereas Bentley often does; and not till the tenth book does he break out with the claim that reason could do it in the end, but there was no room for her to do it in notes reasonably long.

x. 818. Dr. B. would have us throw out this whole Passage as the Editor's : but to approve or disapprove of it, depends on Taste, which is a thing of so nice a Nature, that reasons cannot always be assigned for it, at least in so small a compass as these Notes are commonly drawn up in : and it is a thing in which I fear that the Doctor and I shall hardly ever agree.

Not till the tenth book. It may be worth quoting them both on the ' sound ' issue.

vi. 178.   God and Nature bid the same,
          When he who rules is worthiest, and excells
          Them whom he governs.

Bentley emends *governs* to ' rules,' because ' The word *Rules* in the Repetition has more Force and Rotundity than *Governs*.' Pearce replies that Abdiel here wishes ' to soften the accusation of Servitude '; so that the ruler indeed has a forcible word, but a milder word is used from the point of view of his subjects.

When Bentley destroys the superb words of the Creation—

          Silence, ye troubl'd waves, and thou Deep, peace

with an emendation ' Peace, thou Deep,' Pearce finds a logical objection only : ' better that the most significant and commanding word should stand last in the sentence.' A modern critic would appeal to the sound, but the point about the merit of the sound is best brought out by the appeal to the meaning.

          over head the dismal hiss
          Of fiery Darts in flaming volies flew.

Bentley is sympathetic about this, and does not deny that Milton wrote it; but ' the danger is, of deserting Propriety, while he's hunting after Sound and Tumour,' so he makes the darts fly instead of the hiss. Pearce, with no such reference to sound, and backed by precedents, replies that 'there is a peculiar Force in applying that to the Circumstance of a Thing, which properly belongs to the Thing itself' (it is allied to personification).

In such cases he puts a more exclusive stress on meaning than Bentley himself; it is the more serious that he lost so many points; it had a bad effect on criticism. Reason had to be muzzled, and Bentley hooted as a pedant, because reason obviously gave the wrong answer. This at least Bentley was not; he has ample vigour and good sense and some of his most rousing attacks are against the pedantry of Milton; for instance the comment on the muster-roll of geography in xi. 387-411: 'Very useful, if he was explaining to a young Boy a Sheet Map of the World.' It was not Bentley who found his 'last reward of consummate scholarship' in picking up Milton's learned hints. That his failure was so crashing was a melancholy accident; it was not that his methods were wrong but that the mind of Milton was very puzzling, as his methods showed. I think this topic worth some attention because Bentley has been used as a bogey; he scared later English critics into an anxiety to show that they were sympathetic and did not mind about the sense. One has only to compare such duellists as Pearce and Bentley, who raise questions at every point, however they fail to answer them, which concern the essence of the poetry they are considering, with the mild and tactful hints, the air of a waiter anxious not to interrupt the conversation, of a sensible nineteenth-century editor like Masson.

As a rule, then, I shall try to wipe the eye of both of them, and show that though the question is real the answer justifies Milton. The 'psychological' manner, which

their failure shows to be necessary, may easily be offensive; it implies that Milton wrote in a muddle without
knowing his own mind. As a rule, if Milton's sympathies were divided, he understood the conflict he was
dramatising, and if the result is hard to explain it is easy
to feel. But I shall take first, to win sympathy for the
Doctor, some cases where I think he is right, where there
is a muddle whose effect is unsatisfying. In any case it
is refreshing to see the irruption of his firm sense into
Milton's world of harsh and hypnotic, superb and
crotchety isolation; Sir Walter Raleigh said that there
could not have been a child in *Paradise Lost*, because one
touch of common sense would have destroyed it; it
was left for the great Doctor to take upon himself
this important rôle. Nearly all the critics have shown
faint distress when Raphael is entertained by our parents
at a fruitarian meal with fruit beverages, ' no fear lest
dinner cool,' and ' holds discourse ' about how

> food alike those pure
> Intelligential substances require
> As doth your Rational . . .
> . . . they hear, see, smell, touch, taste,
> Tasting concoct, digest, assimilate,
> And corporeal to incorporeal turn.

' If the Devils want feeding, our Author made poor
provision for them in his Second Book; where they
have nothing to eat but Hell-fire; and no danger of
their dinner cooling.' This is adequate; it sends one back
to the text in a fit state to appreciate poetry when the
author next grants us some; it is a snort worthy of the
nostrils of Milton himself.

Here Milton went on putting concrete for abstract
till it became absurd; sometimes he uses vague poetic

language which conflicts with concrete details already settled. The difficulty is that we are asked to believe the scheme as a whole.

> Such Pleasure took the Serpent to behold
> This Flourie Plat, the sweet recess of Eve
> Thus earlier, thus alone ; her Heav'nly Forme
> Angelic, but more soft, and Feminine,
> Her graceful Innocence, her every Aire
> Of gesture or least action overawd
> His malice.

Angelic. ' So we must suppose, that she has Six Wings, as Raphael had.' *More soft.* (In i. 423 the spirits can assume either sex, are uncompounded, and not manacled with joint or limb). ' If Eve had been more soft . . . than such were, she had been no Fit Mate for her Husband.' Pearce replies ' Why may not Angelic be spoken metaphorically, as well as Heavenly, which certainly is so ? ' but we ought not to have to be fobbed off when there are live walking metaphors just round the corner.

A similar case, where they both shy rightly at Milton's evasive use of language, shows the process of finding concrete for abstract caught half-way ; it has the squalid gelatinous effect of ectoplasm in a flashlight photograph.

> The aggregated Soyle
> Death with his Mace petrific, cold and dry,
> As with a Trident smote, and fix't as firm
> As *Delos* floating once ; the rest his look
> Bound with Gorgonian rigor not to move
> And with Asphaltic slime ; broad as the Gate,
> Deep to the Roots of Hell the gather'd beach
> They fasten'd.

' *Bound with rigor and with slime.* That could not, or at least must not, pass from Milton.' So he emends *and* to ' as,' and Pearce fights a rearguard action to change only the stops. It would be a grand clash in an Elizabethan; they can afford to confuse cause and effect, abstract and concrete, because there is no doubt that they mean something solid, but Milton will see us damned if we don't believe his story, and we expect him to believe it himself.

Pearce insists at one point, with an air of defending Milton against outrageous insult, that his scheme could not possibly be inconsistent if carefully enough considered. I cannot think it an Augustan stupidity to expect this; I too find it irritating when the sun suddenly takes to wheels (v. 140), when prayers are at last found to be as solid as angels (xi. 14), when Hell, in the twelfth book, is replanted inside the earth (41) and heaven placed in reach of Babel (50). There is a touch of the window-dressing of the *Sugar-Cane* about these muddles, which have no purpose, and about the following astronomical ones, whose purpose is disingenuous.

Satan at the top of the universe

> Looks down with wonder on the sudden view
> Of all this world at once ... from pole to pole
> He views its breadth. ...

Then he moves towards it

> Amongst innumerable stars, that shone
> Stars distant, but nearby seemed other worlds.

Raphael from the same place sees the world as

> Not unconform to other shining globes

but can see cedars on it. No doubt the angels have good eyesight, but the purpose is clear. When the Earth is looked at fair and square it is very large and well in the centre of things; only incidentally, to add grandeur and seem up-to-date, is it a small planet attached to one of innumerable stars. Copernicus is too strong to be ignored, so one must show one is broadminded and then have him attacked by Raphael (viii. 73). These are trivial enough points, and Milton is wholly entitled to muddles when serious forces are at work in them, when they carry the complexity of his poetic material; as in some other muddles about stars and perhaps in the many about the sex of the angels. But his mixture of pomposity and evasiveness makes him fair game as soon as they are not justified; he left a grim posterity of shoddy thinking in blank verse.

Given this fundamental sympathy with Bentley's outlook one can view his worst efforts with affection and pleasure, and be properly charmed by the note where Satan, disguised as a familiar toad, is whispering ill dreams to the sleeping Eve. 'Why may I not add *one* Verse to *Milton*, as well as his Editor add so *many*?' inquires Bentley with the innocent wilfulness of the great Victoria:

> Him thus intent Ithuriel with his spear,
> *Knowing no real Toad durst there intrude,*
> Touch'd lightly.

It is the Doctor who dare intrude anywhere and will never whisper any harmful fancies. 'Here, you see, the Versification and Sentiment are quite of a Piece. How naturally does the Movement of the Line imitate the croaking of a Toad!', says Pearce. It is like dogs who cannot bear not to join in the singing. Let me quote the funniest remark of Pearce at once, and have done with this facetious tone.

> out from the ground uprose
> As from his Laire the Wilde Beast where he wonns
> In Forrest wilde

' *Lair* or *Layer* signifies *bed,* the use of which Word is still kept up among us, when we say, that in potted Meats there is a *Lair* of one thing above a *Lair* of another.' One had thought this horror peculiar to modern life.

The most obvious case where neither Bentley nor Pearce can approve Milton's method is where he uses a serious secret pun.

> iv. 264. The Birds thir quire apply; aires, vernal aires,
> Breathing the smell of field and grove, attune
> The trembling leaves.

' *Air,* when taken for the *Element,* has no Plural Number, in *Greek, Latin,* or *English*; where Airs signify *Tunes.* . . . Therefore he must give it here; *Air . . . attunes.*' Pearce gives tolerable authority for taking different airs for different breezes. But it is strange that Bentley should actually use the word *tunes,* and then quote the word *attunes,* and still not see there is a pun. The airs attune the leaves because the air itself is as enlivening as an air; the trees and wild flowers that are smelt on the air match, as if they caused, as if they were caused by, the birds and leaves that are heard on the air; nature, because of a pun, becomes a single organism. A critical theory is powerful indeed when it can blind its holders to so much beauty.

> iv. 555. Thither came Uriel, gliding through the Eev'n
> On a Sun beam.

' I never heard but here, that the *Evening* was a Place or Space to *glide* through. *Evening* implies Time, and he might with equal propriety say: Came gliding though Six a clock. But it's the Printer's Language: the Author gave it, *gliding through the* HEAVEN.' Pearce gives precedent for coming through the evening, and points out that the part of the earth occupied by evening *is* a place, especially to so astronomical a creature. I am glad not to have to tell them what was evidently in Milton's mind; that the angel is sliding, choosing a safe gradient, down a nearly *even* sunbeam; like the White Knight on the poker. But as so often when Milton is on the face of it indefensible the line seems to absorb the harshness of its absurdity; the pun gives both Uriel and the sunset a vast and impermanent equilibrium; it is because of the inevitable Fall of our night that he falls to earth, in the hush and openness of evening, himself in a heroic calm.

> vi. 483.   These in their dark Nativitie the Deep
> Shall yield us, pregnant with infernal flame.

(Satan, while yet in Heaven, in the first triumph of his invention of artillery.) Pearce says 'we may suppose the Epithet *infernal* to have been added to *flame*, that it might stand oppos'd to Heav'n's ray mentioned in l. 480. . . . But (says the Dr.) it is too soon yet for Satan to mention INFERNAL *flame*. That is too hard to be proved: Hell had been mentioned in the speeches of the Combatants on the preceding Day, viz. in v. 186, 276, 291.' Satan says, as a fact, that he will fetch fire 'from below' to answer the fire of God; he says, as a pun and a defiance, if we may suppose him to have understood the previous day's hints about hell, that he will use the fire of punishment as the material of victory, and the voice of Milton behind him assures us that they are *pregnant* with more fire than he has planned.

> This horror will grow mild, this darkness light.

' 'Tis quite too much that the *Darkness* turn into *Light*, 'tis as if he had made *Horror* turn into *Joy*.' ' Surely this was no more than for *Horror* to turn to *Mild*, for both *Mild* and *Light* don't express the highest degree, but only something that, by comparison with what they then suffered, might be called *Mild* and *Light*.' I quote this as a very slight pun which yet has an effect, which Bentley is right in noticing. Both these senses are present, and the combination allows Belial to suggest high hopes without obvious absurdity.

As for the conscious puns of Satan's mockery, of course they both recognise those easily enough. Pearce can ' make no attempt to defend ' the pun about infantry, but Bentley is willing to defend puns so long as they are funny.

> . . . the Passages of Satan and Belial's Jesting have been censured by an Ingenious Gentleman, who had a settled Aversion to all Puns, as they are call'd . . . if that Niceness be carry'd to Extremity, it will depretiate half the good sayings of the old Greek and Latin Wits. . . . He copied those Jocose Sayings from his great predecessor Homer.

Here, as often, Bentley is the more broad-minded of the two.

Another of the main points at issue concerns Milton's rhythm; there seems no doubt that Bentley didn't understand it, but there may be some question whether Pearce did or not. He defended the text, in any case where the rhythm seemed queer to Bentley, by pointing out that it was queer in many other cases as well; it might then, one would suppose, be queer on some system, if such a system could be conceived. ' Milton affected in many places to make such a Roughness as this at the beginning of his Verse.' If the text is frequently rough, and roughness is a fault, that only supports Bentley's view that the text has frequently been corrupted. And even when he attempts more positive approval it is hard to know what is in his mind.

> Half wheeling to the shield, half to the spear.
> Our minds, and teach us to cast off this yoke.

'The bad Measure may be corrected thus,' etc. 'But I see no bad Measure at all in the common Reading; the small stress laid in the pronunciation upon the word *to* does not in my opinion injure the Verse.' Is a stress, even when small, a long syllable, or a short stress a short syllable? The discussion comes to very little conclusion.

At the last moment, however, before his first edition was published, Pearce suddenly understood a Miltonic rhythm, and explained it at the end of the preface; a dramatic affair; it shows that Bentley was some use.

> No sooner had th' Almighty ceas't, but all
> The multitude of Angels with a shout
> Loud as from numbers without number, sweet
> As from blest voices, uttering joy, Heav'n rung
> With Jubilee, and loud Hosannas fill'd
> Th' eternal Regions.

To Bentley this was evidently not grammar, and he let in a couple of main verbs, like ferrets. Pearce could only save the text by putting brackets from *Heaven* to *Hosannas*, so that it is the angels who filled the regions, with a shout. In the preface *angels uttering joy* becomes an ablative absolute, so that the sentence encloses the hierarchy as if with effort and rises through four lines to the main verb.

But though a large-scale rhythm was in reach of discovery he never feels that the iambic beat could be seriously tampered with; both of them find

> Dropped from the Zenith, like a falling star

quite impossible; and it is Bentley who suspects that

the line about the unwieldy elephant may actually be intended to be rough.

People are now agreed in approving Milton's rhythms, and accepting his subdued puns without looking at them closely. I don't know what is the normal view about his vague or apparently disordered grammar, which Bentley thought indefensible; especially the use of *and* or *or* when the sense needs more detailed logical structure. Pearce defended it very little. The chief reason for it is that Milton aims both at a compact and weighty style, which requires short clauses, and a sustained style with the weight of momentum, which requires long clauses.

> vii. 113.   to recount Almightie works
> What words or tongue of Seraph can suffice,
> Or heart of man suffice to comprehend?

Bentley emends to 'words from tongue,' but thereby loses the completeness of the statement; 'How can any stage in the production of the speech of seraphs be adequate; how can they find words, and if they could how could their tongues pronounce them?' But besides this, the merit of *or* is its fluidity; the way it allows 'words from tongue' to be suggested without pausing for analysis, without holding up the single movement of the line.

> xi. 273-285.   O flours,
> That never will in other Climate grow,
> My early visitation, and my last
> At Eev'n, which I bred up with tender hand
> From the first op'ning buds, and gave ye Names,
> Who now shall reare ye to the Sun, or ranke
> Your Tribes, and water from th' ambrosial Fount?

Thee lastly, nuptial Bowre, by mee adornd
With what to sight or smell was sweet; from thee
How shall I part, and whither wander down
Into a lower World, to this obscure
And wilde, how shall we breathe in other Aire
Less pure, acustomed to immortal Fruits?

I have quoted a whole passage to show the accumulation
of its imagery. Bentley objects to the last lines: ' What
do the *Fruits*, now to be parted with, signify to her
Breathing in other Air? There was to be a change of *Diet*
too, as well as of Air'; so he emends it to ' Air less pure?
What eat...' Pearce says, 'To eat (for the future) Fruits
not immortal, and to have Air less pure too, were Circumstances which might well justify her sollicitous enquiry
about her Breathing in the lower World'; indeed the
sense is plain enough. But the effect of Bentley's emendation is to make Eve's pathos into a declamatory piece of
argument. The sliding, sideways, broadening movement,
normal to Milton, is exaggerated into a *non sequitur* to
show a climax; on the other hand, in the tired repeated
rhythm of the last two lines, she leaves floating, as things
already far off, all that makes up for her the 'atmosphere'
of Paradise. There is something like a pun in the way
she is enabled at once to sum up her argument and trail
away in the weakness of her appeal; it is a delicate piece
of brushwork such as seems blurred until you step back.

Pearce is clear about points of fluid grammar, as one
sees from his fondness for brackets to bring out less
obvious connections.

Taste this, and be henceforth among the Gods
Thyself a Goddess, not to Earth confin'd,
But sometimes in the Air, as wee, sometimes
Ascend to Heav'n, by merit thine, and see
What life the Gods live there, and such live thou.

'The Words *as wee*,' remarks Pearce, 'are so plac'd
between the Sentences as equally to relate to both, and
in the first Sentence the Verb *be* is understood. Dr. B.
has altered the passage thus:

> But sometimes range in air, sometimes, as wee,

But in this reading of the Doctor's are not the Angels
excluded from ranging in the Air?' Surely there is
a dramatic reason for the gawkiness of the line here;
the doubt implied as to whether he could go to Heaven
himself shows a natural embarrassment in the disguised
Satan. But the essential step is to notice, as Pearce does,
the fluidity of the grammar.

He also recognises implied conceits of the straightforward kind that would have made an antithesis for
the Augustan couplet.

ix. 631.
> He leading swiftly rowld
> In tangles, and made visible seem strait,
> To mischief swift.

Bentley dislikes the two *swifts*, but 'the Sense rises by
repeating the same word with a new Circumstance
to it.'

> Tangled his coils, and tangled were his wiles,
> And swift he marches, who so swift beguiles.

It is rather pretty to see them fitting the thing into their
more conscious formula.

Bentley's merit as a critic of Milton is of a different
kind; he may only produce a trivial piece of nagging,
but he has a flair for choosing an important place to
do it. Thus his complaint about the first words of
Satan seem to me to draw attention to an unexpected
dramatic subtlety.

If thou beest he; But O how fall'n! how chang'd
From him, who in the happy Realms of Light
Cloth'd with transcendent brightness didst outshine
Myriads though bright: If he whom mutual league,
United thoughts and counsels, equal hope,
And hazard in the Glorious Enterprise,
Joyned with me once, now misery hath joynd
In equal ruin: into what pit thou seest
From what highth fal'n, so much the stronger provd
He with his Thunder; and who knew till then
The force of those due Arms. . . .

Bentley emends *doth joyn And equal ruin*. 'See the series
of the whole sentence: *Whom mutual league, united
counsels, equal hope and hazard in our Revolt, joined with
me* ONCE, viz. in close friendship; *Now Misery hath
join'd*; in what? in closer friendship? no, in equal
Ruin. Great Sense, and great Comfort in this great
Calamity. *Equal Ruin*, in reddition to equal hope, now
again joins us in a *stricter friendship*.' Pearce accepts *and*,
'very right and necessary, I think,' but exclaims 'how
unpoetical is *doth join*.'

The main objection here is that the words claim to
give a source of comfort, and do not. They claim to
give what resolution may be gained from despair. But
I think the shift Bentley describes is part of the thought,
and explains what in such a speaker needs explanation
even at such a moment, the reason why Satan breaks his
sentence. He begins speaking to Beelzebub as an equal,
and then, strengthened by his own rhetoric, feels that
this would be excessive 'comfort' for a rival angel.
If their *hope* (personal advantage hoped for) in the
enterprise was equal they both hoped to rule; if their
ruin (personal loss of glory) is equal they were once
equal in glory. Satan breaks the sentence with *into*

what pit, and their equal ruin (as in *ruining from heaven*), *in* being attracted by *into*, may now only be their equal physical fall. From then on, in his supreme expression of all but lunatic heroism, he speaks only of himself.

Milton's attitude to Satan is a great source of disagreement; Bentley rightly finds something suspicious about the generosity of the language used, and picks out some curious examples of it.

> xi. 101.   Take to thee from among the Cherubim
> Thy choice of flaming Warriors, least the Fiend
> Or on behalf of Man, or to invade
> Vacant possession some new trouble raise.

Bentley emends *or on behalf of man* to ' or in despite to us '; ' Whence came this new Good-will to Man from the Arch-Enemy ? ' The view that there is a calculated progressive decay of Satan is not upheld by this passage; it comes very late and had to be striking for Bentley to bother about it; he is beginning to explain he is old and tired, and repeat his arguments.

> ix. 166.   O foul descent! that I who erst contended
> With Gods to sit the highest, and now constrained
> Into a Beast, and mixt with bestial slime,
> This essence to incarnate and imbrute,
> That to the hight of Deitie aspir'd.

' Milton would not use thus the word *Incarnate*; He knew a higher Essence, than Seraphical, was afterwards Incarnated '; indeed I think one may trace even here that curious parallel between Satan and the Christ, which makes the scenes in Heaven and Hell correspond to one another so closely. But perhaps it is rather Man than the Son of Man who complains in his words.

There is an odd phrase, or as Bentley puts it ' a shocking expression,' in one of these parallel passages, which

seems to show a flash of contempt for the good angels.
Satan in the second book chose to take the risk on his
own shoulders, to go alone to the new world for the
benefit of his party ' or on behalf of man.' God in the
third book tries to make one of the good angels, as a
similar act of public spirit, go to the world to redeem
man ; all of them refuse.

> Say Heav'nly Powers, where shall we find such love,
> Which of ye will be mortal to redeem
> Man's mortal crime, and just th' unjust to save,
> Dwels in all Heaven charity so deare ?

' Lead a perfect human life to save those who are imperfect ' is of course the sense from which this has
diverged, but ' which of ye will be just ' is a piercing
question for the immaculate hierarchy.

> vii. 55.   things to thir thought
> So unimaginable as hate in Heav'n,
> And War so near the Peace of God in bliss
> With such confusion ;

Bentley emends *peace* to ' seat,' because the text implies
that the Peace of God was not incapable of being dis-
turbed. It does indeed ; Milton is at pains to give this
impression, while denying that it is true ; only so can
Satan's heroism be saved from a taint of folly. Perhaps
the strangest means adopted to make one feel this is
the ironical speech which God, ' smiling,' makes to his
Son when the attack is being prepared against them.

> v. 726. Let us advise, and' to this hazard draw
> With speed what ɔrce is left, and all imploy
> In our defence, lest unawares we lose
> This our high place, our Sanctuarie, our Hill.

One accepts this in reading as the brutal mockery of a

much superior force, but it does not seem that of an absolutely superior force, such as there would be no sense in attacking.

Indeed, Satan has a much more plausible defence on grounds of ignorance than Eve had (ix. 775); he does not know whether God is of like nature with the angels (v. 793) and sprang into existence at the same moment (v. 859; but there is a *young* cherub in iii. 637), or whether as he claims he is almighty, their creator, and of absolutely superior nature. Milton himself in ii. 108, God himself in iii. 341, speak of the angels as gods; Milton's language about the creation (vii. 227 and 505) implies, as Bentley pointed out, that they were not created; and Abdiel's official statement in v. 832, that God created them by the instrumentality of the Son, is in flat contradiction with v. 603, where the angels are shown the Son when he is newly begotten. Of course we are supposed to know about God, but there is no clear tradition to tell us how much Satan knows—so far as there is Milton is at pains to muddle it. If Satan believed God to be a usurping angel there is no romantic diabolism at all in giving him our heartiest admiration. I think this is a sharp issue; what the critic has to deal with is not a ' complex personality ' but one plain character superimposed on another quite separate from it.

The most striking single example of this dissolving-view method of characterisation occurs when Satan is struck ' stupidly good ' on his first view of Adam and Eve :

> whom my thoughts pursue
> With wonder, and with love . . .
> whom I could pity thus forlorn
> Though I unpitied. . . .

Milton himself is providing some pity here.

> League with you I seek
> And mutual amity so streight, so close,
> That I with you must dwell, or you with me
> Henceforth ; my dwelling haply may not please
> Like this fair Paradise, your sense, yet such
> Accept your Maker's gift ; he gave it me
> Which I as freely give ; Hell shall unfold
> To entertain you two, her widest Gates,
> And send forth all her kings.

Bentley found the terms inaccurate but the tone
natural—a brutal irony in the style of the address to the
gunners. The gates of hell can no longer be either shut
or opened ' nor need he lie and feign here, for he speaks
to himself only,' and the emendation is arranged to
give ' a Sarcasm rather bitterer.' This seems to be the
accepted view, though a sort of generosity, a sense of
the grandeur of the situation, is admitted from the
parallel in Isaiah. Sir Walter Raleigh, with evasive
humour, said it was ' true hospitality.'

But Satan might mean it as a real offer. It is clear
that the devils can carry life on in hell, and apparently
men can only suffer ; Satan need not know this ; the
irony is that of Milton's appalling God. The two views
of Satan seem actually to be separated to the two ends
of the sentence. The cuddling movement of *mutual
amity*, with the flat mouth of the worm, in *am-*, opening
to feed on them, the insinuating hiss of *so streight, so
close*, full of the delicious softness of the tormentor,
belong to the Satan who will have his guests tortured
by incongruous Furies (ii. 596) ; so the voices whispered
to Bunyan, and he thought his bowels would burst
within him. Then there is a patch of argufying, in which
he seems to feel nothing, as a connection (one might

be sentimentally playful like this before killing a young pig). And only the theory of ignorance provides a character for the last three lines; their melancholy and their grandeur is that of Milton's direct statements; he does not use *all*, his key word, for any but a wholesale and unquestioned emotion; what we are to feel here is the ruined generosity of Satan and the greatness of the fate of man. It seems to me obviously useless to try and fit the two into a consistent character.

The subject of the poem is not a personal Satan but the Fall of Man; the more life Milton could put into our feelings about Satan the better, but his main business was to convey the whole range of feeling inherent in the myth, and the myth clearly involves contradictions. Satan is both a devil and a host who will receive man with honour, because the fall of a man is terrible and yet just this shows that he is important (which makes the belief tolerable). Satan is both the punisher of sin and the supreme sinner (Milton did not invent this, and in neither capacity is Satan ' Milton '); these are combined because ' sin punishes itself and turns to hatred,' because ' it is hard to distinguish sin from independent judgment, courage, the force needed for a full life,' and I think because ' the sinner becomes the judge.' Then perhaps, thirdly, Satan is Milton as rebel and also the paganism Milton had renounced; from the first he has bitterness, from the second the sadism of the Italianate stage villain. Now of course no mere clash between these forces would be a substitute for a conceivable Satan, but the fact that at this crucial point there is a troubling of the surface of the coherent Satan somehow convinces us that they are all at work. It acts not as a puzzle about the person Satan but as a knot, a throttling irony, in the myth; it so sharply concentrates the forces of the story that we are impressed at their not breaking their frame. It looks like a dramatic irony; I think it is more; it is a dramatic failure of character.

Bentley is always ruthless about the large ornamental comparisons, where some incident in the story has a detail in common with, more or less of some quality than, some otherwise irrelevant incident which is described in detail; he classes whole paragraphs of them as 'romantic, and inserted by the editor.' But it is here that Milton shows his attitude to the work as a whole; it is at best mere protection to reply as Pearce did by talking about 'imagination.' I shall take first two more examples about Satan. Satan flying up to the gates of hell

> Now shaves with level wing the Deep, then soares
> Up to the fiery concave touring high.
> As when far off at Sea a Fleet descri'd
> Hangs in the Clouds, by *Aequinoctial* Winds
> Close sailing from *Bengala*, or the Iles
> Of *Ternate* and *Tidore*, whence Merchants bring
> Thir spicie drugs; they on the trading flood
> Through the wide *Ethiopian* to the Cape
> Ply stemming nightly toward the Pole.   So seem'd
> Far off the flying Fiend:

Bentley cuts out the whole passage. Pearce's defence amounts to claiming charity for poets who have classical authority for their licences.

> As to what he adds, *why is this all done nightly, to contradict the whole account, since at that time a sail cannot be descried?* It may be answered, that here is no Contradiction at all; for Milton in his Similitudes (as is the practice of Homer and Virgil too) after he has shown the common resemblance, often takes the liberty of wandering into some unresembling Circumstances: which have no other relation to the Comparison, than that they gave him the Hint, and (as it were) set fire to the Train of his Imagination.

The trouble is that this defends an irrelevant piece of description, one which is merely distracting, as well as one that satisfies the imagination through implied comparisons relevant to the main impulse of the poem.

The description here seems entirely of this second sort. The ships ply nightly because Satan was in the darkness visible of Hell; are far off so that they hang like a mirage and seem flying like Satan (the word *ply,* sounding like ' fly,' ekes this out); and are going towards the Pole because Satan (from inside) is going towards the top of the concave wall of Hell. They carry spices, like those of Paradise, because they stand for paganism and earthly glory, for all that Milton had retained contact with after renouncing and could pile up into the appeal of Satan; Satan is like a merchant because Eve is to exchange these goods for her innocence; and like a fleet rather than one ship because of the imaginative wealth of polytheism and the variety of the world. (It fits in with Satan as a symbol, not as a character.)

> iv. 977.   While thus he spake, th' Angelic Squadron bright
> Turnd fierie red, sharpning in mooned hornes
> Thir Phalanx, and begann to hemm him round
> With ported Spears, as thick as when a field
> Of *Ceres* ripe for harvest waving bends
> Her bearded Grove of ears, which way the wind
> Swayes them ; the careful Plowman doubting stands
> Least on the threshing floore his hopefull sheaves
> Prove chaff.   On th' other side *Satan* allarm'd
> Collecting all his might dilated stood,
> Like *Teneriffe* or *Atlas* unremov'd :

Bentley omits the ploughman sentence.

> The Editor deserts the notion, and from a salutary Gale of Wind
> . . . he passes to a Tempest, and frightens the Husbandman with

the loss of all his Grain. What an Injury is this to the Prior
Comparison? What are Sheaves bound up in a Barn to the
Phalanx, that hem'd Satan?

It certainly makes the angels look weak. If God the
sower is the ploughman, then he is anxious; another
hint that he is not omnipotent. If the labouring Satan
is the ploughman he is only anxious for a moment, and
he is the natural ruler or owner of the good angels.
The main effect is less logical; the homely idea is put
before the description of Satan to make him grander by
contrast, an effect denied to the other angels.

Besides, to suppose a Storm in the Fields of Corn, implies that
the Angels were in a ruffle and hurry about Satan, not in regular
and military Order.

More than that; first the angels lean forward, calm and
eager, in rows, seeming strong; then as the description
approaches Satan, who is stronger, they are in a ruffle
and hurry.

People are by now agreed that Milton partly identified
Satan with part of his own mind, and that the result
though excellent was a little unintentional. But to
say this is to agree with many of Bentley's points; you
can hardly blame him for not admiring what nobody
in his time was prepared to defend; certainly you cannot
blame his methods, as apart from his tone, for they were
surprisingly successful.

A whole series of a particular sort of ornamental
comparison, that which relates a detail of the Biblical
myth to one of a classical myth, is used to convey very
complex feelings about Paradise and also for the vili-
fication of Eve. Bentley is sharp at picking out these
implications, but I think one can carry it further than
he does.

iv. 268.   Not that faire field
Of *Enne*, where *Proserpin* gathring flours
Herself a fairer Floure by gloomie *Dis*
Was gatherd, which cost *Ceres* all that pain
To seek her through the world ; nor that sweet Grove
Of *Daphne* by *Orontes*, and the inspir'd
Castalian Spring might with this Paradise
Of *Eden* strive ; nor that *Nyseian* Ile
Girt with the River *Triton*, where old *Cham*,
Whom Gentiles *Ammon* call and *Libyan Jove*,
Hid *Amalthea* and her Florid Son
Young *Bacchus* from his Stepdame *Rhea's* eye ;
Nor where *Abassin* Kings thir issue Guard,
Mount *Amara*, though this by som suppos'd
True Paradise under the *Ethiop* Line
By *Nilus* head, enclos'd with shining Rock,
A whole dayes journey high, but wide remote
From this *Assyrian* Garden, where the Fiend
Saw undelighted all delight . . .

. . . with a silly thought in the middle, and as sillily conducted in its several parts. *Not Enna, says he, not Daphne, nor Fons Castalus, nor Nysa, nor Mount Amara, could compare with Paradise.* Why, sir, who would have suspected that they could ; though you had never told us of it ?

A man who had given his life to the classics might easily have suspected it ; it is to Milton that the pagan beauty of these gardens has appealed more richly than the perfection of the garden of God. But I want here to play Bentley's trick and bring out the implications against Eve.

Proserpina, like Eve, was captured by the king of Hell, but she then became queen of it, became Sin, then, on Milton's scheme ; Eve, we are to remember, becomes an ally of Satan when she tempts Adam to eat with her. Daphne was not seduced by Apollo as Eve was by Satan (both affairs involve desire, a devil, and a tree) ; Eve might really have done better than a mere pagan nymph; one must class her with the consenting Amalthea. And all the references to guarding children remind us that children were the result of the fall.

In the third comparison Milton takes an unusual version of the myth, on the authority (the sole authority, according to Masson) of Diodorus Siculus, who says that he got it from Dionysius, and that Dionysius got it from a tutor of Hercules. He follows that version of the story, out of his list of versions, with a very fine description of the gardens of the Nyseian isle, but I think one can give a more interesting reason why Milton adopted Bacchus in such a way as to make us confuse him with Jupiter. He wanted a mixed notion for a demigod of the glory and fertility of the earth, because of his pagan feelings about Paradise, and yet for a sky-god, because Adam in spite of this stood for celestial virtue. And the fourth garden was like Eden because the issue of the Abassin kings were kept secluded there like Adam and Eve, but the appeal of the lines is to an idea opposite to that of seclusion. They fling into the scale against Paradise, only still to be outweighed, what many beside Milton would have thought worthy to be put to such a use; the Elizabethan excitement about distant travel and trading, about the discovery of luxury and the sources of the Nile.

Another odd case of Eve-baiting forms a disputed passage.

ix. 503.   Pleasing was his shape,
           And lovely, never since of Serpent kind
           Lovelier, not those that in Illyria chang'd
           Hermione and Cadmus, or the God
           In Epidaurus; nor to which transform'd
           Ammonian Jove, or Capitoline was seen,
           Hee with Olympias, this with her who bore
           Scipio the highth of Rome.

Satan is as beautiful as his creator can make him; you are not to think there is anything low about him even in disguise. Probably he made a very fine toad. But it is remarkable, surely, that the first comparison, as always interpreted, implies that Eve turned into a snake and became Satan's consort, just as the other devils turn into snakes after the fall. *Those,* indeed, may be not the couple named but some serpent gods; Ovid gives the cause (revenge for a killed snake) but no causers of the metamorphosis (from the *Bacchae* they might be the snakes of Bacchus); Milton's grammar may want a comma after *changed.* Even so the last two comparisons treat the Fall as a sexual act after which Eve produced children by Satan, as in the Talmud, which makes her a regular seventeenth-century witch. And again, after the devils have been turned into serpents (an incident which seems to have been invented by Milton to drive these suggestions home) we hear that they

x. 580.   fabled how the Serpent, whom they call'd
Ophion with Eurynome, the wide-
Encroaching Eve perhaps, had first the rule
Of high Olympus, thence by Saturn driven
And Ops, ere yet Dictaean Jove was born.

' *Ophion* the *Serpent* is *Eve's* Husband, and so all Mankind are descended from *Satan,*' remarks Bentley, and no less reasonably ' Where did she encroch, unless to bear children is wide encroching ? ' Pearce's only sensible reply is that in any case it was the spiteful invention of devils. But it was Milton who did the inventing. Pearce indeed catches the infection at one point and uses this trick to defend the text.

Soon had his crew
Op'nd into the Hill a spacious wound
And dig'd out ribs of Gold.

Bentley wanted to read 'seeds of gold,' but the words
here, said Pearce, 'allude to the formation of Eve in
viii. 463.' I call this a profound piece of criticism;
'let none admire; that soil may best Deserve the
precious bane.' It is not specially unkind to Eve; to
connect her with the architecture of Pandemonium
makes her stand for the pride and loyalty that won
grandeur even from the fall. The following passage
goes so far as to suggest that it was she who tempted
Satan and turned him into a serpent. She was not
afraid of him when she saw him in Eden, because she was

ix. 519.   . . . us'd
> To such disport before her through the Field,
> From every Beast, more duteous at her call,
> Than at Circean call the Herd disguis'd.

Samson, too, calls Delilah a sorceress; no doubt he
would have added Circe if he had heard of her.

Even the following comparison, as from the ranging
and pouncing imagination of Dante, shows the same
idea at the back of his mind. The devils when turned
to serpents saw a multitude of trees laden with fruit;

x. 556.   Parcht with scalding thurst and hunger fierce,
> Though to delude them sent, could not abstain,
> But on they rould in heaps, and up the Trees
> Climbing, sat thicker than the snakie locks
> That curld Megaera; greedily they pluck'd
> The Frutage fair to sight, like that which grew
> Neer that bituminous Lake where Sodom flamed:

Eve too, in iv. 307, has curled hair, modest but 'requir-
ing,' that clutches at Adam like the tendrils of a vine.
Eve now then is herself the forbidden tree; the whole
face of Hell has become identical with her face; it is

filled, as by the mockery of the temptress, with her hair that entangled him; all the beauty of nature, through her, is a covering, like hers, for moral deformity. But at least now we have exposed her; her hair is corpse worms; she is the bitter apple of her own crime, kind as the Eumenides. It is a relief to find Bentley snorting at the editor who 'unjudiciously diverts us from the Scene in View, to the snaky curls of a fictitious Fury.'

That Eve was Delilah, the more specious for her innocence, is only one end of Milton's feeling about her; in many of these examples the broad melancholy from the clash of paganism with Paradise is more striking than the snarl at Eve. But the Doctor thought no better of them for that; the snarls were only stupid, the melancholy was infidel; Milton's use of the pagan seemed to him to imply a doubt of the Christian mythology; and for myself I think, not only that he was right, but that the reverberations of this doubt are the real subject of the descriptions of the Garden. 'The description of Heaven,' says an anonymous answerer to Bentley, 'is a beautiful Parody of several Descriptions in the Heathen Poets of the Elysian Fields,' and parody seems an interesting term in this connection. These descriptions have formed our main subsequent poetical tradition of Nature—the Ode to Evening is a cento from Milton; Cowper's need for him is typified by the way *The Sofa* uses a parody of Miltonic blank verse as a starting-handle; Wordsworth's beliefs about Nature were at least in some degree a discovery of the ideas inherent in the style he learned from Milton to describe her—so that this point of literary tact merits some inquiry.

Bentley is very suspicious of the editor's irreligion, and finds evidence of it continually.

> a creature who, not prone
> And brute as other creatures, but endued
> With sanctity of reason, might erect
> His stature, and upright with front serene
> Govern the rest, self-knowing.

' As if his Erection were superadded to his Form by his own Contrivance; not originally made so by his Creator. I remember this senseless Notion spred about, that Man at first was a Quadruped, with a Kentish Tail.' (Kentish men were given tails by Thomas à Becket.) Coleridge makes a similar complaint about the *Essay on Man*; one does not easily realise that a sense of danger from this quarter has been in the air for so long. It is only very faintly hinted by Milton, if at all, but the hint was readily picked up.

The other examples are all classical comparisons. The angels sing to God, at the return of Christ from the Creation, that he is

> greater now in thy return
> Than from the Giant Angels.

This must be altered; it is an indiscreet hint at the Titans. (It seems anyway to show that the good angels admitted the bad ones to be greatly superior.) On the occasion to which they refer he pursued the bad angels

> With terrors and with furies to the bounds
> And Chrystall wall of Heav'n

' This must not pass by any means. We cannot allow *Furies* in Heaven; especially in the Messiah's party.' Pearce agrees but finds furies in Vergil who are only

' inward frights.' The following queer smack at Eve
is a more serious piece of comparative mythology.

> the genial Angel to our Sire
> Brought her in naked beauty more adorn'd
> More lovely than Pandora, whom the Gods
> Endowd with all thir gifts, and O too like
> In sad event, when to the unwiser son
> Of Japhet brought by Hermes, she ensnar'd
> Mankind with her fair looks, to be aveng'd
> On him who had stole Jove's authentic fire.

Not only was Eve not trying to avenge Satan but Pandora
was not trying to avenge Prometheus ; ' to be revenged
on Prometheus—that must be Pandora's revenge, and
yet she had no Thought or Hand in it.' Iapetus is spelt
Japhet, and Epimetheus might well be remembered
as the first man if he lived in the first generation after
the Flood ; there is a neat piece of dovetailing in the
manner of Ralegh's history. Yet Ralegh is a fearful
name in this connection ; Marlowe himself was among
the wild gang of comparative anthropologists he collected
round him in his great days.

Adam and Eve pray together after the fall ; humbly
enough,

> yet thir port
> Not of mean suitors, nor important less
> Seem'd thir Petition, then when th' ancient Pair
> In Fables old, less ancient yet then these,
> Deucalion and chaste Pyrrha to restore
> The race of Mankind drowned, before the Shrine
> Of Themis stood devout.

But was the Man bewitch'd, with his *Old Fables, but not as old
as these* ? Is *Adam* and *Eve's* History an *Old Fable* too, by this
Editor's own Insinuation ?

Pearce makes a case for a grammatical licence, but

it seems clear that they were right to be surprised; Milton intends no unorthodoxy, but feels the poetic or symbolical meaning of the stories to be more important than their truth. The effect is that he compares Christian and pagan views of life as equally solid and possible.

The pamphlets on divorce continually attack, as an obvious absurdity, the idea that the result of the mercy of Christ has been to lay heavier burdens upon the world; if the mercy of Moses would let him divorce Mary Powell how should the harshness of Jesus forbid him? But though he could use this as a weapon and no doubt a belief the paradox he satirises is at the back of all his best poetry. There is a similar puzzle about the gain of knowledge through the fall. Mr. Basil Willey has said that Milton, believing knowledge to be good and by right free, can see no reason why it was withheld or disaster in gaining it; he can only treat the sin of Eve as sensual disobedience. That it is not sensual by normal standards follows, I think, even from the lines he quotes to prove the opposite:

> Reason in man obscured or not obeyed
> Immediately inordinate desires
> And upstart passions catch the Government
> From Reason.

Sensuality here is only an effect, as it is in the story; before the fall it would have no means of attacking so perfect a creature. Milton protests overmuch that there was no danger of sensuality at all among the pleasures of Eden. The Fall is due to carelessness, letting Reason slip for a moment, not living quite for ever as in the great Taskmaster's eye. It is odd to consider that the myth was probably invented to make the frightening and abstract question seem homely and understandable; Milton uses it to give every action a nightmare importance, to hold every instant before the searchlight of the conscious will. It is a terrific fancy, the Western temper at its height; the insane dispro-portion of the act to its effects implies a vast zest for heroic action. But it is too strange and too arid to be more than the official theme of such a poem; the fascination of the thing for Milton is that his feelings continually cry out against his theory in favour of the Biblical implications, that true knowledge was cruel, that sensuality then first became wicked. And the effect of the classical comparisons is to bring out a similar idea, one at the back of all his poetry except perhaps the final *Samson*, that the knowledge of Christianity was cruel because it destroyed paganism; 'on the morning of Christ's nativity' even moderately pagan beauty, flowers, fairies, pastoral, the Elizabethan lyric must be abandoned, and even those stars must fade.

> The lonely mountains o'er
> And the resounding shore
>   A voice of weeping heard and loud lament;
> From haunted spring and dale,
> Edged with poplar pale
>   The parting Genius is with sighing sent,
> With flowre-inwoven tresses torne,
> The Nimphs in twilight shade of tangled thickets mourn.

The whole weight of this feeling is behind all the descrip-tions of Eden.

Milton's language about stars contains two puzzles about them beside the idea that our morning is their evening, and Bentley again puts one on the track of the ideas at work.

The Stars with deep amaze
Stand fixt in steadfast gaze,
 Bending one way their pretious influence,
And will not take their flight,
For all the morning light,
 Or Lucifer that often warned them thence;
But in their glimmering orbs did glow,
Until their Lord himself bespake, and bid them go.

Lucifer, though Satan, cannot lead them away; their *influence* may even have caused the appearance of Christ, but his order must destroy them. Cynthia too, in the next verse, feels that the music at Christ's birth means that 'her part was don'; Elizabeth and her age counted as another paganism. There is an odd doubt about the time at the end of the poem.

 But see the Virgin blest,
 Hath laid her Babe to rest,
  Time is our tedious song should here have ending,
 Heav'ns youngest teemed Star
 Hath fixed her polisht Car,
  Her sleeping Lord with Handmaid Lamp attending:
 And all about the Courtly Stable
 Bright-harnest Angels sit in order serviceable.

It all suggests nightfall; the ending of labour, and a lamp coming to guard a sleeper, now laid to rest. The angels are clearly compared to stars, and show no signs of going. But it is still the Morning—the new star appears and leads up the wise men as the poem ends. When Milton thinks of it as evening he takes the point of view of the stars. It is clear that the stars here stand for something very good; it was no poor thing that the knowledge of Christ destroyed.

 Christ here counts as the sun, but in *Paradise Regained* (i. 294) he becomes Our Morning Star, who is Lucifer,

who is Satan; the doubt about the symbolism fits
Milton's secret parallel between the two. An odd
little emendation in the second edition seems to be
explained by this. The sun lights up the planets:

> Hither as to their Fountain other Starrs
> Repairing, in thir gold'n Urns draw Light,
> And hence the Morning Planet gilds his horns.

The correction puts *her* for *his*; Venus for Christ-Satan.
Satan has not arrived on the world, so Nature may
suggest paganism but not the fall. There is a shade of
doubt about this star even in the prayer of Adam:

> Fairest star of night
> If better thou belong not to the dawn.

It may belong to Christ or Satan, and Satan may
owe to the irony of God what is still left him of his
splendour.

Thirdly, the stars involve the doubts suggested by
Copernican astronomy.

> About him all the Sanctities of Heaven
> Stood thick as Starrs, and from his sight receiv'd
> Beatitude past utterance.

The sun is fixed and the stars move round him; so long
as you think only of the planets the new theory gives a
pleasanter metaphor than the old one. But the fixed
stars (viii. 148, though timidly, and cf. iii. 577) may
themselves be suns; only the small angels move round
God; to those who find stars to be suns reason may
equal God and Satan, Milton and Christ. Donne is
always using the new astronomy to suggest the independence of the individual, and the metaphor here implies
the whole case for Satan.

The description of his revolt is a sustained astronomical metaphor. He plans his revolt

Now ere dim Night had disencumbered Heav'n

and leads off before morning

> an host
> Innumerable as the stars of night,
> Or stars of morning, dewdrops which the sun
> Impearls on every leaf and every flower.

> His count'nance, as the Morning Star that guides
> The starrie flock, allur'd them, and with lyes
> Drew after him the third part of Heav'ns Host.

His angels are called Sons of Morn, rather as Ezekiel (ii. 1) was a Son of Man as well as Christ.

> Meanwhile th' Eternal Eye, whose sight discernes
> Abstrusest thoughts, from forth his holy Mount
> And from within the golden Lamps that burne
> Nightly before him, saw without thir light
> Rebellion rising, saw in whom, how spread
> Among the sons of Morn.

He then, 'smiling,' confesses his anxiety. The picture here takes the lamps round him as the planets; it is the fixed stars beyond them, very possibly as big as the sun, who are the revolted angels of the Morning. The Morning Star itself of course is a planet, but Milton is still keeping to his view that the Morning Stars are not planets when he comes to their 'singing together' at the Creation.

> The Heav'ns and all the Constellations rung,
> The Planets in their stations listening stood,
> While the bright Pomp ascended jubilant.

Bentley complained about the leadership of Satan that the Morning Star disappears last of the stars in the morning, so cannot be said to lead them; Pearce smartly replied that a shepherd walks at the back. But the words are *drew after him,* and the inversion acts as part of the conflict of feeling; he leads them only towards night. Pearce makes a more valuable suggestion in saying that the Morning Star and Evening Star are the same: 'he puts Hesperus as Evening Star; it guides them and comes foremost.' It is as *Hesperus, that led The Starry host,* in the most beautiful of that avenue of descriptions that lead to the nuptial bed of Eden, that he is at the head of his angels in their attack upon the world. I must now try to decide what happens there.

> To Pales, or Pomona, thus adornd,
> Likest she seemed, Pomona when she fled
> Vertumnus, or to Ceres in her Prime,
> Yet Virgin of Proserpina from Jove.

Why was she virgin, and from whom was she flying, Bentley would like to know; and as for *prime*: ' What? have Goddesses the decays of Old Age?' Pearce makes a good case for the façade of the comparison, but the questions deserve an answer that admits their importance. Ceres will decay like the other pagan gods when Christianity comes; the fall from paganism is like the fall from paradise. Eve has insisted on going off alone with her gardening tools to the Temptation; she is flying from the society of Adam and will not fly (it is a reproach against her) from Vertumnus, the god of autumn, of the Fall; the very richness of the garden makes it heavy with autumn. Ceres when virgin of the queen of Hell was already in her full fruitfulness upon the world; Eve is virgin of sin from Satan and of Cain, who in the Talmud was his child. Walking in 'virgin majesty' though not 'ignorant of nuptial rites' she seems at once strong because on Milton's theory freedom does not expose her to sensuality (so Elizabeth might appear, goddess of a paganism now extinguished), hence the more dangerously entitled to the forbidden knowledge, and weak because ignorant of it—she does not know what is at stake, and will fall through triviality. It seems to be ignorance that puts her into the ideal state that is fitted to receive all knowledge. Her lack of shame is felt as a pathetic degree of virginity, and yet it places her with the satyrs outside the Christian world. She and her husband seem great people socially—ambassadors of mankind—and yet savages in a low stage of development. And though she resolves all these opposites, which proves that she is in a state of perfection, the term suggests that there is still something lacking for a full human life. If Milton had been in the Garden, it has been brightly said, he would have eaten the apple at once and written a pamphlet to prove that that was his duty. Another view of the doctrine of the Fall is, I think, somewhere in his mind; that the human creature is essentially out of place in the world and needed no fall in time to make him so.

This very complete ambivalence of feeling is then thrown out and attached to Nature in the garden.

> Thus was this place
> A happy rural seat of various view :
> Groves whose rich Trees wept odorous Gumms and Balme,
> Others whose fruit burnished with Golden Rinde
> Hung amiable, Hesperian fables true,
> If true, here only, and of delicious taste.

Bentley emends *fables* to ' apples,' which makes the idea more obvious. The whole beauty of the thing is a rich nostalgia, but not simply for a lost Eden; sorrow is inherent in Eden itself, as Johnson found it in *L'Allegro*, and that the trees are weeping seems to follow directly from the happiness of the rural seat. The trees that glitter with unheeding beauty and the trees that weep with prescience are alike associated with the tree of knowledge; the same Nature produced the *balm* of healing and the fatal *fruit*; they cannot convey to Adam either its knowledge or the knowledge that it is to be avoided, and by their own nature foretell the necessity of the Fall. The melancholy of our feeling that Eden must be lost so soon, once attached to its vegetation, makes us feel that it is inherently melancholy. These are the same puzzles about the knowledge, freedom, happiness, and strength of the state of innocence, but applied to the original innocence of Nature.

There are three main ideas about Nature, putting her above, equal to, and below man. She is the work of God, or a god herself, and therefore a source of revelation; or she fits man, sympathises with him, corresponds to his social order, has magical connections with him and so forth; or she is not morally responsible so that to contemplate her is a source of relief (this last is Cowper's main business with her, for example). One reason for the force of Milton's descriptions of Eden is that these contradictory ideas can be made there to work together. The apple is a fearful source of revelation. That Nature was magically altered by the fall was part of the tradition that Milton accepted, so we willingly allow her to foresee it and groan as it occurs. To be able to use the supernatural machinery of a

Heroic Poem in this way was in itself a sort of comparison with pagan ideas. And if she is viewed as free from moral responsibility, so, at one end of Milton's feeling, are the sanctified pagans to whom she is fitted.

Wordsworth seems to have two main ways of symbolising Nature, which correspond roughly to father and mother. The mountains of Westmoreland are symbols of morality, the proper and therefore natural way of life, the permanent tradition of the country, not what the French were doing, and so on; they tend to be addressed as local deities, a slip often corrected in later editions, and behind them is God. Nature as a whole appears pantheistically as the nurse of all life, a sustaining rather than moral agent, and one does not feel behind her a personal God who will punish sin. Of course there is no harm in using both conceptions, but Wordsworth seems to have thought them more at home together than they are. It seems possible that one reason for this is that in Milton's blank-verse nature-poetry they really are at home together; before the fall, nature, like man, is not tempted to be wicked, and to adopt pantheism raises no moral problem. And on the other hand, the melancholy of nature in Eden makes her seem not at all unlike nature elsewhere. Nobody could say that Wordsworth was merely imitating Milton, and he was further from him in the first draft of the *Prelude* than in later orthodox revisions, but still the tradition of his medium did not force him to make up his mind on these points.

The trouble about Milton conceived as a writer of pastoral is that he keeps so great a distance between himself and the swain that the more human tricks of the convention cannot work; author and hero seem related as two ambassadors, as Adam is to Raphael. The social feelings that lay behind his politics are allied to this; men ought to be treated as if they had not yet fallen, not out of generosity, but as a painful test of their will, and if they fall it is no fault of the lawgiver. The influence on Wordsworth of this side of Milton is fine so long as the shepherds are gaunt magnified figures striding through the mist, but Wordsworth's descriptions of himself as doing poetic field-work among country people who address him as Sir make a rather different impression. One purpose of the Romantics was to break the class barrier that the Augustans had put into literature; they felt that the couplet was too smart and high-class; surely the democrat Milton, with his sense of the dignity of Man, would be a help here. This part of the program seems to have been a complete failure; only the Tory Scott came near a success independent of class; and the mockery of Gay's Pastorals leaves him obviously more at home with a labourer than the love of Shelley. No doubt the feelings of Milton had a real influence on political theory, but the ' two nations ' of Disraeli came to feel themselves sharply separate while this attempt was being made. Still, so long as Milton is dealing with his first parents, it is fair to say that he has a pastoral sentiment about them. Adam's life is so far from ours that it is necessary to imagine him with dignity from a distance, and Milton seems both to have the double feeling of pastoral, that he is both inferior and superior to Adam, and to be sufficiently at home with it to turn it into poetry.

We first see Paradise through the eyes of the entering

Satan, seated jealously like a cormorant on the Tree of
Life. Like him we are made to feel aliens with a larger
purpose; our sense of its pathos and perfection seems,
as he does, to look down on it from above; the fall has
now happened, and we must avoid this sort of thing
in our own lives. Like so many characters in history
our first parents may be viewed with admiration so
long as they do not impose on us their system of values;
it has become safe to admit that in spite of what is now
known to be the wickedness of such people they had a
perfection which we no longer deserve. Without any
reason for it in Milton's official view of the story this
feeling is concentrated onto their sexual situation, and
the bower where Eve decks their nuptial bed (let not
the reader dare think there is any loss of innocence in
its pleasures) has the most firmly ' pagan ' and I think
the most beautiful of the comparisons.

> In shadier Bower,
> More sacred and sequestered, though but feigned,
> Pan or Sylvanus never slept, nor Nymph
> Nor Faunus haunted.

' *Pan*, *Sylvanus*, and *Faunus*, savage and beastly Deities,
and acknowledg'd *feign'd*, are brought here in Comparison, and their wild Grottos forsooth are Sacred.'
' These three Verses, after all his objections, were certainly Milton's, and may be justified though not perhaps
admired.'

Surely Bentley was right to be surprised at finding
Faunus haunting the bower, a ghost crying in the cold
of Paradise, and the lusts of Pan sacred even in comparison
to Eden. There is a Vergilian quality in the lines,
haunting indeed, a pathos not mentioned because it is
the whole of the story. I suppose that in Satan deter-

mining to destroy the innocent happiness of Eden, for the highest political motives, without hatred, not without tears, we may find some echo of the Elizabethan fulness of life that Milton as a poet abandoned, and as a Puritan helped to destroy.

The Beggar's Opera

Mock-Pastoral as the Cult of Independence

I

SOME queer forces often at work in literature can be seen there unusually clearly; its casualness and inclusiveness allow it to collect into it things that had been floating in tradition. It is both mock-heroic and mock-pastoral, but these take Heroic and Pastoral for granted; they must be used as conventions and so as ways of feeling if they are even to be denied. It would be as reasonable to say that human nature is exalted as that it is debased by this process; it makes Macheath seem like the heroes and swains no less than the heroes and swains like Macheath. If the joke against him is that he is vain to adopt the grand manner of the genteel rakes he at least stands their own final test; he has the courage to sustain it: 'What would you have me say, ladies? You see this affair will soon be at an end, without my disobliging either of you.' Indeed the audience did not want to despise heroic and pastoral but to enjoy them without feeling cheated; to turn them directly onto Marlborough and the contemporary ploughboy did make it feel cheated. The main joke is not against the characters of the play at all, nor does any one in the discussions about its morality seem to have taken it as against the appalling penal code and prison system; it is against the important people who are *like* the characters; the main thing is the political attack and the principles behind it. But pastoral usually works like that; it describes the lives of 'simple' low people to an audience of refined wealthy people, so as to make them think first 'this is true about everyone' and then 'this is specially true about us.' So far as that goes the play is Swift's first conception of it—the pastoral method applied to Newgate.

There is a natural connection between heroic and pastoral before they are parodied, and this gives extra force to the comic mixture. Both when in their full form assume or preach what the parody need not laugh at, a proper or beautiful relation between rich and poor. Hence they belong to the same play—they are the two stock halves of the double plot. It is felt that you cannot have a proper hero without a proper people, even if the book only gives him an implied or magical relation to it; one takes this so much for granted in Sydney's *Arcadia* that the eventual labour trouble over a revolt of Helots seems oddly out of place. I want first to take a few examples of the comic mixture to show the peculiar sort of humour that it can convey.

The most vivid expression in plot of the sentiment that combines heroic and pastoral is the theme of the prince brought up in secret by the peasant (*Winter's Tale* and *Cymbeline*, more or less). Dryden puts the paradox of the idea very neatly (*Marriage à la Mode*):

AMAL. It is not likely . . .
     that such a youth, so sweet, so graceful,
Should be produced from peasants.
  [Evidently not; he has been arrested merely because he
   looks like an aristocrat.]
 HER. [the youth]. Why, nature is the same in villages,
And much more fit to form a noble issue
Where it is least corrupted.
  [So he is certainly a noble; he has the sentiments of pastoral.]
 KING. He talks too like a man that knew the world
To have been long a peasant. But the rack
Will teach him other language. Hence with him.

The ideas are ripe for satire here. Fielding's first note to Tom Thumb has a pretty reflection on the point.

> Corneille recommends some very remarkable day wherein to fix the action of a tragedy. This the best of our tragical writers have understood to mean a day remarkable for the serenity of the sky, or what we call a fine summer's day. So that . . . the same months are proper for tragedy which are proper for pastoral.

Fortunately in this case the weather permitted of the combination.

> GRIZZLE. Oh! Huncamunca, Huncamunca, oh!
> Thy pouting breasts, like kettledrums of brass
> Beat everlasting loud alarums of joy.
> As bright as brass they are, and oh! as hard.
> Oh! Huncamunca, Huncamunca, oh!

The joke is that heroically high people are pastorally low; the very beautiful result reminds one of D. H. Lawrence describing a ' primitive.'

> HUNCA. Ha! Dost thou know me, Princess as I am,
> That thus of me you dare to make your game?
> GRIZZLE. Oh, Huncamunca, well I know that you
> A princess are, and a king's daughter, too.
> But love no meanness scorns, no grandeur fears;
> Love often lords into the cellar bears,
> And bids the sturdy porter come upstairs.
> For what's too high for love, and what's too low?
> Oh! Huncamunca, Huncamunca, oh!

Really heroic love is superior to social convention; it may be pastoral enough to produce bawdy farce. But the striking thing about the result in Fielding is its breadth; he seems to leave room for the ideas he laughs at; there is no private facetiousness about this dance on the grave of heroic tragedy.

Even the aristocratic fool of the Restoration stage has

a touch of the combination; the plays were for a limited social circle, but still clowns have a mock-pastoral tradition. This object of satire, Dryden pointed out, is like the national hero who becomes a symbol of his nation; he 'stands for' the group satirised; he has that hint of parliament which is the dignity of the theatre.

> None Sir Fopling him, or him, can call;
> He's knight of the shire, and represents you all.

One might think that the hearty relation between rich and poor which allowed of tricks between heroic and pastoral belonged mainly to the Elizabethans, and Gay surprisingly refers us back to them. The prologue to the Opera explains that it is a revival of the marriage masques, for the beggar artists (aristocrats no doubt in their own world) James Chanter and Moll Lay; the dance of prisoners in chains is a regular antimasque. Polly indeed views this dance simply as one of the charms of the world, but all its charms just then seem 'an insult on my affliction,' and the antimasque was a sort of symbolic insult.

For the grandest example of the mixture one must go outside England. One cause of the range of *Don Quixote*, the skyline beyond skyline of its irony, is that though mock-heroic it is straight pastoral; only at the second level, rather as the heroic becomes genuine, does the pastoral become mock. Most of the story (' oh basilisk of our mountains ') might be taking place in Sydney's *Arcadia*, and as Quixote himself points out (I. IV. xxiii.; in favour of the boy who was on graceful terms with his goat) the two conventions are alike, so that the book puzzles us between them; we cannot think one fatuous and not the other. A large fraction of it ignores Quixote while the characters tell romantic tales that partake of both; only slightly less romantic tales are part of the main story, and some of the ladies he absurdly fails to help (*e.g.* Dorothea, I. iv. ii.) are actually in need of the sort of help he offers. This makes the satire seem more important by making his heroism less unreal, as do the cautiously implied comparisons of him to Christ, which make him the fool who becomes the judge. And a direct meeting between the two conventions, as in this beautiful and unexpected speech of the innkeeper, always puts knight-errantry back on its horse.

> I have now in the House two or three Books of that kind, which have really kept me, and many others, alive. In Harvest time, a great many of the Reapers come to drink here in the Heat of the Day, and he that can read best among us takes one of these Books, and all the Rest of us, sometimes Thirty or more, sit round him and listen with such Pleasure, that we have neither Sorrow nor Care.

Clearly it is important for a nation with a strong class-system to have an art-form that not merely evades but breaks through it, that makes the classes feel part of a larger unity or simply at home with each other. This may be done in odd ways, and as well by mockery as admiration. The half-conscious purpose behind the magical ideas of heroic and pastoral was being finely secured by the *Beggar's Opera* when the mob roared its applause both against and with the applause of Walpole.

One of the traditional ideas at the back of the hero was that he was half outside morality, because he must be half outside his tribe in order to mediate between it and God, or it and Nature. (In the same way the swain of pastoral is half Man half ' natural.' The corresponding idea in religion is that Christ is the scapegoat.) This in a queer way was still alive in the theatre; no perversion of human feeling might not be justified in the Restoration tragic hero, because he was so ideal, and the Restoration comic hero was a rogue because he was an aristocrat. The process of fixing these forms into conventions, the Tragedy of Admiration and the comedy of the predatory wit, undertaken because the forms had come to seem unreal, for some reason brought out their primitive ideas more sharply. Now on the one hand, this half-magical view seemed to the Augustans wicked as well as ridiculous; all men were men; they had just put down the witch-burnings; to a rational pacificism Marlborough and Alexander were bullies glorified by toadies. On the other hand, they were Tory poets, and the heroic tradition, always royalist (the king's divine right made the best magical symbol), had died on their hands. The only way to use the heroic convention was to turn it onto the mock-hero, the rogue, the man half-justified by pastoral, and the only romance to be extracted from the Whig government was to satirise it as the rogue. The two contradictory feelings were satisfied by the same attitude.

The rogue so conceived is not merely an object of satire; he is like the hero because he is strong enough to be independent of society (in some sense), and can therefore be the critic of it. There was a feeling that the unity of society had become somehow fishy—Hobbes' arguments in its favour, for instance, themselves products of civil war, only affected one the other way; and that the independent individual (the monad, the gravitating particle) was now the only real unit. Hence the ' rogue become judge' formula, with its obscure Christian connections, is used by a long series of writers for almost any purpose in hand. That is why the merchant-pioneer Robinson Crusoe was such a hero and yet must apologise for his life. The interest of the Noble Savage (Dryden's phrase) was that he was another myth about the politically and intellectually free man. Macheath means laird of the open ground where he robs people; he is king of the Waste Land. Dullness to Pope and Dryden is a goddess, so that the theme of human folly is not trivial; she is a hideous danger to civilisation; both she and the hero her representative can tell us with authority who is dull. Moll Flanders in her second robbery is tempted to murder the child robbed, for greater safety; to escape from a moment of horror at herself she becomes indignant with the child's parents, explains how it ought to be looked after, and hopes the robbery will teach them to take better care of it; this makes her touching and competent. All Jonathan Wild's acts, according to himself in Fielding, might be excused in a hero; a denunciation of heroes; it makes him intolerable. Gay has many uses for the formula; a typical joke, that always delights a modern audience, gives its application to marriage, when Peachum says on discovering the marriage of Polly:

> Married! the captain is a bold man, and will risk anything for money; to be sure he thinks her a fortune. Do you think your mother and I should have lived comfortably so long together if we had been married? Baggage!

The point of this is that it is a defence of marriage by one who thinks he is attacking it; marriage is not exalted (one can accept the mockery of the comedies), but it is more stable than its laws. The rogue has only to free it from the offensive approval of society to find it natural.

It may be said that there is no real cult of independence in this, because the irony admits that the hero is not really independent or should not be admired for it. Certainly the irony is necessary; later versions like the raggle-taggle-gypsy business which merely admire the apparently free man obviously leave out part of the truth. But though one may be puzzled by what the *Opera* means, certainly the turns of phrase it uses are pro-independent. The irony may well say that at a higher level the idea of independence is all nonsense; everything is one, all men are dependent on society, man can only be happy through generosity and a good conscience, or what not. But this does not annul the feeling for independence because one is made to feel that at so high a level the common rules of society are nonsense too. (This talk of levels seems evasive; the parallel with extreme pacifism may make it less vague. Granted that it is true that the right thing is for no man to resist another under any circumstances, a man who lives the life of a religious mendicant has or nearly has the right to appeal to it. But a man who allows the police to protect his property, however passively, is already not living by that rule and cannot appeal to it, only to the lower-level idea of justice. Which level is being used is thus a matter of logical consistency.) The feeling of universality given by this ironical method is due to the reader's sense that 'levels' are implied one above another. Not that this is the only way of giving a feeling of universality, which has been

THE BEGGAR'S OPERA

done, I suppose, more strongly by works whose thought
and feeling seem straightforward, but it gives a clear
case open to analysis.

The same feeling for independence comes out in the
Restoration development of an analytic prose with short
sentences; the idea must be purged of associations of
feeling and made to stand on its own (which fitted in,
again, with the rise of the sciences). After what Dryden
called the Deluge, the republic, one could not take the
old symbolisms, even the Elizabethan poetic ones, for
granted; one must go back to the simplest things and
argue from them. So it was in this period that the forms
used in Basic English seemed most attractive to stylists
and were most developed, though I know of none
actually invented then. The assumption of humility
in such flat plain-man writing, together with its analytic
power of generalisation, leads a stylist inevitably to
irony, which was already what they wanted on other
grounds.

I should say then that the essential process behind the
Opera was a resolution of heroic and pastoral into a cult
of independence. But the word is capable of great
shifts of meaning, chiefly because nobody can be independent altogether; Gay meant Peachum to be the
villain, and there is a case for thinking him more independent than Macheath. The animus against him
seems not only that due to a traitor; Gay dislikes him
as a successful member of the shopkeeping middle class,
whereas Macheath is either from a high class or a low
one. After listing the great Robinson among rogues
I had better compare his life to Gay's own.

The first pages of *Crusoe* are a eulogy of the safety
and sanity of the life open to the hero as a shopkeeper;

the description of the forces in his mind that made
him run away to a life of adventure, kept to the tone
that would satisfy the reader intended, is of great subtlety,
follows at once, and makes the best part of the book.
There is no excuse; he ran because of a shameful passion
for new worlds; but he thought there was money in
them too, and no years of solitude can stop him from
keeping his sanity and his accounts. The moral is that
the other sort of independence is the best, but that
Crusoe has somehow proved it by choosing this one;
the qualities that would have made him a good shop-
keeper are those that made him a good pioneer. In
any case this is the proper framework for a story of
adventure (the alternative is the later invention of
making the hero childish). Sindbad the Sailor has the
same shop-keeping background and feels like Crusoe
that he is a black sheep to have left it, but has a grander
way of riding across the conflict of ideals. After wasting
on his pleasures almost all the money his father left
him he remembers some words of Solomon, which seem
to have been misreported; Solomon often gets a fine
effect from putting together two merely contradictory
proverbs, but in the sacred text these particular quota-
tions waste themselves in separation. Sindbad remembered his father saying, 'Three things are better
than other three; the day of death is better than the
day of birth; the grave is better than frustration; and
a live dog is better than a dead lion.' Stirred to manhood
by this wholly contradictory advice (a lesson to the
litterateur) he sold the rest of his property for bales of
goods, and set sail on the voyages that have made him
immortal.

Gay merely escaped to his uncle when apprenticed

to a shop, failed to get the political bribes he thought his due (he is always attacking political bribery), but succeeded in living as a parasite on the nobility (his work is full of horror of parasitism). He went on living with the Queensburies when quite wealthy enough to live on his own, and puzzled his friends by letters full of praise of the state he avoided.

> All the money I get is saving, so that by habit there may be some hopes (if I grow richer) of my becoming a miser. All misers have their excuses. The motive to my parsimony is independence.

Still, a well-protected praise.

> I am every day building villakins, and have given over that of castles. If I were to undertake it [which?] in my present circumstances I should on the most thrifty scheme soon be straitened; and I hate to be in debt, for I cannot bear to pawn five pounds' worth of my liberty to a tailor or butcher. I grant that this is not having the true spirit of modern nobility, but it is hard to cure the prejudice of early education.

He is not easy about it, but the conflict is clear. He preferred to continue as a hanger-on of the aristocracy, and liked Macheath partly because a similar preference was his ruin; but the reason was that it seemed more independent than a moderate independent income. Nobody could make him get out of the South Sea Bubble because it was worth while to make a very large fortune but not worth while to keep what he had won; it would only mean losing the excuse of poverty. One might satirise flattery, but at bottom it was not as sordid as frugality. Here at any rate his life was consistent with his achievement. Every reference to money in the *Opera* carries a satire on the normal attitude to it no less complete than those of Timon of Athens which Marx analysed with so much pleasure.

An interesting family of words deserves to be followed in detail through the shifts of feeling in these ideas; rogue, dog, arch, honest, roguish, dogged, etc. *Rogue* in the sixteenth and *arch* in the seventeenth century appear suddenly with a mystery about their derivation, like the others had a use in describing criminals before developing a use in describing 'good fellows,' and imply courage in both describer and described. After the middle of the eighteenth century the special use of them exchanges this sense of danger for complacence, and becomes silly unless kept for children or young girls. It was the same process that spoilt Poetic Diction. The next development of a queer sort of pastoral, already strong in Wordsworth, triumphant in Lewis Carroll, has accepted this decision that it can be used only on the child.

I should connect this with the Romantic attack on Poetic Diction, conceived as a specially Augustan trait. No doubt all Pope's work claims a dignity that detaches it from the object in the way the Romantics did not want, and Pope himself conventionalised his form in the translations; but the life of this impersonal dignified form was in the play of irony and judgment that could shelter behind it. What the Romantics attacked was the late eighteenth-century emptiness of poetic diction, frequently that of their own early verse. So far from overthrowing it, the Romantic Revival was largely engaged in reviving not only the Augustan cult of independence but the perversions of traditional myth by which it was expressed; the chief difference was that the poet now stole the dignities of the swain and the hero for himself, omitting to add irony, but Pope had started that already. It is clear that the view of the poet as outcast and unacknowledged legislator, equally strong in Byron and Shelley, puts him exactly in the position of the mythical tragic hero. There is a subtler and less assertive version of the myth in the favourite theme of Shelley and Keats, that the poet obtains a vision of eternal extrahuman beauty for an instant, by magic, at great cost, and then faints back to the normal life of the world. Even the poet's more normal relation with Nature in Wordsworth and Coleridge assumes that his main business is to reconcile nature to his tribe. That magical ideas about the poet were inherent in the Romantic Movement is shown very neatly by Gray's *Bard*, in which the last of the Welsh poets, to be killed by the usurper because his political influence is so great, fixes by prophecy the future of English history. Coleridge's Imagination, and the more gradually developed use of the word ' Genius ' about poets, show them trying to live up to this example. Another main romantic element is the development of interest in ' personality '; the style of an author is conceived as ' original,' valuable because different from everybody else's; a character in a novel is treated primarily as an individual, so that the first thing is to show he is different from all other individuals. It seems possible that the machinery by which this idea was produced was not merely a cult of independence but the extension of the magical ideas about the hero to any one who received attention.

To say that a culture has certain fundamental myths, seldom clearly stated, but used in the development of its literature, is not to say much about the product. Nor does it show that any one use of them has much connection with another. But there is, I think, one clear case of influence of the Augustan on the Romantic cult of independence; Byron was fond of praising the Augustans to the disadvantage of his contemporaries and ready enough to throw irony into his self-exaltation; Byronism is almost consciously the Poet as Macheath. Its peculiar mixture of aristocracy and democracy is just that of the mixture of outcasts from heroic and pastoral; the relations of Manfred with the Swiss shepherd on the mountain are those of two demigods above the falsity of civilisation. The importance of incest, so baffling to poor Augusta, was that the hero's family as well as himself must be too great to keep the common rules of humanity, and unable to fit a fit mate elsewhere; an appeal to the Pharaohs rather than the Borgias. One need not pursue the tradition through Baudelaire back to Wilde; it keeps an idea that crimes are the fate of the artist merely because of his greatness, and that to commit hubris is only to admit that one is the tragic demigod. No doubt this ancient dramatic theme becomes a nuisance when the artist persists in acting it all the time, and Byron's own good work was done when he had come at any rate to take it for granted. But in a milder form it is almost the only myth still in active use for poetry.

> Curved like a thin blue scythe, and smoothly reaping
> Their mushroom minarets and toadstool towers,
> My speed has set the steel horizon sweeping
> And mowed the Indies like a field of flowers.

I am not sure how far the ideas I am trying to express are obvious. To me there seems no way of approaching this verse from an excellent traditional poem by Roy Campbell, *The Albatross*, but to say 'The albatross,

THE BEGGAR'S OPERA

tragic and alone like the poet, the figure of pastoral
that corresponds to his position as hero, cleanses the
cluttered world of civilisation by magical influence,
and can do this *because* it is so completely cut off
from it.'

II

The stock device of the play is a double irony like a
Seidlitz powder, piling a dramatic irony onto what was
already an irony. This forces one to read back a more
complex irony onto the first one, and the composure
of language of the characters makes us feel that the
speaker took the whole sense for granted. So he is a
pastoral character; he moves among fundamental
truths. The trick of style that makes this plausible is
Comic Primness, the double irony in the acceptance of
a convention. This is never meant by the speaker as a
single critical irony ('I pretend to agree with this only
to make you use your judgment and see that it is wrong ')
—if an irony does that it does not seem prim—though
the author may mean a critical irony when he assigns
the character a primness. No sentence of the play is
quite free from this trick; one might only doubt over
' bring those villains to the gallows before you and I
am satisfied,' but though there is plain indignation in
both Gay and Macheath, for Macheath to feel it is in
a degree ' rogue-become-judge,' funny because self-
righteous. One might divide Comic Primness with the
usual divisions of comedy, according to the degree to
which the inherent criticism is intended.

It may assume that the conventions are right and that
to be good is to keep them; by applying them unexpectedly a sense of relief is put into their tightness,
though one is still good; they are made to seem deliber-
ately assumed, so that the normal man is unchanged
beneath them, and this gives a sense of power and freedom
just as custard-pie farce does. You may say that this

simple type assumes the others - ' What is an important truth for us would not be true on a higher level; it is good to see the superficiality of the rules we must none the less keep.' But this may be inherent and yet well out of sight. This type goes with ' free ' comedy.

It may imply simply that the conventions are wrong, as a critical irony would, but if it is to remain Comic Primness it must then also imply that the speaker does not feel strong enough, or much desire, perhaps for selfish reasons, to stand up against them; he shelters behind them and feels cosy. One would use this in ' critical ' comedy, but it would be hard to make a complete critical comedy without ever leaving comic primness.

In full Comic Primness (an element of ' full ' comedy) the enjoyer gets the joke at both levels—both that which accepts and that which revolts against the convention that the speaker adopts primly. It is a play of judgment which implies not so much doubt as a full understanding of issues between which the enjoyer, with the humility of impertinence, does not propose to decide. For this pleasure of effective momentary simplification the arguments of the two sides must be pulling their weight on the ironist, and though he might be sincerely indignant if told so it is fair to call him conscious of them. A character who accepts this way of thinking tends to be forced into isolation by sheer strength of mind, and so into a philosophy of Independence.

This may be used for Ironical Humility, whose simplest gambit is to say, ' I am not clever, educated, well born,' or what not (as if you had a low standard to judge by), and then to imply that your standards are so high in the matter that the person you are humbling yourself before

is quite out of sight. This has an amusing likeness to
pastoral; the important man classes himself among
low men, and the effect is to raise his standards, not to
lower them. At the stage of 'device prior to irony'
this is an essential weapon of pastoral. I shall try to
show that Polly uses it in this way. Also there is a feeling
of ironical humility diffused generally through the play,
as if the characters knew they were really much better
than heroes and prime ministers, not merely like them,
though they do not choose to say so clearly; the reason
for this, I think, is that the pretence that Macheath and
Walpole are both heroes is a sort of ironical humility
in the author ('I am easily impressed'), not so much
a critical one as one implying a reserve of force—'by
this means I can understand them completely.' Such an
ironical humility is in effect like the attitude of the
scientist; the observer must not alter what he observes
but shrink to a mere eye. A man like Boswell writes
of himself like this because he wants to keep himself
out of the scene of which in fact he was the stage-
manager. The richness of the ironical humility of
Chaucer is that he combines the truth-seeking feeling
in the trick with its poetical one of pastoral (the notion
that a rightly conducted love affair is a means of understanding the world seems to hold the two together).
The ironical humility of the Victorian Samuel Butler is
more curious. It aims at outflanking the official moralists,
making their pomposity absurd by giving similar but
different moral advice under cover of giving merely
practical advice. 'Every system leads to absurdity in
extreme cases, so we must be careful to keep our system
to plain obvious cases'; 'we must avoid the ideal and
extreme because we have been taught false ideals.'

He cannot help thinking about higher matters than he pretends to, but this acts as a criticism of language; ' the words of all moralists shift as mine do, only they have not the sense to see it. I may not be doing much but I am keeping my head.' That is the force of the perpetual analogy from business to spiritual matters, and the double irony of his sustained praise of the ' mean.' (He does not try to stop altering the field in the course of observing it by making himself small but uses the alterations for further knowledge.) ' Pray let nobody idealise *me* '; the whole charm of his trick, and it is a genuine one, is that he refuses to recognise the grandeur of the senses which he cannot keep out of his words. The figure of pastoral here is *l'homme moyen sensuel*, whom Butler did in fact idealise with painful results in his own life. Butler's small pet list of endurable artists is interesting because they all did the same trick; it seems clear that he was right in feeling that Handel based himself on ironical humility and used it to reconcile the heroic feelings and the Christian ones.

The man who uses the third sort of comic primness need not, however, go off in these directions; he may simply not be interested in the aspect of the matter that makes it a problem. Aristotle's remarks in the *Rhetoric* about how one should treat evidence extracted by torture, according as it is favourable or not, are a good example, because they show how such a man can seem extremely ' innocent ' without seeming silly or ill-informed. The question whether it is stupid to torture witnesses at all has obviously occurred to him but is not the matter in hand. Zuckermann's book on Monkey Hill, and much of Darwin for that matter, give the same effect; one sentence may seem Swift satirising Man

and the next a scientist satirising scientific method, but
the man is keeping himself to one purpose. Even if
he is interested in the matter he may imply a claim that
it is irrelevant without implying a claim to be ignorant
of it. This reserve about the degree to which one has
got the matter in hand is of course a central method
of irony. And the same effect may be given by someone
who has not yet discovered that the problem exists;
this may be called 'genuine innocence' and in a way
returns the third sort of comic primness to the first;
the speaker feels that this is a lively way out, the hearer
that it is rich in contradictions. This again may be
imitated; the ironist may claim that to so good, natural,
innocent, etc., a person as himself the problem in hand
does not arise—what he says satisfies both parties to
the dispute, almost like a pun; there is no way of proving
that he is conscious of the problem—if he is made to
hear of it he will still feel the same. This is best when so
arranged that the other man cannot attempt to call the
bluff without exposing himself, which arises naturally
in the conventional setting of Comic Primness.

It is obvious that the characters of the *Opera* are in
some sense 'artificial,' though to know just how impossible their talk is one would have to inspect the
contemporary Newgate more thoroughly than Gay did
or than we can do. (There is a story in *The Flying Post
or Weekly Medley*, Jan. 11, 1728-9, to which attention
has been drawn recently, showing Gay doing his best
to get information from Peachum, but whether it is
true or not makes no difference to the argument here.)
This feeling of artificiality is, I think, given by the trick
essential to mock-pastoral (or the dignity of style which
allows of it); we are not enabled to know how much

they and how much the author has put into their ironies. The puppets are plausible if they don't mean all that the play puts into their words and delightful if they do, and the shift between the two theories is so easy that we take them as both. One must add doubt about this to the previous doubts about such an irony in plain speech, with which it continually interlocks. To discuss ' what the characters mean ' is therefore a ridiculous occupation. I shall not, however, guard myself against this mistake; the trick would not work unless the audience was able to imagine for itself a level at which the meanings were just plausible and still delightful, and presumably the author does the same. It is clear, for instance, that Polly's remarks are arranged to fit in with a theory of innocence more than Macheath's, and his again more than Peachum's; Peachum would claim that the problem implied was irrelevant rather than unknown. Indeed the critical attack on ' character ' in plays previous to the stress on ' personality ' seems now often pedantic and beyond what a man like Mr. Eliot, who gave the attack its weight, would approve.

> FILCH. Really, madam, I fear I shall be cut off in the flower of my youth, so that, every now and again, since I was pumped, I have thoughts of taking up and going to sea.

The *use* of Filch is that, when you meet young men in other walks of life taking themselves as seriously as he does, you can feel they are like him—unconscious in the way he is. On the other hand (so far as one can separate the feeling of a sentence from the feeling of the whole play), the author means no more by this than to keep up the joke of the style; he does not mean, for instance, that it is always stupid to take oneself seriously.

I should call this the Free sort of comic primness in the author, and mere dignity in the speaker.

> MRS. PEACHUM. You should go to Hockley-in-the-Hole, and to Marlebone, child, to learn valour; these are the schools that have bred so many great men. I thought, boy, by this time, thou hadst lost fear as well as shame. Poor lad! how little does he know yet of the Old Bailey! For the first fact, I'll ensure thee against being hanged; and going to sea, Filch, will come time enough, upon a sentence of transportation. But now, since you have nothing better to do, even go to your book, and learn your catechism; for, really, a man makes but an ill figure in the ordinary's paper who cannot give a satisfactory answer to his questions.

'How little he knows yet of life!'—a simple twist localises each sentence to the sort of life considered. To localise so oddly is in itself to generalise—'One would find a prosing and complacent piety as the basis of feeling in any settled way of life.' The main thing the author wants to say is 'Take these as ordinary people; there is nothing queer about them but their economic conditions.' Mrs. Peachum's kind of piety is indeed put in its place, but we are not told that it need be hypocritical. Yet there seems a touch of archness in 'going to sea, Filch.' One can only say that Mrs. Peachum is between simplicity and the first sort of comic primness, and the author between the first and the third.

> MRS. PEACHUM. How the mother is to be pitied who hath handsome daughters! Locks, bolts, bars, and lectures of morality are nothing to them; they have as much pleasure in cheating a father and mother as in cheating at cards.

(This may look back to the first words of the divine Polly—to 'make a poor hand of her beauty' would be not to cheat with her cards.) The surprise of the

device of rhetoric by which Mrs. Peachum leaps from
the instruments of her trade to a presumption of virtue
makes us feel ' all moral lectures are like locks; all
used to imprison others as much as possible.' By being
a spirited and striking hypocrite she exposes a normal
hypocrisy; the style makes the critic inherent in the
rogue. How far she knows she is amusing for this
reason is a more difficult question; I suppose she has
the first sort of comic primness and the author the third.

> PEACHUM. A lazy dog. . . . This is death, without reprieve.
> I may venture to book him.

There is a conscious contrast between the decision and
the prim caution about keeping the book neat.

> There is not a fellow that is cleverer in his way, and saves
> more goods out of the fire, than Ned.

He took advantage of the fire for robbery; ' saving is
a good act.' Peachum's jokes may well be supposed to
be unconscious from habit, but they imply ' these ideas
are a bit queer, and allow of latitude, but we have just
as much right to them as the others.' One must allow
him the third sort of comic primness as well as his
author, though the author's hatred of him brings in
complications.

One cannot go far into the play without insisting on
the distinction between the two sorts of rogues, which
is made very clearly and gives a rich material for irony.
The thieves and whores parody the aristocratic ideal,
the dishonest prison-keeper and thief-catcher and their
families parody the bourgeois ideal (though the divine
Polly has a foot in both camps); these two ideals are
naturally at war, and the rise to power of the bourgeois

had made the war important. Their most obvious difference is in the form of Independence that they idealise; thus the Peachums' chief objection to Macheath as a son-in-law is that he is a hanger-on of the aristocracy.

> MRS. P. Really, I am sorry, upon Polly's account, the captain hath not more discretion. What business hath he to keep company with lords and gentlemen? He should leave them to prey upon each other.
> P. Upon Polly's account? What the plague does the woman mean?

The discovery follows. The puzzle is that both Peachums feel dicing with the aristocracy might involve independence in their sense as well as his.

> MRS. P. I knew she was always a proud slut, and now the wench hath played the fool and married, because, forsooth, she would do like the gentry! Can you support the expense of a husband, hussy, in gaming, drinking, and whoring? . . . If you must be married, could you introduce nobody into our family but a highwayman? Why, thou foolish jade, thou wilt be as ill-used and as much neglected as if thou hadst married a lord.
> P. Let not your anger, my dear, break through the rules of decency; for the captain looks upon himself in the military capacity as a gentleman by his profession. Besides what he hath already, I know he is in a fair way of getting or dying, and both these, let me tell you, are most excellent chances for a wife. Tell me, hussy, are you ruined or no?
> MRS. P. With Polly's fortune she might very well have gone off to a person of distinction; yes, that you might, you pouting slut.

Decency is the polite tone the bourgeois should keep up towards the wasteful aristocrat he half despises, so it is not clear whether *ruined* means 'married' or 'unmarried'; he is merely, with bourgeois primness, getting the situation clear. But who is a *person of distinction*?

Mrs. Peachum is muddled enough to mean a real lord. (First joke; they will marry anything for money.) But she may mean a wealthy merchant or the squire he could become. (Second joke; this gets at the squires by classing them as bourgeois and at the lords by preferring the squires.) Squire Western, a generation later, was indignant in just this way at the idea of marrying his daughter to a lord.

Gay forced this clash onto his material by splitting up the real Jonathan Wild into Peachum and Macheath, who appear in the story as villain and hero. Swift complained that Gay had wasted a chance of good mock-heroic in Macheath's last speech to the gang; he should have said 'let my empire be to the worthiest' like Alexander. Gay was busy with his real feelings, and Macheath says, 'Bring those villains to the gallows before you, and I am satisfied.' But though he hates Peachum he makes him the parody of a real sort of dignity, that of the man making an independent income in his own line of business, and seems to have been puzzled between the two ideals in his own life. In the play the conflict is hardly made real except in the character of Polly; the fact that both parties are compared to Walpole serves to weaken it to the tone of comedy.

The ironies of the two parties are naturally of different intentions.

JEMMY. . . . Why are the laws levelled at us? Are we more dishonest than the rest of mankind? What we win, gentlemen, is our own, by the law of arms and the right of conquest.

[This specially heroic member peached.]

CROOK. Where shall we find such another set of practical philosophers, who, to a man, are above the fear of death?

WAT. Sound men, and true.

ROBIN. Of tried courage, and indefatigable industry.

NED. Who is there here that would not die for his friend?

HARRY. Who is there here that would betray him for his interest?

MAT. Show me a gang of courtiers that can say as much.

BEN. We are for a just partition of the world, for every man hath a right to enjoy life.

The main effect of this mutual comparison, of the assumption of a heroic manner here, is to make the aristocrats seem wicked and the thieves vain. But even for this purpose it must act the other way, and make both charming by exchanging their virtues; that the aristocrats can be satirised like this partly justifies the thieves, and to extend to Walpole's government the sort of sympathy it was generous to feel for the thieves was strong satire precisely because it was gay. The author means the passage hardly less than the thieves do as a statement of an attitude admittedly heroic; Ben Budge anticipates Jefferson, and the whole complaint against the morality of the play was that they are too hard to answer. No doubt there is a further critical irony in the author—' the whole business of admiring Marlborough and Alexander is nonsense '; and in people like thieves, in whom heroism does so much less harm than politicians, Gay is ready enough for an irresponsible sort of admiration. It seems enough, if one requires a tidy formula, to say that the thieves have both grandeur and the first sort of comic primness and their author the third.

The political ironies of Peachum and Lockit are of a different sort. The difficulty in saying whether they mean their ironies does not arise because they are simpleminded but because they are indifferent; they bring out the justification that they are necessary to the state

and partake of its dignity firmly and steadily, as a habitual
politeness, and this goes on till we see them as por-
tentous figures with the whole idea of the state, sometimes
a cloud that's dragonish, dissolving in their hands.

> PEACHUM. In one respect indeed we may be reckoned dis-
> honest, because, like great statesmen, we encourage those who
> betray their friends.
> LOCKIT. Such language, brother, anywhere else might turn to
> your prejudice. Learn to be more guarded, I beg you.

Either ' it is not safe to accuse the great ' or ' it is bad
for any man's credit to admit that in anything he is as
bad as they are.' But there is no sense of surprise in
this double meaning; the primness of caution is merely
indistinguishable from the primness of superior virtue.

> PEACHUM. 'Tis for our mutual interest, 'tis for the interest of
> the world that we should agree. If I said anything, brother, to
> the prejudice of your credit, I ask pardon.

Credit is used both about business and glory—' that
fellow, though he were to live these six months, will
never come to the gallows with any credit.' *The world*
may be the whole of society or Society, the only people
who are ' anybody,' the rich who alone receive the
benefits of civilisation. The traditional hero has a
magical effect on everything; the Whig politicians act
like tradesmen but affect the whole country; Lockit
and Peachum have the heroic dignity of the great
because they too have a calculating indifference to other
men's lives. The point of the joke is that the villains
are right, not that they are wrong; ' the root of the
normal order of society is a mean injustice; it is ludicrous
to be complacent about this; but one cannot conceive
its being otherwise.' The conclusion is not that society

should be altered but that only the individual can be admired.

This double-irony method, out of which the jokes are constructed, is inherent in the whole movement of the story. We feel that Macheath's death is not 'downright deep tragedy,' nor his reprieve—a sort of insult to the audience not made real in the world of the play—a happy ending, because, after all, the characters, from their extraordinary way of life, are all going to die soon anyway; then this turns back and we feel that we are all going to die soon anyway. One of the splendid plain phrases of Macheath brings out the feeling very sharply:

> A moment of time may make us unhappy for ever.

The antithesis might make *for ever* 'in the life of eternity' from a speaker who expected such a thing, or as derived from heaven 'in one of those moments whose value seems outside time.' His life seems the more dazzlingly brief because 'for ever' assumes it is unending.

> That Jemmy Twitcher should peach me I own surprised me. 'Tis a plain proof that the world is all alike, and that even our gang can no more trust one another than other people; therefore, I beg you, gentlemen, to look well to yourselves, for, in all probability, you may live some months longer.

'And no more; take care because you are in danger' is the plain sense; but the turn of the phrase suggests 'You may live as long as several months, so it is worth taking trouble. If you were dying soon like me you might be at peace.' It is by these faint double meanings that he gets genuine dignity out of his ironical and genteel calm.

An odd trick is used to drive this home; as most

literature uses the idea of our eventual death as a sort of frame or test for its conception of happiness, so this play uses hanging.

> Lucy. How happy am I, if you say this from your heart! For I love thee so, that I could sooner bear to see thee hanged than in the arms of another.

It is true enough, but she means merely 'dead' by *hanged*; no other form of death occurs to her.

> Mrs. P. Away, hussy. Hang your husband, and be dutiful.

Hang here has its real sense crossed with the light use in swearing—'don't trouble about him; he's a nuisance; be dutiful to your parents.'

> Polly. And will absence change your love?
> Mach. If you doubt it, let me stay—and be hanged.

'Whatever happens' or even 'and be hanged to you,' but he really would be hanged.

> Macheath (in prison). To what a woeful plight have I brought myself! Here must I (all day long, till I am hanged) be confined to hear the reproaches of a wench who lays her ruin at my door.

His natural courage, and the joke that the scolding woman is a terror to which all others are as nothing, give 'till I am hanged' the force of 'for the rest of my life,' as if he was merely married to her. Finally as a clear light use:

> Peachum. Come home, you slut, and when your fellow is hanged, hang yourself, to make your family some amends.

Hanging in the songs may even become a sort of covert metaphor for true love. 'Oh twist thy fetters about me, that he may not haul me from thee,' cries

Polly very gracefully, but her song while her father is hauling carries a different suggestion.

> No power on earth can e'er divide
> The knot that sacred love hath tied.
> When parents draw against our mind
> The true love's knot they faster bind.

It is the hangman's knot, and the irony goes on echoing through the play. The songs can afford to be metaphysical poetry in spite of their date because they are intended to be comically 'low'; only an age of reason could put so much beauty into burlesque or would feel it needed the protection; they take on the vigour of thought which does not fear to be absurd. This excellence depends on the same ironical generosity—a feeling that life is fresh among these people—as lies behind Gay's whole attitude to his characters. (The point that genuine pastoral could then only be reached through burlesque was indeed made clearly by Johnson about Gay's own admirable *Pastorals*.)

There are two elements in the joke of this. One comes from the use of the local details of a special way of life for poetry regardless of how they seem to outsiders, like Johnson's *Rambler* showing how an Esquimaux would take metaphors for his love-rhetoric from seal-blubber. This in itself is satisfying to the age of reason because it shows the universal forces at work. Secondly it uses the connection between death (here hanging) and the sexual act, which is not merely a favourite of Freud but a common joke of the period; the first effect of this is to give an odd ironical courage to the wit of the characters.

> Here ends all dispute, for the rest of our lives,
> For this way, at once, I please all my wives.

> Which way shall I turn me, how can I decide?
> Wives, the day of our death, are as fond as a bride.

The joke need not be given the additional deathliness of the joke against marriage:

> MRS. TRAPES. If you have blacks of any kind, brought in of late, mantoes, velvet scarfs, petticoats, let it be what you will, I am your chap, for all my ladies are very fond of mourning.

Both the ladies want to be hanged 'with' Macheath, in the supreme song of the play; 'but hark,' he replies, there is the bell; this is real death, which one dies alone.

A song by Mrs. Peachum, that lady of easy sentiment, introduced early to make us clear on the point, shows the range of ideas in this direct and casual comedy.

> If any wench Venus' girdle wear,
> Though she be never so ugly,
> Lilies and roses will quickly appear,
> And her face look wondrous smugly.

A rich irony identifies the beauty created by desire in the eye of the beholder with self-satisfaction. The last word admits and enjoys the banality of the preceding flower-symbols.

> Behind the left ear so fit but a cord
> (A rope so charming a zone is!)

Monks use them as zones; they stand for asceticism.

> The youth in his cart hath the air of a lord,

Macheath is a 'captain'; it is the military hero's chariot of triumph. (When the cart is driven away he is left hanging.)

> And we cry, There dies an Adonis!

> —Whose annual wound in Lebanon allured
> The Syrian damsels to lament his fate
> In amorous ditties all a summer's day—

—Whose tragic sacrifice, every spring, like Christ, makes

the crops grow. It is a rare case of the full use of the
myth.

At Mrs. Peachum's first entry she finds her husband
deciding which thief to hang next sessions; her cue is
the end of the laugh at a string of aliases for Walpole.

> MRS. P. What of Bob Booty, husband? I hope nothing bad
> hath betided him. You know, my dear, he's a favourite customer
> of mine—'twas he, made me a present of this ring.
> P. I have set his name down in the black list, that's all, my
> dear; he spends his life among women, and, as soon as his money
> is gone, one or other of the ladies will hang him for the reward,
> and there's forty pound lost to us for ever!
> MRS. P. You know, my dear, I never meddle in matters of
> death; I always leave those affairs to you. Women, indeed, are
> bitter bad judges in these cases; for they are so partial to the brave,
> that they think every man handsome who is going to the camp,
> or the gallows.

The song follows. ' Spends his life among women '
means among prostitutes; not to say so implies that
they are what all women are. Mrs. P.'s callous squeam-
ishness only points the moral; the reason that all women
are bitter bad judges about killing men by treachery is
that they find so much interest in doing it to their lovers.
It is the first hint of that eerie insistence on the sex war
by which the play makes betrayal itself a lascivious act.

Perhaps the most grisly version of this notion is the
one lapse into sentiment of the great Peachum. By
this time Mrs. Peachum (who pleaded for a brave man
before) is firmly entrenched in brutality behind her
bourgeois ' duty.'

> MRS. PEACHUM, PEACHUM, POLLY listening.
> MRS. P. The thing, husband, must and shall be done. For
> the sake of intelligence we must take other measures and have
> him peached the next session without her consent. If she will
> not know her duty we know ours.

P. But, really, my dear! it grieves one's heart to take off a great man. When I consider his personal bravery, his fine stratagems, how much we have already got by him, and how much more we may get, methinks I can't find it in my heart to have a hand in his death : I wish you could have made Polly undertake it.

MRS. P. But in a case of necessity—our own lives are in danger.

P. Then indeed we must comply with the customs of the world, and make gratitude give way to interest.

Then indeed—when not heroic one can always be sure to be respectable, because bourgeois, because self-seeking. She started with the insinuating pomp of the language of diplomacy. Their lives are in no danger; they only think Macheath will betray them because they think he is like Peachum. To be heroic would be to hang on for what they can get. Warmed into feelings of generosity by this situation, and fretfully wishing that Polly might save him the moral effect of deciding to violate them, he shows a fleeting sympathy with romantic love, which so often kills its loved one, and of which at other times, in his bourgeois virtue, he disapproves. Swift is beaten clean off the field here.

The same idea is implicit in one of the purest of Polly's fancies.

LUCY, MACHEATH, POLLY. (The condemned Hold.)

POLLY (entering). Where is my dear husband? Was ever a rope intended for this neck! Oh, let me throw my arms about it, and throttle thee with love. . . . What means my love? not one kind word! not one kind look! Think what thy Polly suffers to see thee in this condition!

> Thus when the swallow, seeking prey,
>   Within the sash is closely pent,
> His consort with bemoaning lay
>   Without sits pining for the event.
> Her chattering lovers round her skim;
> She heeds them not, poor bird, her soul's with him.

Her first words say that her love is death; her love has caused his arrest; the presence of her love here only makes it impossible for him to be saved by the love of Lucy. 'Think what your Polly suffers'; even without these accidents her love would be mere additional torture. And for what *event* is the consort (which also seeks *prey*) of this swallow *pining*? *Event* may mean 'whatever happens,' but the sense thrown at us is 'the thing happening,' the exciting thing; they both mean to be in at the death.

> Lucy. Am I then bilked of my virtue?

'The thing I have *paid* for?'—the slang verb drags in a ludicrous and frightfully irrelevant bit of money-satire. Only the unyielding courage of Macheath, who keeps the thing firmly on the level of the obvious, gives one the strength to take it as comedy or even to feel the pathos of the appeal of Polly.

> Lucy. Hadst thou been hanged five months ago, I had been happy.
> Polly. And I too. If you had been kind to me till death, it would not have vexed me—and that's no very unreasonable request (though from a wife) to a man who hath not above seven or eight days to live.

He takes so completely for granted their state of self-centredness tempered by blood-lust that the main over-tone of her speech is that so often important to the play—'we have all very few days to live, and must live with spirit.' The selfishness of her remarks reconciles us to his selfish treatment of her, and the idea behind their pathos to his way of life.

So that to follow up the ideas of 'love-betrayal-death,' the sacred delight in the tragedy of the hero, is to reach those of 'pathetic right to selfishness,' the ideal of Independence. This comes out more clearly in the grand betrayal scene of the second act, of Macheath by the prostitutes. The climax is one of the double ironies.

> JENNY. These are the tools of a man of honour. Cards and dice are only fit for cowardly cheats, who prey on their friends.
>
> (She takes up the pistol; Tawdry takes up the other.)

(First laugh; the great are like the rogues but more despicable.) Having got his pistols she calls in the police. (Second laugh; the rogues are after all as despicable as the great.) But this is not merely a trick of surprise because she means it; 'we are better than the others only because we know the truth about all human beings'; the characters are always making this generalisation. 'Of all beasts of prey,' remarks Lockit, 'mankind is the only sociable one.' The play only defends its characters by making them seem the norm of mankind and its most informed critics, and does this chiefly by the time-interval in their ironies.

> JENNY. I must and will have a kiss to give my wine a zest.
>
> (They take him about the neck, and make signs to the constables, who rush in upon him.)
>
> PEACHUM. I seize you, sir, as my prisoner.

It is the kiss of Judas, an expression of love with a parallel to hanging in it, like Polly's, that gives zest. Wine is normally used as a symbol of spiritual intoxication, but in this play the spirit is a sinister one, rather as the word *pleasure*, which it uses continually, always refers to the pleasures ('mystical' because connected with death-wishes) of cheating, or cruelty, or death.

The five other uses, counting *pleased*, that I don't quote, are all of this sort. The doubtful one is Lockit's—

> Bring us then more liquor. To-day shall be for pleasure, to-morrow for business.

He has told the audience that he will make Peachum drunk and so have the pleasure of cheating him.

The more sinister because by making the pleasure of betrayal a mere condiment she claims that to her the affair is trivial—' What you can be made to feel heart-breaking I have the strength to judge rightly.' Anyway the *zest* keeps us from thinking her so stupid as to be mercenary about it, which would be to feel nothing.

Peachum treats Macheath here with a sinister respect not chiefly intended as mockery; all politeness has an element of irony, but this is a recognition of the captain's claims; he is now half divine because fated to sacrifice.

> P. You must now, sir, take your leave of the ladies; and, if they have a mind to make you a visit, they will be sure to find you at home [and sure of the ' last pleasure ' of seeing the execu-tion. The preliminaries of death are a failure in the sex war, since the ladies can no longer be deceived, even if death itself is a triumph in it]. The gentleman, ladies, lodges in Newgate. Constables, wait upon the captain to his lodgings.

> MAC. At the tree I shall suffer with pleasure,
> At the tree I shall suffer with pleasure ;
>   Let me go where I will
>   In all kinds of ill
> I shall find no such furies as these are.

He can't go where he will—he expects to leave prison only for Hell. The half-poetical, half-slang word *tree* applies both to the gibbet and to the cross, where the supreme sacrificial hero suffered, with ecstasy.

PEACHUM. Ladies, I'll take care the reckoning shall be discharged.

(Exit Macheath, guarded, with Peachum and constables.)

He, not they, is the fury, the avenging snake-goddess; to look after the reckoning is his whole function towards both parties. The delicacy of his irony (this, I think, is a rule about good ironies) is that it can safely leave you guessing about both parties' consciousness of it; the more sincerely he treats Macheath as an aristocrat the more cruelly he isolates him—

(In the condemned Hold.)

LOCKIT. Do but examine them, sir—never was better work —how genteelly they are made. They will fit as easily as a glove, and the nicest gentleman in England *might* not be ashamed to wear them. (He puts on the chains.) If I had the best gentleman in the land in my custody, I could not equip him more handsomely. And so, sir, I now leave you to your private meditations.

—the less sincerely, the more he mocks—but at the whole notion of aristocracy that Macheath has aped into disaster. Thus even if the insincerity was expressed grossly, so that Macheath could appeal through it to his audience ('obviously you mean this, and it is unfair') he could still not appeal against it as a personal insult ('I really *have* the virtues of the aristocrat'); they would then be mocked, and he would have confessed he was not one of them. Such an irony is a sort of intellectual imitation of more valuable states of mind. To the opponent, there is no practical use in distinguishing between whether the man is conscious or unconscious of his meaning—if he isn't he will be when he is told. 'Oh, so you thought that funny, did you? Well, I wasn't thinking of that special case, but it seems to apply to that all right.' The force of irony is its claim to innocence; the reason for its wide usefulness is that the claim may still be plausible when the man's consciousness of his irony is frank—'This is the normal thing to feel; I felt this before I had met people like you.'

Overpoliteness is a form of comic primness worth looking at for a momen* in general. The original sense is 'I respect you too much to be less formal,' and the effect is to shut you out from intimacy; 'I want you to be formal too.' This may be a coy claim to attention, since to be shut out suggests a desire to come in, or an insult, since you may be below the intimacy not above it. The combination says, 'Notice that I would like to insult you but will not grant you even that form of intimacy.' However, the politeness accepts you as a civilised person, since otherwise it would be no use; 'You ought to know already that we can't be intimate.' This also allows of irony: 'I am polite on principle even to people like you; the best people do this, because any one may deserve it; but it is curious to reflect that even you may.' And it may show that it is not trying to hide these meanings or that it thinks you too much of a fool to see them. The last, I think, is what makes Pope's *Epistle to Augustus* so peculiarly insulting: 'I am safe in saying this, though you would persecute me if you could understand it, because you can't.'

I must go back to the betrayal scene.

> MACHEATH. Was this well done, Jenny? Women are decoy ducks, who can trust them? Beasts, jades, jilts, harpies, furies, whores.

He may mean that these women are whores, which is no discovery, or that all women are, which is made plausible only by being half-said. The climax, the worst he can say of them, is the obvious, which brings back a sort of comedy to the strain of the scene. But its trenchant flatness also makes us feel that the second meaning is obvious, though it would contradict the first (he could not blame them for being like everybody). Even this is a sort of double irony.

' Was this well done ? ' belongs to Cleopatra in all the versions of her story. It does not matter whether we take Macheath as quoting it (he quotes Shakespeare a moment before) or re-inventing it, but it would be wrong to take it only as a comic misuse of heroic dignity like Ancient Pistol's; however queer the logic may be there should be a grand echo in one's mind from the reply of Charmian:

> It is well done, and fitting for a princess
> Descended from so many mighty kings.

—indeed Peachum drives the point home at once:

Your case, Mr. Macheath, is not particular; the greatest heroes have been undone by women.

The pleasure in seeing that two systems so different to emotion or morality as Antony and Macheath work in the same way is connected with the Royal Society, but there are queerer forces in it than that.

Grand only by simplicity and concentration, and only by this grandeur not normal colloquial English (so that it is a reliable phrase for Macheath), the question owes its tenseness to its peculiar assumptions; if it is fitting the other person must have thought the act good, not merely allowable, and yet must be capable of being made to see that it is wrong by a mere appeal. So there must be a powerful and obvious clash of two modes of judgment. When it is used to Cleopatra one must remember that by choosing this death she destroys her children only to avoid a hurt to her pride (not till her being carted in the triumph becomes certain does the world become empty for her without Antony); that the soldier who speaks feels that she has broken her word to Caesar; that Shakespeare's play has made us suspect her of planning to betray Antony, and that some of her tantrums—dragging the messenger about by the hair—can only have seemed comic, vulgar and wicked. Only by a magnificent forcing of the sympathies of the audience is she made a tragic figure in the last act. The sentence, then, used to her, means 'You have cheated Caesar and destroyed yourself; you think this heroic but it is childish; it is like the way you cheated Antony till you destroyed him.' It is because of this suggestion that the answer of Charmian seems to call back and justify Cleopatra's whole life; all her acts were indeed like this one; all therefore fitting for a princess. It is a measure of the queerness of this alarming tragedy (no one can say how much irony there is in the barge speech) that the effect of the question is very little altered when it is 'parodied' for the comic opera; both uses give a quasi-mystical 'justification by death' which does not pretend to justify by normal standards.

So to explain the effect of the phrase here (it is a great effect) one has to invent queer but plausible reasons for thinking 'This was well done.' The most obvious is that the betrayal is poetic justice on him for being unfaithful to Polly; the structure of the play indeed insists on this. The first act gives the personal situation; we meet Polly, her parents at their business, finally Macheath, secretly married to her and hiding in the house. From his richly-prepared entry to the end of the first act he goes on swearing eternal faithfulness

to her—'if you doubt it, let me stay—and be hanged.'
Two grand scenes of the second act then introduce us
to the tribe of which these two are symbolic heroes,
the society of which they are flowers (for Polly, unlike
her parents, is 'aristocratic' as well as 'bourgeois')
—to the eight thieves of Macheath's gang, which he
dare not join since Polly's father is now his enemy,
then to the eight whores he collects because he must
be idle.

> I must have women—there is nothing unbends the mind like
> them; money is not so strong a cordial for the time.

Cordial, medicine for the heart, implies drink, which
gives courage—love is an intoxication. To unbend
your mind is to loosen the strong bow of your thought
so that it will be strong in the next demand on it; a
statesman's excuse for pleasure (indeed *the time* seems
to imply 'this unfortunate but no doubt brief period
of history'); used here with a ludicrous or pathetic
dignity whose very untruth has the gay dignity of
intentional satire. Macheath, like Antony, like the
ambitious politician, must unbend his mind because he
must forget his fears. Into his statement of this fact,
whose confession of fear frees it from bravado, he
throws a further comparison to the avarice inherent in
the life of safety he despises (so that these few words
include both bourgeois and aristocrat); 'to those who
live within the law the mere possession of money is a
sufficient intoxication.' But however well he talks he
is treating Polly with contempt:

> What a fool is a fond wench! Polly is most confoundedly
> bit. I love the sex; and a man who loves money might as well
> be contented with one guinea, as I with one woman.

(Satire on money justifies anything.)

> Do all we can, women will believe us; for they look upon a promise as an excuse for following their own inclinations.

('However frankly theatrical we make our professions of heroic love, professions which necessarily have the irony inherent in all fixed rules of politeness, such as are essential to civilisation.') It was the innocence and pathos of Polly in 'oh ponder well,' we are told, that swung round the audience on the first night. From the standpoint of heroic love the act was well done.

In any case the woman who really undoes him is not Jenny but Polly, however much against her will; unselfish love leads to honest marriage, and therefore Polly's father is determined to have him killed. It is love at its best that is the most fatal. This forces her to be like Cleopatra, and may make it poetic justice that he should betray her; anyway it removes much of the guilt from Jenny. And there is always, since this brings the thing nearer to a stock tragedy, the idea that it is in a fundamental way 'well done' to cause the hero's death because it is necessary to the play.

But there is a more curious pathos in the question if one forgets about Polly, as Macheath has done. It is the questioner here who has both answers to the question in his mind. The 'compliments' of the ladies to one another, through which he has sat placidly drinking, treat just such betrayals by Jenny only as acts of heroic self-control.

> MRS. COAXER. If any woman hath more art than another, to be sure 'tis Jenny Diver. Though her fellow be never so agreeable, she can pick his pocket as coolly as if money were her only pleasure. Now that is a command of the passions uncommon in a woman.

JENNY. I never go to a tavern with a man but in the way of business. I have other hours, and other sort of men, for my pleasure. But had I your address, madam—

(On the face of things a prostitute is unlike other women in only wanting money. In this satire a prostitute is an independent woman who wants all the nobility included in the idea of freedom, and a chaste genteel woman only wants a rich marriage. If you hate Jenny for betraying the hero then she is actually as bad as a good woman, but Mrs. Coaxer assumes that she obviously can't be, and therefore that her behaviour on the crucial issue of money shows nobility; she is faithful to her sorority when she acts like this. Jenny's reply shows the humility of a truly heroic soul.)

MACHEATH. Have done with your compliments, ladies, and drink about. You are not so fond of me, Jenny, as you used to be.

JENNY. 'Tis not convenient, sir, to show my fondness before so many rivals. 'Tis your own choice, and not my inclination, that will determine you.

He cannot say she has deceived him. ' What,' he says as she enters :

And my pretty Jenny Diver too! as prim and demure as ever! There is not any prude, however high bred, hath a more sanctified look, with a more mischievous heart : ah, thou art a dear artful hypocrite!

He loves her for having the power to act as she so soon acts to him (there is a bitter gentility in it which he too feels to be heroic) both as a walking satire on the claims to delicacy of the fine ladies and as justified in her way of life by her likeness to the fine ladies, whose superiority he half admits.

MACHEATH. . . . If any of the ladies choose gin, I hope they will be so free as to call for it.

JENNY. You look as if you meant me. Wine is strong enough for me. Indeed, sir, I never drink strong waters but when I have the colic.

MACHEATH. Just the excuse of the fine ladies! why, a lady of quality is never without the colic.

The colic as a justification for drinking is a disease like the spleen, half-mental, caused by a life of extreme refinement, especially as expressed by tight-lacing. It is because he so fully understands and appreciates her half-absurd charm that he is so deeply shocked by what should have been obvious, that it is a weapon frankly used against himself.

His respect for her is very near the general respect for independence; the main conflict in his question is that between individualism and the need for loyalty. In being a 'beast of prey,' the play repeats, she is like all humanity except in her self-knowledge and candour, which make her better. She is the test and therefore somehow the sacrifice of her philosophy; quasi-heroic because she takes a theory to its extreme; if wrong then because she was 'loyal' to it. Macheath's question becomes 'It is a fine thing when individuals like us can sustain themselves against society. But for that very reason we ought to hold together; surely it is not well done of you to prey upon *me* '—with the idea ' I thought I could make her love me so much that I could disarm her.' Jenny's answer is supplied by Mrs. Slammekin in her complaint at not sharing in the profits; ' I think Mr. Peachum, after so long an acquaint-ance, might have trusted me as well as Jenny Diver'; she owes as much faith to the professional betrayer as to Macheath in his capacity of genteel rake, ' martyr to the fair.'

But Macheath does not believe in individualism in this sense; honour among thieves is taken for granted and only a boast by contrast with politicians. He believes his second arrest to be due to Jemmy Twitcher, and this seems really to shock him. The question does not simply mean (what is inherent in it) 'we believe in all against all, but now I am horrified by it.' It is only in matters of love that he has so nearly believed in all against all as to put a real shock into the question. He has really a sort of love for her (partly because she is against all). He has of course treated her with more contempt than Polly. So that the more serious you make their feelings for each other the more strongly you invoke the other notion, which applies also to Polly; not Independence but Love-Betrayal-Death; ' it is especially in all lovers that we see that all human beings, being independent, are forced to prey upon one another.'

These notions must now be pursued into the character of Polly, where their irony is more subtle. She has been idealised ever since her first night. In the self-righteous sequel named after her, when they are all transported, Gay made Macheath a weak fish permanently in the clutches of Jenny Diver and Polly the only civilised character able to sustain the high tone demanded by the Noble Savage. Her first words in the play, at an entry for which our curiosity has been worked up for two and a half pages, make a rather different impression. She uses the same comic primness as her father and his clients—a friend of Richardson's told him he was too fond of 'tarantalising' like Polly—and this delicate device in a dramatist may wish one to feel any shade of sympathy towards the speaker. You may say that this is a bold and subtle trick to defeat the tone of the play and bring on a real good heroine (if she is not careful she will seem a prig), or that she is defending her lover by a process unusual to her; so that the audience will have a pleasant surprise on discovering her true character. There is more in it than that.

> POLLY. I know as well as any of the fine ladies how to make the most of myself and of my man too. A woman knows how to be mercenary, though she hath never been in a court or at an assembly. We have it in our natures, papa. If I allow Captain Macheath some trifling liberties, I have this watch and other visible marks of his favour to show for it. A girl who cannot grant some things, and refuse what is most material, will make a poor hand of her beauty, and soon be thrown upon the common.

(The common is the heath that her husband rules.) This might be an attack on her under both heads, as making a false fine-lady claim and having real shop-keeper vices. She has two songs, and there are near two pages, containing the discovery that she is married, before she can safely be let speak again.

Peachum's remarks about her do not make up our minds for us—

> If the girl had the discretion of a court lady, who can have a dozen young fellows at her ear without complying with one, I should not matter it.

It is her innocence, which he admits, that is untrustworthy; it is a form of sensuality; especially because certain to change.

She does not say what is 'most material,' either from the modesty of virtue, the slyness of evil, or the necessity of deceiving her father; her real object may be to reform Macheath and make him an honest shopkeeper.

One may take either way her classing the unmentioned marriage lines with the flaunted watch, and the dignity of its appearance among general terms may be pathetic from avarice or from a simple pride. ' *We* have it in our natures, papa,' either because theft is in our blood, or because our nature is to be intelligent as well as good, and could not reliably be good otherwise. This is an early example of the joke from comic primness about the innocent young girl, which runs on through Sheridan, Thackeray, Dodgson, and Wilde—that it is only proper for her to be worldly, because she, like the world, should know the value of her condition, and that there must be no question of whether she is conscious or not of being worldly, so that she is safe (much too safe) from your calling the bluff of her irony, because she deserves either not to be told of the cold judgments of the world or not to be reminded of them. ' Make the most of my man ' may mean ' make the most money possible out of the man I am working on now ' or ' have the best influence I can on this man to whom my life is now bound '; nor would it be graceful in her to claim that the second is wholly unselfish and so distinguish it from the first. If she is able to deceive her father by this phrase it is a perquisite rightly due to the language of delicacy and understanding. Yet on the highest view of her she is absurd; what could any woman ' make ' of Macheath, already a limited perfection? To make him honest would be to make him mercenary. She might indeed (I suspect Gay ran away from this very ironical theme in *Polly*) make him a Virginian squire after transportation, as Moll Flanders did her ' very fine gentleman, as he really is.' The exquisite sense of freedom in one of the ballad lines used by the songs—' over the hills and

far away '—is twisted into a romantic view of transportation by a remark of Polly just before. But she
doesn't see her way to that now; she is not so placed as
to have one purpose and one meaning.

Indeed the fascination of the character is that one has
no means of telling whether she is simple or ironical;
not merely because if ironical she would speak as if
simple, but because if simple it would be no shock to her,
it would be a mere shift of the conscious focus, to be told
her meanings if ironical. The effect is that ' the contradictions do not arise for her; she is less impeded
than we are.' This sort of thing usually requires complacence, and the Victorians did it very well, as in the
mellowness of the jumps from spirituality to intrigue
in Trollope's clerical death-scenes. Polly accepts her
parents' wise advice, though she cannot live up to it, as
readily as their high moral tone, as readily as she makes
herself useful by telling lies to their customers; that
she is so businesslike makes us believe in the vigour of
her goodness; ' real goodness knows that if its practice
in an imperfect world is to be for the best its acts
must be imperfect.' She grants fully that her love is a
weakness; her excuse for marriage even in a song
has a delicate reserve in its double use of the inevitable
criteria:

I thought it both safest and best

is as near as a lyric will carry her to a moral claim.
You may always think her as bad as they are. Her most
shocking effects of pathos, like the play's best jokes,
come from a firm acceptance of her parents' standards,
which gives her the excuse always needed by poetry
for a flat statement of the obvious. Circumstances make

the low seem to her the normal, so she can use without affectation the inverted hypocrisy of Swift.

> PEACHUM. And had you not the common views of a gentle-woman in your marriage, Polly?
>
> POLLY. I don't know what you mean, sir.
>
> PEACHUM. Of a jointure, and of being a widow. . . . Since the thing sooner or later must happen, I daresay the captain himself would like that we should get the reward for his death sooner than a stranger. . . .
>
> MRS. PEACHUM. But your duty to your parents, hussy, obliges you to hang him. What would many a wife give for such an opportunity!
>
> POLLY. What is a jointure, what is widowhood, to me? I know my heart, I cannot survive him.

No less rich background of irony would let us feel that this was true, and a discovery, and a confession, and yet not be too burlesque for us to feel seriously about her.

> MRS. P. What! is the wench in love in earnest then? I hate thee for being particular. Why, wench, thou art a shame to thy sex.
>
> POLLY. But, hear me, mother—if you ever loved——
>
> MRS. P. These cursed playbooks she reads have been her ruin. One word more, hussy, and I shall knock your brains out, if you have any.

This playbook itself, as the moralists insisted, is as likely as the others, like them through its very idealism, to bring ruin. Mrs. Peachum does well to be angry and is right in her suspicion ('I find in the romance you lent me, that none of the great heroes was ever false in love'). But the objection to love is not merely that of Puritan virtue or bourgeois caution; independence is involved. Because love puts this supreme virtue in danger good faith is there most of all necessary, but because of 'love-betrayal-death' is there least obtained.

A still more searching point is made in dealing with the weaker and more violent Lucy.

> LOCKIT. And so you have let him escape, hussy—have you?
>
> LUCY. When a woman loves, a kind word, a tender look, can persuade her to anything, and I could ask no other bribe. [Love is a form of money, as contemptible and as easy to cheat with as another.]
>
> LOCKIT. Thou wilt always be a vulgar slut, Lucy. If you would not be looked upon as a fool, you should never do anything but upon the foot of interest. Those that act otherwise are their own bubbles.
>
> LUCY. But love, sir, is a misfortune that may happen to the most discreet woman, and in love we are all fools alike. Notwithstanding all that he swore, I am now fully convinced that Polly Peachum is actually his wife. Did I let him escape, fool that I was! to go to her? Polly will wheedle herself into his money; and then Peachum will hang him, and cheat us both.

One might think Independence a brutish ideal imposed by a false intellectualism. Lockit makes it a polite social trick, a decent hiding of the reality, to *pretend* that one is a beast of prey. It is from a social criterion that Lucy is told to be anti-social and not ' vulgar.' You may call this an admission that the ideal, as a defence of selfishness, does not meet the facts of human nature; the joke is that as a cynicism the thing refutes itself; but there is a joke too against Lockit and the conventions. We are left with an acceptance of Egoist ethical theory. And the philosophical joke fits naturally onto the social one; only the rogue or the aristocrat, only the independent character, can afford to see the truth about the matter.

We return here to the Senecan remark of Peachum: ' Of all beasts of prey, mankind is the only sociable one.' The reason for the breadth of this remark, its wide use for a cult of independence, is that it gives two contradictory adjectives to man. One cannot reduce it to a

gangster blow-the-gaff sentiment, implying ' see how
tough I am.' In the first place it may involve an appeal
to individualist theory—' all actions apparently altruistic
must have a solid basis in the impulses of the individual,
and only so can be understood. They can only be
based on self-love, because the individual is alone;
there is merely nothing else for them to be based on.
Only by facing this, by understanding the needs of
the individual, can society be made safe.' Secondly
there is a more touching and less analytic idea—' all
life is too painful for the impulses of altruism to be
possible. To refuse to accept this is to judge your
fellow creatures unjustly.' That man should be made
unique in this way is indeed a boast about his reason and
the power that it gives to be independent; all the rami-
fications of irony that drive home and generalise this
idea relate it to the central cult of the man who can
stand alone. Of course the claim to be such a man is as
pathetic in an Augustan thief as a Chicago tough, but
the play makes us feel that.

For there is no doubt about the sociability. One of
the most terrible of these comic scenes is that between
Lucy and Polly, one attempting murder, the other
suspecting it, and yet each finding ' comfort ' in each
other's company. The play has made the word ready
for them to wring the last ironies from it.

PEACHUM. But make haste to Newgate, boy, and let my friends
know what I intend; for I love to make them easy, one way or
the other.

FILCH. When a gentleman is long kept in suspense, penitence
may break his spirit ever after. Besides, certainty gives a man a
good air upon his trial, and makes him risk another without fear
or scruple. But I'll away, for 'tis a pleasure to be a messenger of
comfort to friends in affliction.

245

Death is the comfort, for most, and it is a pleasure to tell them of it. Polly tells her mother she has married for love; she faints, thinking the girl had been better bred:

> PEACHUM. See, wench, to what a condition you have reduced your poor mother! A glass of cordial this instant! How the poor woman takes it to heart!
>
> [POLLY goes out, and returns with it.]
>
> Ah hussy, now this is the only comfort your mother has left.
>
> POLLY. Give her another glass, sir; my mother drinks double the quantity whenever she is out of order.

When she isn't, it is still her chief comfort. All this leads up to Lucy's great scene.

> LUCY. . . . I have the ratsbane ready—I run no risk; for I can lay her death upon the gin, and so many die of that naturally, that I shall never be called in question. But say I were to be hanged—I never could be hanged for anything that would give me greater comfort than the poisoning that slut.

Death is certain anyhow, and its name is hanging throughout the play.

> [Enter POLLY.]
>
> . . . Dear madam, your servant. I hope you will pardon my passion when I was so happy to see you last—I was so overrun with the spleen, that I was perfectly out of myself; and really when one hath the spleen, everything is to be excused by a friend.

The spleen is aristocratic, so her use of poison is also to be excused. Their faults are always the result of their greatness of soul.

> LUCY. When a wife's in her pout
>   (As she's sometimes, no doubt)
>   The good husband, as meek as a lamb,
>   Her vapours to still,
>   First grants her her will,
>   And the quieting draught is a dram;
>   Poor man! and the quieting draught is a dram.

I wish all our quarrels might have so comfortable a recon-
ciliation.

POLLY. I have no excuse for my own behaviour, madam, but
my misfortunes—and really, madam, I suffer too upon your
account.

Polly's polite claim to altruism, whether or not it has
a sincerity which would only be pathetic, acts as an
insult, and the dram ('in the way of friendship') is
immediately proposed. Lucy is leading up to the poison
in the song, but her diplomacy is so stylised as to become
a comment of the author's. The quieting draught is
death; no other medicine will bring peace or comfort
to so restless a fragment of divinity. It is also alcohol;
peace can only be obtained from what gives further
excitement, because simple peace is not attainable in the
world. Gin alone, however, she has just pointed out, is
often enough quieting in the fullest sense, and the
poetic connection between death and intoxication gives
a vague rich memory of the blood of the sacrament
and the apocalyptic wine of the wrath of God.

Poor man. He is a martyr to the fair, so that his
weaknesses are due to his modish greatness of spirit;
when a man takes this tone about himself he means
that he considers himself very successful with women,
and pays them out. Lucy is boasting of the strength
of the spleen as a weapon against him. Poor man,
more generally, because of the fundamental human
contradictions that are displayed; he is a beast of prey
forced to be sociable. And 'poor man, in the end he
kills her, and is no doubt hanged'—for the force of
and, prominent and repeated, is to make giving a quieting
draught something quite different from, and later than,
the attempt to 'give her will'—it might be only drink

she willed for, and the attempt to give it once for all
was anyway hopeless. The comparison of the dramatic
and condemned thing—murder by poison—to the dull
and almost universal one—quieting by drink—is used
to show that the dramatic incident is a symbol or analysis
of something universal. Afterwards (the double irony
trick) this both refutes itself and insists on its point
more suggestively (appears analysis not symbol) by
making us feel that the dramatic thing is itself universal
—the good meek husband, whether by poison or plain
gin, is as much a murderer as Lucy. From whatever
cause there is a queer note of triumph in the line.

The attempted murder is called a ' comfort ' chiefly
because it is no more; to kill Polly won't get her back
Macheath. And it fails because she finds Polly is not
happy enough to deserve it; at the crucial moment
Macheath is brought back in chains. There is no more
need for murder in Lucy, because Macheath seems to
have despised Polly's help, and anyway is separated
from her. There is no more hope of ' comfort ' for
Polly; she tosses gin and death together to the floor.
So both women are left to poison his last moments.
The playwright then refuses to kill Macheath, from the
same cheerful piercing contempt; he is not dignified
enough, he tells the audience, ' though you think he is,'
to be made a tragic hero. Lucy's attempt is useless
except for its ill-nature, which makes it seem a ' typically
human ' and therefore pathetic piece of folly; she takes
up an enthusiasm for murder because otherwise she
would have to admit the facts (which the human
creature can never afford to do) and give way to the
' spleen ' and despair—the spleen which is the despair
of the most innocent and highly refined characters

because to such characters this existence is essentially inadequate. Lucy's comic vanity in taking this tone (as in Macheath's different use of the device) is displayed only to be justified; 'what better right has anyone else to it?'; it is not denied, such is the pathos of the effect, that the refined ladies may well take this tone, but they must not think it a specially exalted one. (To the Freudian, indeed, it is the human infant to whose desires this life is essentially inadequate; King Lear found a mystical pathos in the fact that the human infant, alone among the young of the creatures, is subject to impotent fits of fury.) It is this clash and identification of the refined, the universal, and the low that is the whole point of pastoral.

For the final meaning of this play, whose glory it is to give itself so wholeheartedly to vulgarisation, I can only list a few approaches to its irony. 'I feel quite grateful to these fools; they make me feel sure I am right because they are so obviously wrong' (in this hopeful form satire is widely used to 'keep people going' after loss of faith); 'having got so far towards sympathy with the undermen, *non ragioniam di lor*, lest we come down to the *ultima ratio*' (Voltaire not talking politics to his valet); 'one can see how impossible both the thieves and the politicians are if one compares them to heroes' (the polite literary assumption; the pose of detachment); 'low as these men are, the old heroes were like them, and one may well feel the stronger for them; life was never dignified, and is still spirited.' (The good spirits of Fielding making a Homeric parody of a village scuffle.) 'The old heroes were much more like the modern thief than the modern aristocrat; the present order of society is based on an inversion of real

values' (Pope sometimes made rather fussy local satire
out of this); 'this is always likely to happen; everything spiritual and valuable has a gross and revolting
parody, very similar to it, with the same name; only
unremitting effort can distinguish between them'
(Swift); 'this always happens; no human distinction
between high and low can be accepted for a moment;
Christ on earth found no fit company but the thieves'
(none of them accepted the full weight of the anarchy
of this, but none of them forgot it; perhaps the mere
easiness of Gay makes one feel it in him most easily).
It is a fine thing that the play is still popular, however
stupidly it is enjoyed.

Alice in Wonderland

The Child as Swain

IT must seem a curious thing that there has been so little serious criticism of the Alices, and that so many critics, with so militant and eager an air of good taste, have explained that they would not think of attempting it. Even Mr. De La Mare's book, which made many good points, is queerly evasive in tone. There seems to be a feeling that real criticism would involve psycho-analysis, and that the results would be so improper as to destroy the atmosphere of the books altogether. Dodgson was too conscious a writer to be caught out so easily. For instance it is an obvious bit of interpretation to say that the Queen of Hearts is a symbol of ' uncontrolled animal passion ' seen through the clear but blank eyes of sexlessness ; obvious, and the sort of thing critics are now so sure would be in bad taste ; Dodgson said it himself, to the actress who took the part when the thing was acted. The books are so frankly about growing up that there is no great discovery in translating them into Freudian terms ; it seems only the proper exegesis of a classic even where it would be a shock to the author. On the whole the results of the analysis, when put into drawing-room language, are his conscious opinions ; and if there was no other satisfactory outlet for his feelings but the special one fixed in his books the same is true in a degree of any original artist. I shall use psycho-analysis where it seems relevant, and feel I had better begin by saying what use it is supposed to be. Its business here is not to discover a neurosis peculiar to Dodgson. The essential idea behind the books is a shift onto the child, which Dodgson did not invent, of the obscure tradition of pastoral. The formula is now 'child-become-judge,' and if Dodgson identifies himself with the child so does the writer of the primary sort of pastoral with his magnified version of the swain. (He took an excellent photograph, much admired by Tennyson, of Alice Liddell as a ragged beggar-girl, which seems a sort of example of the connection.) I should say indeed that this version was more open to neurosis than the older ones; it is less hopeful and more a return into oneself. The analysis should show how this works in general. But there are other things to be said about such a version of pastoral; its use of the device prior to irony lets it make covert judgments about any matter the author was interested in.

There is a tantalising one about Darwinism. The first Neanderthal skull was found in 1856. *The Origin of Species* (1859) came out six years before *Wonderland*, three before its conception, and was very much in the air, a pervading bad smell. It is hard to say how far Dodgson under cover of nonsense was using ideas of which his set disapproved; he wrote some hysterical passages against vivisection and has a curious remark to the effect that chemistry professors had better not have laboratories, but was open to new ideas and doubted the eternity of hell. The 1860 meeting of the British Association, at which Huxley started his career as publicist and gave that resounding snub to Bishop Wilberforce, was held at Oxford where Dodgson was already in residence. He had met Tennyson in '56, and we hear of Tennyson haranguing him later on the likeness of monkeys' and men's skulls.

The only passage that I feel sure involves evolution comes at the beginning of *Wonderland* (the most spontaneous and 'subconscious' part of the books) when Alice gets out of the bath of tears that has magically released her from the underground chamber; it is made clear (for instance about watering-places) that the salt water is the sea from which life arose; as a bodily product it is also the amniotic fluid (there are other forces at work here); ontogeny then repeats phylogeny, and a whole Noah's Ark gets out of the sea with her. In Dodgson's own illustration as well as Tenniel's there is the disturbing head of a monkey and in the text there is an extinct bird. Our minds having thus been forced back onto the history of species there is a reading of history from the period when the Mouse 'came over' with the Conqueror; questions of race turn into the questions of breeding in which Dodgson was more frankly interested, and there are obscure snubs for people who boast about their ancestors. We then have the Caucus Race (the word had associations for Dodgson with local politics; he says somewhere, 'I never go to a Caucus without reluctance '), in which you begin running when you like and leave off when you like, and all win. The subtlety of this is that it supports Natural Selection (in the offensive way the nineteenth century did) to show the absurdity of democracy, and supports democracy (or at any rate liberty) to show the absurdity of Natural Selection. The race is not to the swift because idealism will not let it be to the swift, and because life, as we are told in the final poem, is at random and a dream. But there is no weakening of human values in this generosity; all the animals win, and Alice because she is Man has therefore to give them comfits, but though they demand this they do not fail to recognise that she is superior. They give her her own elegant thimble, the symbol of her labour, because she too has won, and because the highest among you shall be the servant of all. This is a solid piece of symbolism; the politically minded scientists preaching progress through 'selection' and *laissez-faire* are confronted with the full anarchy of Christ. And the pretence of infantilism allows it a certain grim honesty; Alice is a little ridiculous and discomfited, under cover of charm, and would prefer a more aristocratic system.

In the *Looking-Glass* too there are ideas about progress at an early stage of the journey of growing up. Alice goes quickly through the first square by railway, in a carriage full of animals in a state of excitement about the progress of business and machinery; the only man is Disraeli dressed in newspapers—the new man who gets on by self-advertisement, the newspaper-fed man who believes in progress, possibly even the rational dress of the future.

> . . . to her great surprise, they all *thought* in chorus (I hope you understand what *thinking in chorus* means—for I must confess that *I* don't), 'Better say nothing at all. Language is worth a thousand pounds a word.'
> 'I shall dream of a thousand pounds to-night, I know I shall,' thought Alice.
> All this time the Guard was looking at her, first through a telescope, then through a microscope, and then through an opera-glass. At last he said, 'You're travelling the wrong way,' and shut up the window and went away.

This seems to be a prophecy; Huxley in the Romanes lecture of 1893, and less clearly beforehand, said that the human sense of right must judge and often be opposed to the progress imposed by Nature, but at this time he was still looking through the glasses.

> But the gentleman dressed in white paper leaned forwards and whispered in her ear, 'Never mind what they all say, my dear, but take a return ticket every time the train stops.'

In 1861 'many Tory members considered that the prime minister was a better representative of conservative opinions than the leader of the opposition' (*D.N.B.*). This seems to be the double outlook of Disraeli's conservatism, too subtle to inspire action. I think he turns up again as the unicorn when the Lion and the Unicorn are fighting for the Crown; they make a great dust and nuisance, treat the commonsense Alice as entirely mythical, and are very frightening to the poor king to whom the Crown really belongs.

> 'Indeed I shan't,' Alice said rather impatiently. 'I don't belong to this railway journey at all—I was in a wood just now—and I wish I could get back there!'

When she gets back to the wood it is different; it is Nature in the raw, with no names, and she is afraid of it. She still thinks the animals are right to stay there; even when they know their names 'they wouldn't answer at all, if they were wise.' (They might do well to write nonsense books under an assumed name, and refuse to answer even to that.) All this is a very Kaffka piece of symbolism, less at ease than the preceding one; *Wonderland* is a dream, but the *Looking-Glass* is self-consciousness. But both are topical; whether you call the result allegory or 'pure nonsense' it depends on ideas about progress and industrialisation, and there is room for exegesis on the matter.

The beginning of modern child-sentiment may be

SOME VERSIONS OF PASTORAL

placed at the obscure edition of *Mother Goose's Melodies*
(John Newbury, 1760), with 'maxims' very probably
by Goldsmith. The important thing is not the rhymes
(Boston boasts an edition of 1719. My impression is
that they improved as time went on) but the appended
maxims, which take a sophisticated pleasure in them.
Most are sensible proverbs which the child had better
know anyway; their charm (mainly for the adult)
comes from the unexpected view of the story you must
take if they are not to be irrelevant.

Amphion's Song of Eurydice.
I won't be my Father's Jack,
I won't be my Father's Jill,
I won't be the Fiddler's Wife,
And I will have music when I will.

T'other little Tune,
T'other little Tune,
Prithee Love play me
T'other little Tune.

MAXIM.—Those Arts are the most valuable which are of the
greatest Use.

It seems to be the fiddler whose art has been useful in
controlling her, but then again she may have discovered
the art of wheedling the fiddler. The pomp of the
maxim and the childishness of the rhyme make a
mock-pastoral compound. The pleasure in children
here is obviously a derivative of the pleasure in Macheath;
the children are 'little rogues.'

Bow wow wow
Whose dog art Thou?
Little Tom Tinker's Dog.
Bow wow wow.

Tom Tinker's Dog is a very good Dog; and an honester Dog
than his Master.

Honest (' free from hypocrisy ' or the patronising tone to a social inferior) and *dog* (' you young dog ') have their *Beggar's Opera* feelings here; it is not even clear whether Tom is a young vagabond or a child.

This is a pleasant example because one can trace the question back. Pope engraved a couplet ' on the collar of a dog which I gave to His Royal Highness '—a friendly act as from one gentleman to another resident in the neighbourhood.

> I am his Highness' dog at Kew.
> Pray tell me, sir, whose dog are you?

Presumably Frederick himself would be the first to read it. The joke carries a certain praise for the underdog; the point is not that men are slaves but that they find it suits them and remain good-humoured. The dog is proud of being the prince's dog and expects no one to take offence at the question. There is also a hearty independence in its lack of respect for the inquirer. Pope took this from Sir William Temple, where it is said by a fool: ' I am the Lord Chamberlain's fool. And whose are you? ' was his answer to the nobleman. It is a neat case of the slow shift of this sentiment from fool to rogue to child.

Alice, I think, is more of a ' little rogue ' than it is usual to say, or than Dodgson himself thought in later years:

> loving as a dog . . . and gentle as a fawn; then courteous,— courteous to *all*, high or low, grand or grotesque, King or Caterpillar . . . trustful, with an absolute trust. . . .

and so on. It depends what you expect of a child of seven.

> . . . she had quite a long argument with the Lory, who at last turned sulky, and would only say, ' I am older than you, and

must know better'; and this Alice would not allow without knowing how old it was, and as the Lory positively refused to tell its age, there was no more to be said.

Alice had to be made to speak up to bring out the points—here the point is a sense of the fundamental oddity of life given by the fact that different animals become grown-up at different ages; but still if you accept the Lory as a grown-up this is rather a pert child. She is often the underdog speaking up for itself.

A quite separate feeling about children, which is yet at the back of the pertness here and in the Goldsmith, since it is needed if the pertness is to be charming, may be seen in its clearest form in Wordsworth and Coleridge; it is the whole point of the *Ode to Intimations* and even of *We are Seven*. The child has not yet been put wrong by civilisation, and all grown-ups have been. It may well be true that Dodgson envied the child because it was sexless, and Wordsworth because he knew that he was destroying his native poetry by the smugness of his life, but neither theory explains why this feeling about children arose when it did and became so general. There is much of it in Vaughan after the Civil War, but as a general tendency it appeared when the eighteenth-century settlement had come to seem narrow and unescapable; one might connect it with the end of duelling; also when the scientific sort of truth had been generally accepted as the main and real one. It strengthened as the aristocracy became more puritan. It depends on a feeling, whatever may have caused that in its turn, that no way of building up character, no intellectual system, can bring out all that is inherent in the human spirit, and therefore that there is more in the child than any man has been able to keep. (The child is a microcosm like Donne's world, and Alice too is a stoic.) This runs through all Victorian and Romantic literature; the world of the adult made it hard to be an artist, and they kept a sort of tap-root going down to their experience as children. Artists like Wordsworth and Coleridge, who accepted this fact and used it, naturally come to seem the most interesting and in a way the most sincere writers of the period. Their idea of the child, that it is in the right relation to Nature, not dividing what should be unified, that its intuitive judgment contains what poetry and philosophy must spend their time labouring to recover, was accepted by Dodgson and a main part of his feeling. He quotes Wordsworth on this point in the ' Easter Greeting '—the child feels its life in every limb; Dodgson advises it, with an infelicitous memory of the original poem, to give its attention to death from time to time. That the dream books are

> Like Pilgrim's withered wreaths of flowers
> Plucked in a far-off land

is a fine expression of Wordsworth's sense both of the poetry of childhood and of his advancing sterility. And the moment when she finds herself dancing with Tweedledum and Tweedledee, so that it is difficult to introduce herself afterwards, is a successful interruption of Wordsworthian sentiment into his normal style.

. . . she took hold of both hands at once; the next moment they were dancing round in a ring. This seemed quite natural (she remembered afterwards), and she was not even surprised to hear music playing: it seemed to come from the tree under which they were dancing, and it was done (as well as she could make out) by the branches rubbing one against another, like fiddles and fiddle-sticks. . . . ' I don't know when I began it, but somehow I felt as if I had been singing it a long long time.'

261

This is presented as like the odd behaviour of comic objects such as soup-tureens, but it is a directer version of the idea of the child's unity with nature. She has been singing a long long time because she sang with no temporal limits in that imperial palace whence she came. Yet it is the frank selfishness of the brothers, who being little boys are horrid, are made into a satire on war, and will only give her the hands free from hugging each other, that forces her into the ring with them that produces eternity. Even here this puts a subtle doubt into the eternities open to the child.

For Dodgson will only go half-way with the sentiment of the child's unity with nature, and has another purpose for his heroine; she is the free and independent mind. Not that this is contradictory; because she is right about life she is independent from all the other characters who are wrong. But it is important to him because it enables him to clash the Wordsworth sentiments with the other main tradition about children derived from rogue-sentiment. (For both, no doubt, he had to go some way back; the intervening sentiment about children is that the great thing is to repress their Original Sin, and I suppose, though he would not have much liked it, he was among the obscure influences that led to the cult of games in the public schools.)

One might say that the Alices differ from other versions of pastoral in lacking the sense of glory. Normally the idea of including all sorts of men in yourself brings in an idea of reconciling yourself with nature and therefore gaining power over it. The Alices are more self-protective; the dream cuts out the real world and the delicacy of the mood is felt to cut out the lower classes. This is true enough, but when Humpty Dumpty says that glory means a nice knock-down argument he is not far from the central feeling of the book. There is a real feeling of isolation and yet just that is taken as the source of power.

The obvious parody of Wordsworth is the poem of the White Knight, an important figure for whom Dodgson is willing to break the language of humour into the language of sentiment. It takes off *Resolution and Independence*, a genuine pastoral poem if ever there was one; the endurance of the leechgatherer gives Wordsworth strength to face the pain of the world. Dodgson was fond of saying that one parodied the best poems, or anyway that parody showed no lack of admiration, but a certain bitterness is inherent in parody; if the meaning is not ' This poem is absurd ' it must be ' In my present mood of emotional sterility the poem will not work, or I am afraid to let it work, on *me*.' The parody here will have no truck with the dignity of the leechgatherer, but the point of that is to make the unworldly dreaminess of the Knight more absurd; there may even be a reproach for Wordsworth in the lack of consideration that makes him go on asking the same question. One feels that the Knight has probably imagined most of the old man's answers, or anyway that the old man was playing up to the fool who questioned him. At any rate there is a complete shift of interest from the virtues of the leechgatherer onto the childish but profound virtues of his questioner.

The main basis of the joke is the idea of absurd inventions of new foods. Dodgson was well-informed about food, kept his old menus and was wine-taster to the College; but ate very little, suspected the High Table of overeating, and would see no reason to deny that he connected overeating with other forms of sensuality. One reason for the importance of rich food here is that it is the child's symbol for all luxuries reserved for grown-ups. I take it that the fascination of Soup and of the Mock Turtle who sings about it was that soup is mainly eaten at dinner, the excitingly grown-up meal eaten after the child has gone to bed. When Alice talks about her dinner she presumably means lunch, and it is rather a boast when she says she has already met whiting. In the White Knight's song and conversation these little jokes based on fear of sensuality are put to a further use; he becomes the scientist, the inventor, whose mind is nobly but absurdly detached from interest in the pleasures of the senses and even from ' good sense.'

' How *can* you go on talking so quietly, head downwards ? ' Alice asked, as she dragged him out by the feet, and laid him in a heap on the bank.

The Knight looked surprised at the question. ' What does it matter where my body happens to be ? ' he said. ' My mind goes on working all the same. In fact, the more head downwards I am, the more I keep inventing new things.'

' Now the cleverest thing that I ever did,' he went on after a pause, ' was inventing a new pudding during the meat-course.'

This required extreme detachment; the word ' clever ' has become a signal that the mind is being admired for such a reason. The more absurd the assumptions of the thinking, for instance those of scientific materialism, the more vigorous the thought based upon it. ' Life is so strange that his results have the more chance of being valuable because his assumptions are absurd, but we must not forget that they are so.' This indeed is as near the truth as one need get about scientific determinism.

One reason for the moral grandeur of the Knight, then, is that he stands for the Victorian scientist, who was felt to have invented a new kind of Roman virtue; earnestly, patiently, carefully (it annoyed Samuel Butler to have these words used so continually about scientists) without sensuality, without self-seeking, without claiming any but a fragment of knowledge, he goes on labouring at his absurd but fruitful conceptions. But the parody makes him stand also for the poet, and Wordsworth would have been pleased by this; he considered that the poet was essentially one who revived our sense of the original facts of nature, and should use scientific ideas where he could; poetry was the impassioned expression of the face of all science; Wordsworth was as successful in putting life into the abstract words of science as into 'the plain language of men,' and many of the Lyrical Ballads are best understood as psychological notes written in a form that saves one from forgetting their actuality. The Knight has the same readiness to accept new ideas and ways of life, such as the sciences were imposing, without ceasing to be good and in his way sensible, as Alice herself shows for instance when in falling down the rabbit-hole she plans a polite entry into the Antipodes and is careful not to drop the marmalade onto the inhabitants. It is the childishness of the Knight that lets him combine the virtues of the poet and the scientist, and one must expect a creature so finely suited to life to be absurd because life itself is absurd.

The talking animal convention and the changes of relative size appear in so different a children's book as *Gulliver*; they evidently make some direct appeal to the child whatever more sophisticated ideas are piled onto them. Children feel at home with animals conceived as human; the animal can be made affectionate without its making serious emotional demands on them, does not want to educate them, is at least unconventional in the sense that it does not impose its conventions, and does not make a secret of the processes of nature. So the talking animals here are a child-world; the rule about them is that they are always friendly though childishly frank to Alice while she is small, and when she is big (suggesting grown-up) always opposed to her, or by her, or both. But talking animals in children's books had been turned to didactic purposes ever since Aesop; the schoolmastering tone in which the animals talk nonsense to Alice is partly a parody of this—they are really childish but try not to look it. On the other hand, this tone is so supported by the way they can order her about, the firm and surprising way their minds work, the abstract topics they work on, the useless rules they accept with so much conviction, that we take them as real grown-ups contrasted with unsophisticated childhood. 'The grown-up world is as odd as the child-world, and both are a dream.' This ambivalence seems to correspond to Dodgson's own attitude to children; he, like Alice, wanted to get the advantages of being childish and grown-up at once. In real life this seems to have at least occasional disadvantages both ways; one remembers the little girl who screamed and demanded to be taken from the lunch-table because she knew she couldn't solve his puzzles (not, apparently, a usual, but one would think a natural reaction to his mode of approach) —she clearly thought him too grown-up; whereas in the scenes of jealousy with his little girls' parents the grown-ups must have thought him quite enough of a child. He made a success of the process, and it seems clear that it did none of the little girls any harm, but one cannot help cocking one's eye at it as a way of life.

The changes of size are more complex. In *Gulliver* they are the impersonal eye; to change size and nothing else makes you feel ' this makes one see things as they are in themselves.' It excites Wonder but of a scientific sort. Swift used it for satire on science or from a horrified interest in it, and to give a sort of scientific authority to his deductions, that men seen as small are spiritually petty and seen as large physically loathsome. And it is the small observer, like the child, who does least to alter what he sees and therefore sees most truly. (The definition of potential, in all but the most rigid text-books of electricity, contents itself with talking about the force on a *small* charge which doesn't alter the field *much*. The objection that the small alteration in the field might be proportional to the small force does not occur easily to the reader.) To mix this with a pious child's type of Wonder made science seem less irreligious and gave you a feeling that you were being good because educating a child; Faraday's talks for children on the chemical history of a candle came out in 1861, so the method was in the air. But these are special uses of a material rich in itself. Children like to think of being so small that they could hide from grown-ups and so big that they could control them, and to do this drama-tises the great topic of growing up, which both Alices keep to consistently. In the same way the charm of Jabberwocky is that it is a code language, the language with which grown-ups hide things from children or children from grown-ups. Also the words are such good tongue-gestures, in Sir Richard Paget's phrase, that they seem to carry their own meaning; this carries a hint of the paradox that the conventions are natural.

SOME VERSIONS OF PASTORAL

Both books also keep to the topic of death—the first
two jokes about death in *Wonderland* come on pages
3 and 4—and for the child this may be a natural connection; I remember believing I should have to die in order
to grow up, and thinking the prospect very disagreeable.
There seems to be a connection in Dodgson's mind
between the death of childhood and the development
of sex, which might be pursued into many of the details
of the books. Alice will die if the Red King wakes up,
partly because she is a dream-product of the author and
partly because the pawn is put back in its box at the end
of the game. He is the absent husband of the Red
Queen who is a governess, and the end of the book
comes when Alice defeats the Red Queen and ' mates '
the King. Everything seems to break up because she
arrives at a piece of *knowledge*, that all the poems are
about fish. I should say the idea was somehow at work
at the end of *Wonderland* too. The trial is meant to be
a mystery; Alice is told to leave the court, as if a child
ought not to hear the evidence, and yet they expect her
to give evidence herself.

' What do you know about this business? ' the King said to
Alice.
' Nothing,' said Alice.
' Nothing *whatever*? ' persisted the King.
' Nothing whatever,' said Alice.
' That's very important,' the King said, turning to the jury.
They were just beginning to write this down on their slates,
when the White Rabbit interrupted: ' *Un*important, your
Majesty means, of course,' he said in a very respectful tone, but
frowning and making faces as he spoke.
' *Un*important, of course, I meant,' the King hastily said, and
went on to himself in an undertone, ' important—unimportant—
unimportant—important—' as if he were trying which word
sounded best.

There is no such stress in the passage as would make one feel there must be something behind it, and certainly it is funny enough as it stands. But I think Dodgson felt it was important that Alice should be innocent of all knowledge of what the Knave of Hearts (a flashy-looking lady's-man in the picture) is likely to have been doing, and also important that she should not be told she is innocent. That is why the king, always a well-intentioned man, is embarrassed. At the same time Dodgson feels that Alice is right in thinking ' it doesn't matter a bit ' which word the jury write down ; she is too stable in her detachment to be embarrassed, these things will not interest her, and in a way she includes them all in herself. And it is the refusal to let her stay that makes her revolt and break the dream. It is tempting to read an example of this idea into the poem that introduces the *Looking-Glass*.

> Come, hearken then, ere voice of dread,
>   With bitter summons laden,
> Shall summon to unwelcome bed
>   A melancholy maiden.

After all the marriage-bed was more likely to be the end of the maiden than the grave, and the metaphor firmly implied treats them as identical.

The last example is obviously more a joke against Dodgson than anything else, and though the connection between death and the development of sex is I think at work it is not the main point of the conflict about growing up. Alice is given a magical control over her growth by the traditionally symbolic caterpillar, a creature which has to go through a sort of death to become grown-up, and then seems a more spiritual creature. It refuses to agree with Alice that this process is at all peculiar, and clearly her own life will be somehow like it, but the main idea is not its development of sex. The butterfly implied may be the girl when she is ' out ' or her soul when in heaven, to which she is now nearer than she will be when she is ' out '; she must walk to it by walking away from it. Alice knows several reasons why she should object to growing up, and does not at all like being an obvious angel, a head out of contact with its body that has to come down from the sky, and gets mistaken for the Paradisal serpent of the knowledge of good and evil, and by the pigeon of the Annunciation, too. But she only makes herself smaller for reasons of tact or proportion; the triumphant close of *Wonderland* is that she has outgrown her fancies and can afford to wake and despise them. The *Looking-Glass* is less of a dream-product, less concentrated on the child's situation, and (once started) less full of changes of size; but it has the same end; the governess shrinks to a kitten when Alice has grown from a pawn to a queen, and can shake her. Both these clearly stand for becoming grown-up and yet in part are a revolt against grown-up behaviour; there is the same ambivalence as about the talking animals. Whether children often find this symbolism as interesting as Carroll did is another thing; there are recorded cases of tears at such a betrayal of the reality of the story. I remember feeling that the ends of the books were a sort of necessary assertion that the grown-up world was after all the proper one; one did not object to that in principle, but would no more turn to those parts from preference than to the ' Easter Greeting to Every Child that Loves Alice ' (Gothic type).

To make the dream-story from which *Wonderland*

was elaborated seem Freudian one has only to tell it. A fall through a deep hole into the secrets of Mother Earth produces a new enclosed soul wondering who it is, what will be its position in the world, and how it can get out. It is in a long low hall, part of the palace of the Queen of Hearts (a neat touch), from which it can only get out to the fresh air and the fountains through a hole frighteningly too small. Strange changes, caused by the way it is nourished there, happen to it in this place, but always when it is big it cannot get out and when it is small it is not allowed to; for one thing, being a little girl, it has no key. The nightmare theme of the birth-trauma, that she grows too big for the room and is almost crushed by it, is not only used here but repeated more painfully after she seems to have got out; the rabbit sends her sternly into its house and some food there makes her grow again. In Dodgson's own drawing of Alice when cramped into the room with one foot up the chimney, kicking out the hateful thing that tries to come down (she takes away its pencil when it is a juror), she is much more obviously in the foetus position than in Tenniel's. The White Rabbit is Mr. Spooner to whom the spoonerisms happened, an undergraduate in 1862, but its business here is as a pet for children which they may be allowed to breed. Not that the clearness of the framework makes the interpretation simple; Alice peering through the hole into the garden may be wanting a return to the womb as well as an escape from it; she is fond, we are told, of taking both sides of an argument when talking to herself, and the whole book balances between the luscious nonsense-world of fantasy and the ironic nonsense-world of fact.

I said that the sea of tears she swims in was the amniotic

fluid, which is much too simple. You may take it as Lethe in which the souls were bathed before re-birth (and it is their own tears; they forget, as we forget our childhood, through the repression of pain) or as the ' solution ' of an intellectual contradiction through Intuition and a return to the Unconscious. Anyway it is a sordid image made pretty; one need not read Dodgson's satirical verses against babies to see how much he would dislike a child wallowing in its tears in real life. The fondness of small girls for doing this has to be faced early in attempting to prefer them, possibly to small boys, certainly to grown-ups; to a man idealising children as free from the falsity of a rich emotional life their displays of emotion must be particularly disconcerting. The celibate may be forced to observe them, on the floor of a railway carriage for example, after a storm of fury, dabbling in their ooze; covertly snuggling against mamma while each still pretends to ignore the other. The symbolic pleasure of dabbling seems based on an idea that the liquid itself is the bad temper which they have got rid of by the storm and yet are still hugging, or that they are not quite impotent since they have at least ' done ' this much about the situation. The acid quality of the style shows that Dodgson does not entirely like having to love creatures whose narcissism takes this form, but he does not want simply to forget it as he too would like a relief from ' ill-temper '; he sterilises it from the start by giving it a charming myth. The love for narcissists itself seems mainly based on a desire to keep oneself safely detached, which is the essential notion here.

The symbolic completeness of Alice's experience is I think important. She runs the whole gamut; she is a father in getting down the hole, a foetus at the bottom, and can only be born by becoming a mother and producing her own amniotic fluid. Whether his mind played the trick of putting this into the story or not he has the feelings that would correspond to it. A desire to include all sexuality in the girl child, the least obviously sexed of human creatures, the one that keeps its sex in the safest place, was an important part of their fascination for him. He is partly imagining himself as the girl-child (with these comforting characteristics) partly as its father (these together make *it* a father) partly as its lover—so it might be a mother—but then of course it is clever and detached enough to do everything for itself. He told one of his little girls a story about cats wearing gloves over their claws: 'For you see, " gloves " have got " love " inside them—there's none outside, you know.' So far from its dependence, the child's independence is the important thing, and the theme behind that is the self-centred emotional life imposed by the detached intelligence.

The famous cat is a very direct symbol of this ideal of intellectual detachment; all cats are detached, and since this one grins it is the amused observer. It can disappear because it can abstract itself from its surroundings into a more interesting inner world; it appears only as a head because it is almost a disembodied intelligence, and only as a grin because it can impose an atmosphere without being present. In frightening the king by the allowable act of looking at him it displays the soul-force of Mr. Gandhi; it is unbeheadable because its soul cannot be killed; and its influence brings about a short amnesty in the divided nature of the Queen and Duchess. Its cleverness makes it formidable—it has very long claws

and a great many teeth—but Alice is particularly at
home with it; she is the same sort of thing.

The Gnat gives a more touching picture of Dodgson;
he treats nowhere more directly of his actual relations
with the child. He feels he is liable to nag at it, as a
gnat would, and the gnat turns out, as he is, to be
alarmingly big as a friend for the child, but at first it
sounds tiny because he means so little to her. It tries
to amuse her by rather frightening accounts of other
dangerous insects, other grown-ups. It is reduced to
tears by the melancholy of its own jokes, which it
usually can't bear to finish; only if Alice had made
them, as it keeps egging her on to do, would they be
at all interesting. That at least would show the child
had paid some sort of attention, and he could go away
and repeat them to other people. The desire to have
jokes made all the time, he feels, is a painful and obvious
confession of spiritual discomfort, and the freedom of
Alice from such a feeling makes her unapproachable.

'Don't tease so,' said Alice, looking about in vain to see where
the voice came from; 'if you're so anxious to have a joke made,
why don't you make one yourself?'
The little voice sighed deeply: it was *very* unhappy, evidently,
and Alice would have said something pitying to comfort it, 'if
it would only sigh like other people!' she thought. But this
was such a wonderfully small sigh, that she wouldn't have heard
it at all, if it hadn't come *quite* close to her ear. The consequence
of this was that it tickled her ear very much, and quite took off
her thoughts from the unhappiness of the poor little creature.
'*I know you are a friend,*' the little voice went on; '*a dear friend,
and an old friend. And you won't hurt me, though I am an insect.*'
'What kind of insect?' Alice inquired a little anxiously.
What she really wanted to know was, whether it could sting or
not, but she thought this wouldn't be quite a civil question to ask.
'*What, then you don't—*' the little voice began. . . .

'Don't know who I am! Does anybody not know who
I am?' He is afraid that even so innocent a love as his,
like all love, may be cruel, and yet it is she who is able
to hurt him, if only through his vanity. The implications
of these few pages are so painful that the ironical calm
of the close, when she kills it, seems delightfully gay
and strong. The Gnat is suggesting to her that she
would like to remain purely a creature of Nature and
stay in the wood where there are no names.

> '. . . That's a joke. I wish *you* had made it.'
> 'Why do you wish *I* had made it?' Alice asked. 'It's a very
> bad one.'
> But the Gnat only sighed deeply, while two large tears came
> rolling down its cheeks.
> 'You shouldn't make jokes,' Alice said, 'if it makes you so
> unhappy.'
> Then came another of those melancholy little sighs, and this
> time the poor Gnat really seemed to have sighed itself away,
> for, when Alice looked up, there was nothing whatever to be
> seen on the twig, and, as she was getting quite chilly with sitting
> so long, she got up and walked on.

The overpunctuation and the flat assonance of 'long—on'
add to the effect. There is something charmingly prim
and well-meaning about the way she sweeps aside the
feelings that she can't deal with. One need not suppose
that Dodgson ever performed this scene, which he can
imagine so clearly, but there is too much self-knowledge
here to make the game of psycho-analysis seem merely
good fun.

The scene in which the Duchess has become friendly
to Alice at the garden-party shows Alice no longer
separate from her creator; it is clear that Dodgson would
be as irritated as she is by the incident, and is putting
himself in her place. The obvious way to read it is as

the middle-aged woman trying to flirt with the chaste young man.

> ' The game seems to be going on rather better now,' she said.
> ' 'Tis so,' said the Duchess; ' and the moral of it is—" Oh, 'tis love, 'tis love, that makes the world go round ! " '
> ' Somebody said,' whispered Alice, ' that it's done by everybody minding their own business ! '
> ' Ah, well ! It means much the same thing,' said the Duchess, digging her sharp little chin into Alice's shoulder as she added, ' and the moral of *that* is—" Take care of the sense, and the sounds will take care of themselves." '
> ' How fond she is of finding morals in things,' Alice thought to herself.

Both are true because the generous and the selfish kinds of love have the same name; the Duchess seems to take the view of the political economists, that the greatest public good is produced by the greatest private selfishness. All this talk about ' morals ' makes Alice suspicious; also she is carrying a flamingo, a pink bird with a long neck. ' The chief difficulty Alice found at first was in managing her flamingo . . . it *would* twist itself round and look up in her face.'

> ' I dare say you're wondering why I don't put my arm round your waist,' the Duchess said after a pause: ' the reason is, that I'm doubtful about the temper of your flamingo. Shall I try the experiment ? '
> ' He might bite,' Alice cautiously replied, not feeling at all anxious to have the experiment tried.
> ' Very true,' said the Duchess: ' flamingoes and mustard both bite. And the moral of that is—" Birds of a feather flock together." '

Mustard may be classed with the pepper that made her ' ill-tempered ' when she had so much of it in the soup, so that flamingoes and mustard become the desires of the two sexes. No doubt Dodgson would be indignant at having this meaning read into his symbols, but the meaning itself, if he had been intending to talk about the matter, is just what he would have wished to say.

The Duchess then jumps away to another aspect of the selfishness of our nature.

> 'It's a mineral, I *think*,' said Alice.
> 'Of course it is,' said the Duchess, who seemed ready to agree to everything that Alice said; 'there's a large mustard-mine near here. And the moral of that is—" The more there is of mine, the less there is of yours." '

One could put the same meanings in again, but a new one has come forward : ' Industrialism is as merely greedy as sex ; all we get from it is a sharper distinction between rich and poor.' They go off into riddles about sincerity and how one can grow into what one would seem to be.

This sort of ' analysis ' is a peep at machinery ; the question for criticism is what is done with the machine. The purpose of a dream on the Freudian theory is simply to keep you in an undisturbed state so that you can go on sleeping ; in the course of this practical work you may produce something of more general value, but not only of one sort. Alice has, I understand, become a patron saint of the Surrealists, but they do not go in for Comic Primness, a sort of reserve of force, which is her chief charm. Wyndham Lewis avoided putting her beside Proust and Lorelei to be danced on as a debilitating child-cult (though she is a bit of pragmatist too) ; the present-day reader is more likely to complain of her complacence. In this sort of child-cult the child, though a means of imaginative escape, becomes the critic ; Alice is the most reasonable and responsible person in the book. This is meant as charmingly pathetic about

her as well as satire about her elders, and there is some
implication that the sane man can take no other view
of the world, even for controlling it, than the child
does; but this is kept a good distance from sentimental
infantilism. There is always some doubt about the
meaning of a man who says he wants to be like a child,
because he may want to be like it in having fresh and
vivid feelings and senses, in not knowing, expecting,
or desiring evil, in not having an analytical mind, in
having no sexual desires recognisable as such, or out of
a desire to be mothered and evade responsibility. He is
usually mixing them up—Christ's praise of children,
given perhaps for reasons I have failed to list, has made
it a respected thing to say, and it has been said often and
loosely—but he can make his own mixture; Lewis's
invective hardly shows which he is attacking. The
praise of the child in the Alices mainly depends on a
distaste not only for sexuality but for all the distortions
of vision that go with a rich emotional life; the opposite
idea needs to be set against this, that you can only understand people or even things by having such a life in
yourself to be their mirror; but the idea itself is very
respectable. So far as it is typical of the scientist the books
are an expression of the scientific attitude (*e.g.* the bread-
and-butter fly) or a sort of satire on it that treats it as
inevitable.

The most obvious aspect of the complacence is the
snobbery. It is clear that Alice is not only a very well-
brought-up but a very well-to-do little girl; if she has
grown into Mabel, so that she will have to go and live
in that poky little house and have next to no toys to
play with, she will refuse to come out of her rabbit-hole
at all. One is only surprised that she is allowed to meet

Mabel. All through the books odd objects of luxury are viewed rather as Wordsworth viewed mountains; meaningless, but grand and irremovable; objects of myth. The whiting, the talking leg of mutton, the soup-tureen, the tea-tray in the sky, are obvious examples. The shift from the idea of the child's unity with nature is amusingly complete; a mere change in the objects viewed makes it at one with the conventions. But this is still not far from Wordsworth, who made his mountains into symbols of the stable and moral society living among them. In part the joke of this stands for the sincerity of the child that criticises the folly of convention, but Alice is very respectful to conventions and interested to learn new ones; indeed the discussions about the rules of the game of conversation, those stern comments on the isolation of humanity, put the tone so strongly in favour of the conventions that one feels there is nothing else in the world. There is a strange clash on this topic about the three little sisters discussed at the Mad Tea-party, who lived on treacle. ' They couldn't have done that, you know,' Alice gently remarked, ' they'd have been ill.' ' So they were,' said the Dormouse, ' *very* ill.' The creatures are always self-centred and argumentative, to stand for the detachment of the intellect from emotion, which is necessary to it and yet makes it childish. Then the remark stands both for the danger of taking as one's guide the natural desires (' this is the sort of thing little girls would do if they were left alone ') and for a pathetic example of a martyrdom to the conventions; the little girls did not mind *how* ill they were made by living on treacle, because it was their rule, and they knew it was expected of them. (That they are refined girls is clear from the fact that they do allegorical sketches.) There is an obscure connection here with the belief of the period that a really nice girl is ' delicate ' (the profound sentences implied by the combination of meanings in this word are (*a*) 'you cannot get a woman to be refined unless you make her ill ' and more darkly (*b*) ' she is desirable because corpse-like '); Dodgson was always shocked to find that his little girls had appetites, because it made them seem less pure. The passage about the bread-and-butter fly brings this out more frankly, with something of the wilful grimness of Webster. It was a creature of such high refinement that it could only live on weak tea with cream in it (tea being the caller's meal, sacred to the fair, with nothing gross about it).

A new difficulty came into Alice's head.

' Supposing it couldn't find any ? ' she suggested.
' Then it would die, of course.'
' But that must happen very often,' Alice remarked thoughtfully.
' It always happens,' said the Gnat.
After this, Alice was silent for a minute or two, pondering.

There need be no gloating over the child's innocence here, as in Barrie; anybody might ponder. Alice has just suggested that flies burn themselves to death in candles out of a martyr's ambition to become Snap-dragon flies. The talk goes on to losing one's name, which is the next stage on her journey, and brings freedom but is like death; the girl may lose her personality by growing up into the life of convention, and her virginity (like her surname) by marriage; or she may lose her ' good name ' when she loses the conventions ' in the woods '—the animals, etc., there have no names because they are out of reach of the controlling reason; or when she develops sex she must neither understand nor name her feelings. The Gnat is weeping and Alice is afraid of the wood but determined to go on. 'It always dies of thirst' or 'it always dies in the end, as do we all'; 'the life of highest refinement is the most deathly, yet what else is one to aim at when life is so brief, and when there is so little in it of any value.' A certain ghoulishness in the atmosphere of this, of which the tight-lacing may have been a product or partial cause,[1] comes out very strongly in Henry James; the decadents pounced on it for their own purposes but could not put more death-wishes into it than these respectables had done already.

The blend of child-cult and snobbery that Alice shares with Oscar Wilde is indeed much more bouncing and cheerful; the theme here is that it is proper for the well-meaning and innocent girl to be worldly, because she, like the world, should know the value of her condition. 'When we were girls we were brought up to know nothing, and very interesting it was'; 'mamma, whose views on education are remarkably strict, has brought me up to be extremely short-sighted; so do you mind my looking at you through my glasses?' This joke seems to have come in after the Restoration dramatists as innocence recovered its social value; there are touches in Farquhar and it is strong in the *Beggar's Opera*. Sheridan has full control of it for Mrs. Malaprop.

I don't think so much learning becomes a young woman. . . . But, Sir Anthony, I would send her, at nine years old, to a boarding school, in order to learn a little ingenuity and artifice. Then, sir,

---

[1] It was getting worse when the Alices were written. In what Mr. Hugh Kingsmill calls 'the fatal fifties' skirts were so big that the small waist was not much needed for contrast, so it can't be blamed for the literary works of that decade.

she should have a supercilious knowledge in accounts; and as she grew up, I would have her instructed in geometry, that she might learn something of the contagious countries; but above all, Sir Anthony, she should be mistress of orthodoxy, that she might not mis-spell, and mispronounce words so shamefully as girls usually do; and likewise that she might reprehend the true meaning of what she is saying.

Dodgson has an imitation of this which may show, what many of his appreciators seem anxious to deny, that even *Wonderland* contains straight satire. The Mock Turtle was taught at school

Reeling and Writhing, of course, to begin with, and then the different branches of Arithmetic—Ambition, Distraction, Uglification, and Derision . . . Mystery, ancient and modern, with Seaography; then Drawling—the Drawling-master used to come once a week; *he* taught us Drawling, Stretching, and Fainting in Coils.

Children are to enjoy the jokes as against education, grown-ups as against a smart and too expensive education. Alice was not one of the climbers taught like this, and remarks firmly elsewhere that manners are not learnt from lessons. But she willingly receives social advice like 'curtsey while you're thinking what to say, it saves time,' and the doctrine that you must walk away from a queen if you really want to meet her has more point when said of the greed of the climber than of the unselfseeking curiosity of the small girl. Or it applies to both, and allows the climber a sense of purity and simplicity; I think this was a source of charm whether Dodgson meant it or not. Alice's own social assumptions are more subtle and all-pervading; she always seems to raise the tone of the company she enters, and to find this all the easier because the creatures are so rude to her. A central idea here is that the perfect lady can gain all the advantages of contempt without soiling herself by expressing or even feeling it.

> This time there could be no mistake about it; it was neither more nor less than a pig, and she felt that it would be quite absurd for her to carry it any further. So she set the little creature down, and felt quite relieved to see it trot quietly away into the wood. 'If it had grown up,' she said to herself, 'it would have made a dreadfully ugly child, but it makes rather a handsome pig, I think.' And she began thinking over other children she knew, who might do very well as pigs, and was just saying to herself, 'if only one knew the right way to change them—' when she was a little startled by seeing the Cheshire Cat on the bough of a tree a few yards off.
>
> The Cat only grinned when it saw Alice. It looked good-natured, she thought: still it had very long claws and a great many teeth, so she felt that it ought to be treated with respect.

The effect of cuddling these mellow evasive phrases— 'a good deal'—'do very well as'—whose vagueness can convey so rich an irony and so complete a detachment, while making so firm a claim to show charming good-will, is very close to that of Wilde's comedy. So is the hint of a delicious slavishness behind the primness, and contrasting with the irony, of the last phrase. (But then Dodgson feels the cat deserves respect as the detached intelligence—he is enjoying the idea that Alice and other social figures have got to respect Dodgson.) I think there is a feeling that the aristocrat is essentially like the child because it is his business to make claims in advance of his immediate personal merits; the child is not strong yet, and the aristocrat only as part of a system; the best he can do if actually asked for his credentials, since it would be indecent to produce his pedigree, is to display charm and hope it will appear unconscious, like the good young girl. Wilde's version of this leaves rather a bad taste in the mouth because it is slavish; it has something of the naïve snobbery of the high-class servant. Whistler meant this by the most crashing of his insults—'Oscar now stands forth unveiled as his own "gentleman"'—when Wilde took shelter from a charge of plagiarism behind the claim that a gentleman does not attend to coarse abuse.

Slavish, for one thing, because they were always juggling between what they themselves thought wicked and what the society they addressed thought wicked, talking about sin when they meant scandal. The thrill of *Pen, Pencil and Poison* is in the covert comparison between Wilde himself and the poisoner, and Wilde certainly did not think his sexual habits as wicked as killing a friend to annoy an insurance company. By their very hints that they deserved notice as sinners they pretended to accept all the moral ideas of society, because they wanted to succeed in it, and yet society only took them seriously because they were connected with an intellectual movement which refused to accept some of those ideas. The Byronic theme of the man unable to accept the moral ideas of his society and yet torn by his feelings about them is real and permanent, but to base it on intellectual dishonesty is to short-circuit it; and leads to a claim that the life of highest refinement must be allowed a certain avid infantile petulance.

Alice is not a slave like this; she is almost too sure that she is good and right. The grown-up is egged on to imitate her not as a privileged decadent but as a privileged eccentric, a Victorian figure that we must be sorry to lose. The eccentric though kind and noble would be alarming from the strength of his virtues if he were less funny; Dodgson saw to it that this underlying feeling about his monsters was brought out firmly by Tenniel, who had been trained on drawing very serious things like the British Lion weeping over Gordon, for *Punch*. Their massive and romantic nobility is, I think, an important element in the effect; Dodgson did not get it in his own drawings (nor, by the way, did he give all the young men eunuchoid legs) but no doubt he would have done if he had been able. I should connect this weighty background with the tone of worldly goodness, of universal but not stupid charity, in Alice's remarks about the pig: 'I shall do my best even for you; of course one will suffer, because you are not worth the efforts spent on you; but I have no temptation to be uncharitable to you because I am too far above you to need to put you in your place'—this is what her tone would develop into; a genuine readiness for self-sacrifice and a more genuine sense of power.

The qualities held in so subtle a suspension in Alice are shown in full blast in the two queens. It is clear that this sort of moral superiority involves a painful isolation, similar to those involved in the intellectual way of life and the life of chastity, which are here associated with it. The reference to *Maud* (1855) brings this out. It was a shocking book; mockery was deserved; and its improper freedom was parodied by the flowers at the beginning of the *Looking-Glass*. A taint of fussiness hangs over this sort of essay, but the parodies were assumed to be obvious (children who aren't forced to learn Dr. Watts can't get the same thrill from parodies of him as the original children did) and even this parody is not as obvious as it was. There is no doubt that the

flowers are much funnier if you compare them with
their indestructible originals.

> whenever a March-wind sighs
> He sets the jewel-print of your feet
>   In violets blue as your eyes . . .
>   the pimpernel dozed on the lea ;
> But the rose was awake all night for your sake,
>   Knowing your promise to me ;
> The lilies and roses were all awake . . .
> Queen rose of the rose-bud garden of girls. . . .
>
> There has fallen a splendid tear
>   From the passion-flower at the gate.
> She is coming, my dove, my dear ;
>   She is coming, my life, my fate ;
> The red rose cries, ' She is near, she is near ' ;
>   And the white rose weeps, ' She is late ' ;
> The larkspur listens, ' I hear, I hear ' ;
>   And the lily whispers, ' I wait.'

'It isn't manners for us to begin, you know,' said the Rose,
' and I really was wondering when you'd speak.' . . . 'How is it
that you all talk so nicely ? ' Alice said, hoping to get it into a
better temper by a compliment. . . . 'In most gardens,' the
Tiger-Lily said, ' they make the beds too soft, so that the flowers
are always asleep.' This sounded a very good reason, and Alice
was quite pleased to know it. ' I never thought of that before ! '
she said. ' It's *my* opinion you never think *at all*,' the Rose said
in rather a severe tone. ' I never saw anybody that looked
stupider,' a Violet said, so suddenly, that Alice quite jumped ;
for it hadn't spoken before. . . . ' She's coming ! ' cried the Lark-
spur. ' I hear her footstep, thump, thump, along the gravel-
walk ! ' Alice looked round eagerly, and found that it was the
Red Queen—

the concentrated essence, Dodgson was to explain, of all
governesses. The Tiger-Lily was originally a Passion-
Flower, but it was explained to Dodgson in time that

the passion meant was not that of sexual desire (which he
relates to ill-temper) but of Christ; a brilliant recovery
was made after the shock of this, for *Tiger-Lily* includes
both the alarming fierceness of ideal passion (chaste till
now) and the ill-temper of the life of virtue and self-
sacrifice typified by the governess (chaste always). So
that in effect he includes all the flowers Tennyson named.
The willow-tree that said Bough-Wough doesn't come
in the poem, but it is a symbol of hopeless love anyway.
The pink daisies turn white out of fear, as the white
ones turn pink in the poem out of admiration. I don't
know how far we ought to notice the remark about
beds, which implies that they should be hard because
even passion demands the virtues of asceticism (they are
also the earthy beds of the grave); it fits in very well
with the ideas at work, but does not seem a thing Dodgson would have said in clearer language.

But though he shied from the Christian association in
the complex idea wanted from 'Passion-Flower' the
flowers make another one very firmly.

> 'But that's not *your* fault,' the Rose added kindly: 'you're
> beginning to fade, you know—and then one can't help one's
> petals getting a little untidy.' Alice didn't like this idea at all:
> so, to change the subject, she asked 'Does she ever come out
> here?' 'I daresay you'll see her soon,' said the Rose. 'She's
> one of the thorny kind.' 'Where does she wear the thorns?'
> Alice asked with some curiosity. 'Why, all round her head, of
> course,' the Rose replied. 'I was wondering *you* hadn't got
> some too. I thought it was the regular rule.'

Death is never far out of sight in the books. The Rose
cannot help standing for desire but its thorns here stand
for the ill-temper not so much of passion as of chastity,
that of the governess or that involved in ideal love.
Then the thorns round the Queen's head, the 'regular

287

rule' for suffering humanity, not yet assumed by the child, stand for the Passion, the self-sacrifice of the most ideal and most generous love, which produces ugliness and ill-temper.

The joke of making romantic love ridiculous by applying it to undesired middle-aged women is less to be respected than the joke of the hopelessness of idealism. W. S. Gilbert uses it for the same timid facetiousness but more offensively. This perhaps specially nineteenth-century trick is played about all the women in the Alices—the Ugly Duchess who had the aphrodisiac in the soup (pepper, as Alice pointed out, produces 'ill-temper') was the same person as the Queen in the first draft ('Queen of Hearts and Marchioness of Mock Turtles') so that the Queen's sentence of her is the suicide of disruptive passion. The Mock Turtle, who is half beef in the picture, with a cloven hoof, suffers from the calf-love of a turtle-dove; he went to a bad school and is excited about dancing. (He is also weeping for his lost childhood, which Dodgson sympathised with while blaming its exaggeration, and Alice thought very queer; this keeps it from being direct satire.) So love is also ridiculous in young men; it is felt that these two cover the whole field (Dodgson was about thirty at the time) so that granted these points the world is safe for chastity. The danger was from middle-aged women because young women could be treated as pure like Alice. Nor indeed is this mere convention; Gilbert was relying on one of the more permanent jokes played by nature on civilisation, that unless somewhat primitive methods are employed the specific desires of refined women may appear too late. So far as the chaste man uses this fact, and the fact that men are hurt by permanent chastity less than women, in order to insult women, no fuss that he may make about baby women will make him dignified. Dodgson keeps the theme fairly agreeable by connecting it with the more general one of self-sacrifice—which may be useless or harmful, even when spontaneous or part of a reasonable convention, which then makes the sacrificer ridiculous and crippled, but which even then makes him deserve respect and may give him unexpected sources of power. The man playing at child-cult arrives at Sex War here (as usual since, but the comic Lear didn't), but not to the death nor with all weapons.

The same ideas are behind the White Queen, the emotional as against the practical idealist. It seems clear that the *Apologia* (1864) is in sight when she believes the impossible for half an hour before breakfast, to keep in practice; I should interpret the two examples she gives as immortality and putting back the clock of history, also Mass occurs before breakfast. All through the Wool and Water chapter (milk and water but not nourishing, and gritty to the teeth) she is Oxford; the life of learning rather than of dogmatic religion. Every one recognises the local shop, the sham fights, the rowing, the academic old sheep, and the way it laughs scornfully when Alice doesn't know the technical slang of rowing; and there are some general reflections on education. The teacher wilfully puts the egg a long way off, so that you have to walk after it yourself, and meanwhile it turns into something else; and when you have 'paid for' the education its effects, then first known, must be accepted as part of you whether they are good or bad. Oxford as dreamy may be half satire half acceptance of Arnold's 'adorable dreamer' purple patch (1865).

Once at least in each book a cry of loneliness goes up from Alice at the oddity beyond sympathy or communication of the world she has entered—whether that in which the child is shut by weakness, or the adult by the renunciations necessary both for the ideal and the worldly way of life (the strength of the snobbery is to imply that these are the same). It seems strangely terrible that the answers of the White Queen, on the second of these occasions, should be so unanswerable.

> By this time it was getting light. 'The crow must have flown away, I think,' said Alice: 'I'm so glad it's gone. I thought it was the night coming on.'

Even in the rhyme the crow may be fear of death. The rhymes, like those other main structural materials, chess and cards, are useful because, being fixed, trivial, odd, and stirring to the imagination, they affect one as conventions of the dream world, and this sets the tone about conventions.

> 'I wish I could manage to be glad!' the Queen said. 'Only I never can remember the rule. You must be very happy, living in this wood, and being glad whenever you like.'

So another wood has turned out to be Nature. This use of 'that's a rule' is Sheridan's in *The Critic*; the pathos of its futility is that it is an attempt of reason to do the work of emotion and escape the dangers of the emotional approach to life. There may be a glance at the Oxford Movement and dogma. Perhaps chiefly a satire on the complacence of the fashion of slumming, the remark seems to spread out into the whole beauty and pathos of the ideas of pastoral; by its very universality her vague sympathy becomes an obscure self-indulgence.

' Only it is so very lonely here ! ' Alice said in a melancholy voice ; and at the thought of her loneliness two large tears came rolling down her cheeks.

' Oh, don't go on like that,' cried the poor Queen, wringing her hands in despair. ' Consider what a great girl you are. Consider what a long way you've come to-day. Consider what o'clock it is. Consider anything, only don't cry ! '

Alice could not help laughing at this, even in the midst of her tears. ' Can you keep from crying by considering things ? ' she asked.

' That's the way it's done,' the Queen said with great decision ; ' nobody can do two things at once, you know. Let's consider your age to begin with—how old are you ? '

We are back at once to the crucial topic of age and the fear of death, and pass to the effectiveness of practice in helping one to believe the impossible; for example that the ageing Queen is so old that she would be dead. The helplessness of the intellect, which claims to rule so much, is granted under cover of the counter-claim that since it makes you impersonal you can forget pain with it; we do not believe this about the queen chiefly because she has not enough understanding of other people. The jerk of the return to age, and the assumption that this is a field for polite lying, make the work of the intellect only the game of conversation. Humpty Dumpty has the same embarrassing trick for arguing away a suggestion of loneliness. Indeed about all the rationalism of Alice and her acquaintances there hangs a suggestion that these are after all questions of pure thought, academic thought whose altruism is recognised and paid for, thought meant only for the upper classes to whom the conventions are in any case natural habit; like that suggestion that the scientist is sure to be a gentleman and has plenty of space which is the fascination of Kew Gardens.

The Queen is a very inclusive figure. ' Looking before and after ' with the plaintive tone of universal altruism she lives chiefly backwards, in history; the necessary darkness of growth, the mysteries of self-knowledge, the self-contradictions of the will, the antinomies of philosophy, the very Looking-Glass itself, impose this; nor is it mere weakness to attempt to resolve them only in the direct impulse of the child. Gathering the more dream-rushes her love for man becomes the more universal, herself the more like a porcupine. Knitting with more and more needles she tries to control life by a more and more complex intellectual apparatus—the ' progress ' of Herbert Spencer; any one shelf of the shop is empty, but there is always something very interesting—the ' atmosphere ' of the place is so interesting—which moves up as you look at it from shelf to shelf; there is jam only in the future and our traditional past, and the test made by Alice, who sent value through the ceiling as if it were quite used to it, shows that progress can never reach value, because its habitation and name is heaven. The Queen's scheme of social reform, which is to punish those who are not respectable before their crimes are committed, seems to be another of these jokes about progress :

> ' But if you *hadn't* done them,' the Queen said, ' that would have been better still ; better, and better, and better ! ' Her voice went higher with each ' better ' till it got to quite a squeak at last.

There is a similar attack in the Walrus and the Carpenter, who are depressed by the spectacle of unimproved nature and engage in charitable work among oysters. The Carpenter is a Castle and the Walrus, who could eat so many more because he was crying behind his handkerchief, was a Bishop, in the scheme at the beginning of the book. But in saying so one must be struck by the depth at which the satire is hidden; the queerness of the incident and the characters takes on a Wordsworthian grandeur and aridity, and the landscape defined by the tricks of facetiousness takes on the remote and staring beauty of the ideas of the insane. It is odd to find that Tenniel went on to illustrate Poe in the same manner; Dodgson is often doing what Poe wanted to do, and can do it the more easily because he can safely introduce the absurd. The Idiot Boy of Wordsworth is too milky a moonlit creature to be at home with Nature as she was deplored by the Carpenter, and much of the technique of the rudeness of the Mad Hatter has been learned from Hamlet. It is the ground-bass of this kinship with insanity, I think, that makes it so clear that the books are not trifling, and the cool courage with which Alice accepts madmen that gives them their strength.

This talk about the snobbery of the Alices may seem a mere attack, but a little acid may help to remove the slime with which they have been encrusted. The two main ideas behind the snobbery, that virtue and intelligence are alike lonely, and that good manners are therefore important though an absurd confession of human limitations, do not depend on a local class system; they would be recognised in a degree by any tolerable society. And if in a degree their opposites must also be recognised, so they are here; there are solid enough statements of the shams of altruism and convention and their horrors when genuine; it is the forces of this conflict that make a clash violent enough to end both the dreams. In *Wonderland* this is mysteriously mixed up with the trial of the Knave of Hearts, the thief of love, but at the end of the second book the symbolism is franker and more simple. She is a grown queen and has acquired the conventional dignities of her insane world; suddenly she admits their insanity, refuses to be a grown queen, and destroys them.

> 'I can't stand this any longer!' she cried, as she seized the table-cloth in both hands: one good pull, and plates, dishes, guests, and candles came crashing down together in a heap on the floor.

The guests are inanimate and the crawling self-stultifying machinery of luxury has taken on a hideous life of its own. It is the High Table of Christ Church that we must think of here. The gentleman is not the slave of his conventions because at need he could destroy them; and yet, even if he did this, and all the more because he does not, he must adopt while despising it the attitude to them of the child.

INDEX

Alexander, 200, 220
Amenemhat III, 72
Aristotle, *Rhetoric*, 213
Arnold, 289
Augustus, 3
Aurelius, Marcus, 73, 85

Bacon, 77
Baudelaire, 208
Beaumont, *Knight of the Burning Pestle*, 70
Becket, Thomas à, 178
Bentley, 149-91
Bissill, George, 8
Border Ballads, 6
Boswell, 212
Bradbrook, M. C., 127
Britton, Lionel, *Hunger and Love*, 7
Brooke, Rupert, 59, 64
Browne, Sir Thomas, 77
Bunyan, 168
Butler, 63, 102, 213, 265
Butler, Samuel, the elder, 77
Byron, 122, 207, 208

Campbell, Roy, *The Albatross*, 208

Carew, 83
Carroll, Lewis (*see* Dodgson)
Céline, *Voyage au Bout de la Nuit*, 10-11
Chapman, 37, 39, 85, 139
Chaucer, 35, 212
Coleridge, 79, 122, 207, 260
  The Ancient Mariner, 120-1
Cornford, F. M., *From Religion to Philosophy*, 78
Cowper, 188
  The Sofa, 177
Crashaw, *The Weeper*, 83

Dante, 176
Darwin, 213
  Origin of Species, 254
Defoe, 58
  Robinson Crusoe, 203-4
De La Mare, W., 253
Disraeli, 189, 256, 257
Dodgson, 206, 207, 241, 253
  Alice in Wonderland, 18, 20, 253-94
  Through the Looking-Glass, 256, 257, 270, 285-7
Don Quixote, 198

295

INDEX